Expositions
Exhibits
Industrial and Trade Fairs

Wolfgang Clasen

Expositions
Exhibits
Industrial and Trade Fairs

Frederick A. Praeger, Publishers
New York · Washington

BOOKS THAT MATTER

Published in the United States of America in 1968
by Frederick A. Praeger, Inc., Publishers
111 Fourth Avenue, New York, N. Y. 10003
Copyright in Stuttgart, Germany, 1968, by Verlag Gerd Hatje, Stuttgart
All rights reserved
Library of Congress Catalog Card Number: 68-19846
Translation into English by E. Rockwell
Printed in Germany

Contents

Inhalt

6

Introduction

Architectural documentation is particularly important when dealing with a category of works of architecture which are not built to last (fig. 1). Among these categories are most exhibitions as well as shop window or showcase displays. Our collection has however been limited in two ways: First, all kinds of window displays have been omitted since, as they remain purely decorative, they are not directly related to architecture. Second, the book does not deal with multi-purpose exhibition buildings which, like permanent exhibition or assembly halls, merely serve as a venue for any kind of display. On the other hand, we have included a number of buildings of the pavilion type which were erected for certain sponsors (public authorities, associations, companies) to last for a longer period of time (pages 44, 48, 60). Although the exhibitions held in such buildings are generally concerned with the same subject – as, for example, in a trade fair pavilion – so that the exhibits remain basically the same, the design of the stand, i.e. the presentation of the exhibits, is liable to vary.

Over the period of time with which this book is concerned – from about 1961 onwards – the standard of exhibition design has greatly improved. Certain fundamental findings, technical conditions and design features which, even ten years ago, were still regarded as almost revolutionary, are now taken for granted, e.g. the application of a module system to an exhibition stand (fig. 2) or the design of display units for travelling exhibitions, so that they can be easily dismantled and packed within a minimum space (fig. 3).

Klaus Franck was right when, in his work on the same subject published in 1961, he took the technical conditions, display systems, designs and units as his starting point and, as it were, assembled those units into full-size exhibitions. (Klaus Franck: "Exhibitions", London–New York–Stuttgart, 1961). To-day, new possibilities have emerged, new problems and questions have arisen which make it appear desirable to reverse the process and to begin the series of examples with the large exhibitions.

This already indicates the principle which has here been followed in arranging the material. Existing literature is not lacking in theoretical discussions of exhibition problems, or in attempts at systematisation. A frequent approach is to divide exhibitions by their functions into representative, informative and commercial events. But which representative display could dispense with information or sales intentions even if the exhibits are confined to cultural items? Which informative exhibition could succeed without representative design? Which commercial show could make do without information or without stressing the image of the firm?

In any case, such a systematisation would yield no clues as to what the design can and must achieve. A logical classification can only be based on very simple, practical considerations. Beginning with the most extensive examples, the book will therefore first of all deal with entire exhibitions, i.e. exhibitions where the architectural treatment of the premises has been governed by the exhibits and has been conceived as an entity. This will be followed by pavilions for changing exhibitions displaying identical or at least similar subjects. The book will then turn to exhibitions in 'neutral' exhibition buildings and halls, beginning with those which – mainly sponsored by public authorities – were originally designed for a specific event; it will then deal with smaller exhibitions of the kind often sponsored by companies and as travelling exhibitions, and finally with the larger and smaller exhibition stands and with display systems and units where these are novel or of particular interest.

During the period covered by the book, three World Exhibitions took place: One on a limited scale at Seattle, Washington, in 1962; a large exhibition – though not officially recognised as a World Fair – in New York in 1964–65; finally, in 1967, on the occasion of Canada's centenary celebrations, the great official World Exhibition at Montreal; thus all three of them took place in North America. In reviewing these exhibitions, the critics again and again referred to the World Exhibition held in Brussels in 1958 which was, as it were, taken as a reference basis and scale. In retrospect, it must be acknowledged that the designers of the Brussels exhibition had in fact succeeded in finding a felicitous synthesis between the traditional display of national vanities which had become a habit at World Exhibitions, and the successful mastery not only of the overall design – achieved through adroit arrangement of the buildings in open landscape settings – but also of the design of the more prominent individual contributions. This effect was undoubtedly attributable to architecture: it was this which dominated the overall impression. Although the imitative structure of the "Atomium" might by some be regarded as an aberration,

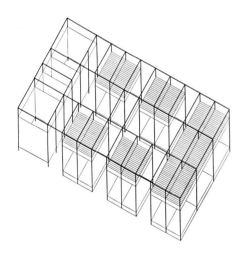

1. Expo '67, Montreal. Exhibition buildings on the Ile de Notre-Dame.
2. Isometric view of a Fair Stand of the Sonor Company at the International Fair, Frankfurt, 1960. Design: Otl Aicher and "Entwicklungsgruppe 5" of the College for Design, Ulm, Germany.

1. Expo '67 in Montreal: Ausstellungsbauten auf der Ile Notre-Dame.
2. Isometrie eines Messestandes für die Firma Sonor, Internationale Frankfurter Messe, 1960. Entwurf: Otl Aicher und »Entwicklungsgruppe 5« der Hochschule für Gestaltung, Ulm.

3. Travelling Exhibition "Forms from Israel", 1958–1960. Design: Nathan H. Shapira.

3. Wanderausstellung »Formen aus Israel«, 1958–1960. Entwurf: Nathan H. Shapira.

the incentive of competition generally resulted in a consistently high standard of quality. With Brussels as a starting point, several new avenues were open. One of them was followed at Seattle. It led to stricter discipline and greater concentration – in size, in thematic scope and, not least, in design. For instance, national considerations receded in the background in relation to the general theme of technical and scientific progress. Admittedly, however, the architectural creations – still in existence as part of Seattle's 'Civic Center' – revealed somewhat too ostentatiously the urge to achieve artistic significance (fig. 4) so that they fell victim to that artificial trend which has, in recent years, led to a kind of exaggerated technological craftsmanship recognisable in a whole series of cultural buildings in America.

In New York, on the other hand, the show business of the county fair was given free rein (fig. 5). Here, it was mainly the large industrial corporations which grasped the opportunity of world-wide publicity. Among the stunts were, for example, monumentalised road cruisers, gigantic domes with decorations reminiscent of the surface of the moon (fig. 6); roofs looking like clusters of children's balloons. And even such a prominent architect as Saarinen was not above crowning the IBM Pavilion by a gigantic typewriter matrix. Not without justification, the critics singled out the Spanish Pavilion as the architecturally most significant building (page 32) which, following in this respect entirely in the wake of the Brussels exhibition, combined modern structural and design features with a distinctly national atmosphere and was content with an informal presentation of individual exhibits of high quality. This was completely in contrast to the general tendency which was otherwise apparent in New York and, in somewhat different form, also at Seattle, namely to intensify, dramatise, dynamise the exhibition so that the visitor was induced to take a more active part in it. At Seattle, for example, the centre of the Science Pavilion was taken up by an ovoid theatre with simultaneous film projections on six screens. Or take the large Coliseum where the visitors were taken to the "World of Tomorrow" section in the "Bubbleator" – large plastic globes sliding on an inclined ramp (fig. 7). In keeping with the concept of a complete free-for-all, the exhibitors at the New York Fair tried to excel each other by sensational attractions, with dioramas depicting the world of yesterday or that of the day after to-morrow which the visitor was able to view sliding in a motor car or being carried in armchairs or on conveyor belts. They perfected the technique of multiple projection to which Charles and Ray Eames with their IBM Pavilion – already preceded by the Science Pavilion at Seattle – made a significant contribution (page 62).

If, in this connection, Brussels is again recalled, the principle of providing general information had already been abandoned even then (with the exception of the Russian Pavilion which still had the bazaar character of a Fair) in favour of a greater emphasis on interesting and essential features. But more extreme possibilities were only apparent to a modest extent; that spiral passage of the Brazilian Pavilion which, rather ingeniously, ended at a bar; the fashion show in the centre of the American rotunda and the all-round projection show in an ancillary building; not least, Le Corbusier's bold tent constructed of prestressed concrete where, in the interior, picture, light and acoustics were combined to provide a new audio-visual overall effect (fig. 8).

Meanwhile, it has come to be quite generally accepted that the visitor to an exhibition

4. World Exhibition, Seattle, 1962. In the foreground the U.S. group of Science Pavilions (Architect: Minoru Yamasaki) which now serves as a Civic Center. In the background, John Graham's "Space Needle".

4. Weltausstellung 1962 in Seattle. Die US-Pavillongruppe der Wissenschaften (Architekt: Minoru Yamasaki), die heute als Civic Center dient, dahinter die »Space Needle« von John Graham.

should not be overstrained, that he should be guided without noticing any constraint, yet should also be enabled to visualize even the most complicated processes. This finding applies to the exhibition as a whole (pages 24–43) just as much as to the small stand. Visitors are guided by a suitable placing of wall panels and by the geographical sequence of individual rooms or corridors. Orientation is aided by providing specific accents which attract particular attention – such as special shows and, particularly, cinematic projections ranging from simple slides and films to increasingly sophisticated multiple-screen projections.

As the examples illustrated on pages 62–75 show, it is quite feasible for entire exhibitions or, at least, certain sections of exhibitions to be concentrated around such a major screen show. Here, variety can be obtained even by varying the type and arrangement of the screens: the all-round projection, already seen in the '360° theatre' in Brussels; the display of thematically associated pictures and scenes on parts of a large screen (Eames in New York, page 62, or the Czechoslovak 'Diapolyecran' system, page 70); projections on main and ancillary screens at different points in the room (Dutch Pavilion at the International Transport Exhibition, page 64); an extensive, synchronised programme comprising several successive projection strips (Pavilion of the German Federal Railway at the same exhibition, page 66); finally, the projection of stills and films on screens arranged at different angles and on different levels ('Alarm' at Stockholm, page 68).

At Montreal, the visitor would have been able to spend 183 days merely in viewing films; in other words, hardly any of the exhibitors and hardly any of the exhibitions were able to dispense with films or film-like projections. Here, not only ordinary films but even the older methods of multiple-screen projection were regarded as conventional, if not outdated. New possibilities were found, climaxing in the "multi-media happening" which was experienced in its most exaggerated form in the "Gyrotron" – a space flight ending in the crater of a vulcano. This particular experience was, admittedly, confined to the 'Fun Fair' section of the 'Expo'. But its creator, the well-known stage designer Ire Sean Kenny, was also responsible for the design of a similarly multifarious, blazing, growling, glittering show depicting the history of Great Britain in the basement of the tower of the British Pavilion. Or the "percorso-plurimo-luce" happening created by Vedova for the Italian Pavilion, where rotating colour patterns were conjured up on the walls of grottos by a dozen projectors in an electronically controlled rhythm. Or the "Polytope" created by Xenakis, which provided in the staircase of the French Pavilion an electrically produced audio-visual show with scientific undertones. Or in the Russian Pavilion, where models of power stations and factories moved and hammered away with austere purposefulness, fascinating like a toy railway. A real toy railway, scurrilously persiflaged by Stoeckl, rolled through the landscape of German souls – one of the few touches of humour in the German exhibition.

Even purely cinematic techniques had something new to offer. The truly labyrinthine display of the National Film Board of Canada, consisting in continuous and – at the end – five-fold film projections on screens arranged on five different levels, depicted the "History of Man". The Czechs showed a film where the visitors were able, by pressing a button, to influence the unravelling of the plot; as a rule, the happy end prevailed.

5. A view of the New York World Exhibition, 1964–1965.

5. Blick auf die New Yorker Weltausstellung, 1964–1965.

9

All this might give rise to the impression that the 'Expo' at Montreal was if anything more dynamic – though no doubt of higher quality – than the show business in New York. However, even the boldest "happenings" took place in buildings which dominated the scene mainly through their architecture (fig. 1). It would therefore seem that – apart from the bolder and more ambitious scale befitting a vast and young country – Expo '67 was after all more in line with the good tradition of Brussels, reflected in that contest between nations for which, at Montreal, the leitmotif was provided by Saint Exupéry's "La Terre des Hommes" (a motif, incidentally, which the Churches were the only ones not to interpret in a purely optimistic spirit).

This tradition was apparent even from details. Again – though separated by a wide canal, yet linked by a 'bridge of peace' – the American and Russian Pavilions were facing each other. Again, the Russians provided, albeit this time in better taste, a Super-Fair though they left the design and erection of the hall to the Italians. Again, the Americans opted for the circle, though this time in a more perfect and consistent manner in the shape of the ingenious spherical design created by Buckminster Fuller (page 24). And again, the interiors were characterized by unimpeded spaciousness, even in the dominating display of space travel, free from heavy-handed propaganda, and so sparkling in its irony that conservative American Members of Congress were provoked into harsh criticism. Even the British were highly critical of their bunker stronghold with its tower of painted plaster, especially as the self-irony of the exhibits was in fact somewhat heavy-handed. The French again provided a department store which – though distinguished by elegant architectural treatment – displayed industrial products and Gloire but reached a really high standard in the Art Gallery only. The "Museum without Muff" also formed the attractive centre of the German exhibition (page 28) which was otherwise excessively overloaded by ideology, condescension and conflicting group interests though its shell, that characteristic tent designed by Frei Otto and Rolf Gutbrod, was admired not only by his countrymen. In any case, the visitors to the German Pavilion were given a good chance to move about whilst, in certain other Pavilions, the recent general trend towards stricter guidance resulted in unpleasant traffic congestion. As an architectural idea pure and simple, bold in conception yet not sterile, the thematic buildings of the Canadians themselves – wooden pagodas (fig. 9) and steel lattice work (fig. 10) – must not be forgotten. By and large, one would not be wrong in regarding the quality of its architecture as the permanent bonus of this world exhibition.

Although, or perhaps just because, there had been a lack of experiments in recent years, the most important European event in the history of great exhibitions has been the Swiss National Exhibition, held in Lausanne in 1964 – that comprehensive self-portrait of Switzerland which became a worthy successor to others of its kind. The particularly attractive feature of the "Expo '64" was the careful and balanced planning of the exhibition as a whole (fig. 11), its division into different sections dealing with interesting specific themes, the assignment of individual sectors to different teams of designers. Even by this policy alone, the kind of schematism liable to result from excessively disciplined planning was avoided. Even within each sector, a logical subdivision and a high quality of design provided the image which the Swiss are not alone in linking with their country.

6. World Exhibition 1964–1965, New York. On the right, the dome of the Travel and Transport Pavilion, covered by a moon landscape. On the left, the Chrysler Pavilion in the shape of a motor car engine.
7. World Exhibition, Seattle, 1962. In the "Bubbleator", the visitors were taken to the "World of Tomorrow".

6. Weltausstellung 1964–1965 in New York. Rechts die mit einer Mondlandschaft überzogene Kuppel des Pavillons für Reise und Transport, links der in die Form eines Automotors gekleidete Chrysler-Pavillon.
7. Weltausstellung 1962 in Seattle. Mit dem »Bubbleator« gelangten die Besucher in die »Welt von morgen«.

8. World's Fair, Brussels, 1958. "Visions" from the 'electronic poem' in Le Corbusier's Philips Pavilion. The open hand symbolizes "Give and Take".

8. Weltausstellung 1958 in Brüssel. »Visionen« aus dem elektronischen Gedicht in Le Corbusiers Philips-Pavillon (die offene Hand als Symbol für Geben und Empfangen).

Particularly convincing was the interplay of the architectural design – which was deliberately kept simple in technical and structural respects and temporary in character, using mainly wood, plastic foils, and tent roofs (fig. 12) – with the contents of the exhibition. "The Way of Switzerland" (page 36) defied any temptations to display a jingoist patriotism. "The Art of Living" (page 38) was amiable and attractive. In the technical and economic sectors, monotony was avoided by providing informal, selective information. Particularly comprehensive was the range of transport and traffic facilities. The "Telecanape" carried the visitor from the entrance to the centre, affording a first impression. The "Monorail", raised above ground by columns, connected the different sectors and permitted rapid orientation without impeding the pedestrians – an advantage which led to the re-utilisation of the same system at Montreal (fig. 13). In each sector of the exhibition, the visitor had the choice of a rapid synoptic walk or a more leisurely perambulation enabling him to appreciate even the details (fig. 14).

In the group in which several minor exhibitions were integrated (pages 44–61), further examples were combined which differed in their design just as much as major exhibitions although the buildings themselves mainly consisted of prefabricated assemblies – generally metal or wood structures with panelling of metal, plastics, wood, glass or textile materials. Even the roof of the IRI Pavilion (page 48) was assembled from prefabricated parts. This building shared with the Aluminium Pavilion at Hanover (page 44) not only the boldness of its design but also its claim to permanency. With other examples, including those provided by the German Industrial Fair at Khartoum (page 40) and of course with the tents designed by Kuhn (page 52), the advantages of assembly construction methods were utilized; these methods are particularly well suited for travelling exhibitions as they permit rapid erection and dismantling as well as variety of design. Such designs are most successful where exhibits and surrounding architecture can be attuned to each other. This may already be achieved by skilful arrangement of the lighting. Sometimes, the design of the display units inside the building is based on the same principles as that of the structure itself (pages 44, 52); in other cases, the panel walls complementing the framework structure are also used as display panels (pages 56, 58). But in these cases, too, facilities for guiding the visitors are kept in mind; a particularly clear example is provided by Ionel Schein's small Timber Pavilion in Paris for the French Ministry of Building Construction (page 60).

Exhibitions without a specific architectural frame of their own (pages 76–133) must somehow come to terms with their architectural setting. It is only in very rare cases that the exhibition building itself can be used as a design feature; frequently, one may even seek to screen the existing shell so that the exhibition can be given an integrated form. Among the technical means to achieve such screening are lighting effects which concentrate the attention of visitors on the exhibits and display units and, in the process, almost conceal the surrounding architecture (pages 98, 108, 110); systems and combinations of scaffolding which form self-contained suites of rooms (pages 104, 122); tent roofs spanned out like sails (page 106); finally, recourse to major structural measures and conversions. With the exception of the latter, these means have the advantage that they can easily be erected and dismantled, so that they are particularly well suited for travelling exhibitions.

More elaborate shells are mainly provided for great exhibitions of international character which must be housed in existing exhibition halls, e.g. the Milan Triennale (page 76), or the "Italia 61" in Turin (page 88), or the 1965 International Transport Exhibition in Munich (page 64). As a rule, exhibitions of this kind are divided into sections which are generally sponsored by different countries or at least by national associations or organisations. As with the national pavilions at World Exhibitions, this practice permits the discovery of certain national characteristics. The Italians, for example, are particularly skilful in using dynamic, dramatic effects (pages 72, 84, 114). France, on the other hand, has hardly made any contribution to international exhibition techniques. The British, in their turn, have developed a number of interesting and practical systems (pages 104, 108, 118) and are, apart from the Scandinavians (page 134), among those most apt to include certain contemporary artistic trends such as Pop Art (page 130). Some Finnish examples (pages 80, 82, 98) combine simplicity of means with imaginative conception; an interesting comparison is afforded between two Finnish contributions to the theme of leisure time (pages 80, 82) and a British essay on the same theme (page 76).
The designers of German exhibitions, especially the Munich Transport Exhibition (pages 90, 94, 96), do make use of dynamic accents without, however, going in for unduly dramatic effects. Over the attractions of the show itself, they do not forget the task of providing instructive information without becoming long-winded or tedious (pages 86, 102, 112). The participation of the United States in foreign exhibitions with cultural themes has greatly declined in recent years. But the few examples (pages 124, 128) available are

still convincing through the perfection of their programme as well as through the quality of their technique and design.

The design aids employed for such large constituent exhibitions held in an existing architectural setting are much akin to those already referred to in connection with integral exhibitions. Here, too, is a distinct trend towards intensifying the exhibits and inducing the visitor to more active participation. There is now hardly any major exhibition in which the visitor is not guided, seemingly without compulsion, from room to room, from accent to accent, from object to object. The accents are provided by projections, shows, live models, tableaux vivants and mirror effects.

The greatest ingenuity in this respect has been displayed by the Italians. The entrance to the XIIIth Triennale (page 72) was a veritable composition of projections, mirror reflections and acoustic effects. In another example, the Olivetti contribution to the "Italia 61" (page 84), the exhibits were paraded past the visitor. The use of specific materials, even of the simplest kind, can provide an optical bracket for even such a major show as the Waterways Exhibition in Milan (page 114). Much attention is paid, quite generally, to the arrangement and control of lighting. It is to lighting that the German contributions to the Munich Transport Exhibition mainly owe their success. The Finns have developed display panels illuminated from inside (page 98). The Anglo-Saxons are prone to use spotlights which are concentrated on precious or particularly delicate or noteworthy objects (pages 104, 108). An evenly lit exhibition room is becoming increasingly rare (pages 80, 102); even here, the accentuation designed to attract the visitor is obtained by the arrangement of the exhibits. As to visitors' guidance, attention may be drawn to some German examples (pages 86, 112, 116). In these cases, the visitor had to be confronted with some rather unyielding material, basically capable of diagrammatic presentation only, and calling for a given viewing sequence. Even so, success was achieved by the sculptural and informal treatment of the wall panels and by a skilful layout. Practical demonstrations, either in a special auditorium or in an open section of the exhibition (fig. 15), are among the most prominent characteristics of the American examples (pages 124, 128).

The following group of exhibitions held in existing premises (pages 134–155) differs from the preceding group in that they are fewer in number, and are sponsored not so much by public organisations but by industrial undertakings and associations. All these exhibitions are mainly concerned with objective information though this may well be combined with commercial image-building. Nowhere, however, are the exhibitors' products pushed into the foreground ostentatiously. The design of such exhibitions is hardly different from that of 'neutral' exhibitions. But here again, certain national traits can be detected, such as the predilection of the Italians for dramatic stage-setting (pages 146, 148, 150) which may tell the story of petroleum in ingenious tableaux or compel the visitor's attention by unconventionally designed luminous showcases and displays. An impressive company image is reflected in Burtin's spherical structures (page 140), whilst his fascinating scientific large-scale models (page 138) have a highly propagandist effect just because the sponsor and his products are kept in the background. They may be regarded as a particularly bold and exhaustive synthesis of up-to-date scientific knowledge and potentialities, of exhibition techniques, and of formative arts (Op Art, kinetics). With great deliberation, Pop Art features have been used for a Scandinavian exhibition (page 134), wittily demonstrating a dry company history. The picture is rounded off by more objective but by no means unimaginative exhibitions of well-known Swiss quality (pages 142, 156) and by the Dutch display of high-quality printed matter (page 154).

As far as design is concerned, large-size exhibition stands (pages 156–187) are hardly different from minor company exhibitions. In the case of the latter, the informative-cum-representative character might be said to prevail over the commercial-cum-representative character, and the show is more self-contained. In contrast, exhibition stands tend to form clusters or chains. During the past decade, the structural systems based on module units – of the type already introduced earlier by progressive manufacturers such as Braun AG (fig. 16) – have become so successful that such stands are nowadays the rule rather than the exception. Admittedly, this again entails the risk of a certain monotony which can, in individual cases, only be avoided by introducing distinctive accentuating features unless one has the courage and opportunity of abandoning the module design in spite of its great advantages in regard to space utilisation. Some fairs, such as the Cologne Furniture Exhibition in 1966, have already introduced permanent stands of standard design. Others like the Motor Shows, can afford virtually to forgo an architectural treatment of the stands because the exhibits themselves are sufficiently attractive in their own right. Altogether, the simplicity and reticence of the stands is found to increase as the exhibits themselves become more distinctive.

The programme of a normal exhibition stand is fixed (fig. 17). The outsides and peripheral zones are used for commercial publicity displays; these surround a core which is reserved

9. Expo '67, Montreal. Canadian Pavilion on the theme 'Man in the Community'.

9. Expo '67 in Montreal: Kanadischer Themen-pavillon »Der Mensch in der Gemeinschaft«.

10. Expo '67, Montreal. Canadian Pavilion on the theme 'Man the Producer'.

10. Expo '67 in Montreal: Kanadischer Themenpavillon »Der Mensch als Erzeuger«.

for deeper information and often contains secluded booths for confidential negotiations. Position and proportion of the different components depend on the size and situation of the stand which may, for instance, be open on one or several or possibly all sides, or may be contiguous with other stands on one or more sides. The larger the stand, the more clearly can the different functions (display - information - negotiations) be separated from each other and the easier becomes the task of providing centres of gravity by the prominent display of new products (page 162). The conception of the stand is also influenced by the type of exhibition; Specialised exhibitions require more space for negotiations and less for display; for trade fairs open to the public at large, facilities for display and shows are of greater importance. Even these fundamental considerations alone give rise to a great variety of alternatives, even if the – by now conventional – module principle is preserved and fashionable excesses are avoided.

Another problem frequently encountered at exhibition stands is the screening of the stand from the architectural setting of the hall. Apart from the usual roofing with textile materials or plastic foils – which are, however, not ideal for ventilation – the devices most frequently used are lattice work ceilings of timber boards placed on edge (page 162) or metal structures. Often, all or at least some of the ceiling panels remain open so that one is content with a merely optical roofing in the interest of adequate ventilation. There are, however, also compromise solutions which offer a relatively enclosed ceiling with more favourable ventilation conditions. Among these solutions are tent structures assembled from metal bars (page 170) where ventilation gaps are kept open between saddle-shaped roofings, or stands with rhythmically alternating ceiling units and with light fittings of unorthodox design (page 164) which give the entire stand an unmistakable character. In addition, a number of methods have been developed which – using prefabricated components and requiring comparatively little technical effort – permit the erection of full-size roof shells (page 160) of prismatic roof units lit from above (page 168). Further possibilities in this direction are offered by the cocoon spraying method (page 204).

If it is decided to renounce the rectangular module system and, albeit at the expense of some useful additional floor space, to adopt a circular, oval, or diagonal layout plan (pages 176, 182, 184), this will in itself represent a distinguishing feature of the stand. On the other hand, more informal layout plans of this kind might lead to certain difficulties in displaying the exhibits if these are relegated to the periphery by the comparatively large space taken up by interview booths or special prestige displays in the centre.

With rectangular stands, even of smaller size, it is important to design the structural elements, for a given suitable layout, in such a way that a distinctive effect is obtained. Apart from technical details, these structural units are generally very similar to each other. They usually consist of a scaffolding in or on which the display panels and wall units are mounted (fig. 18). Metal scaffolds are particularly light and transparent in appearance and suggest technical precision. But many designers prefer, for such scaffoldings, the more compact and warmer wood. Others prefer to renounce solid wall panels if it is desired merely to hint at a sub-division of the room without, however, impeding the view across the stand. Loose textiles, wood mattings, metal grilles or lattice walls are better suited for this purpose. As to details, it is left to the designer's imagination to enhance the publicity effect of an exhibition stand by distinctive features such as a graphic symbol (page 184), a wall of wine glasses (page 180), or a display element which, by its very shape, symbolises the products of the exhibitor (page 166).

The last category is represented by structures and display supports, designed for easy dismantling and packing and therefore specially suited for travelling exhibitions (pages 188–205). Some of the design principles and display systems for many different applications have already been referred to, such as Kuhn's three-dimensional structures or Zerning's cocoon-sprayed ceiling units. For minor exhibits and all types of documents, domed showcases have proved to be a good solution (page 188). Demountable units which can be assembled to form showcases or coherent display areas permit interesting layouts especially for travelling exhibitions (page 196, 198). With most of these systems, the light fittings are among the standard components. Even for display systems working exclusively with panels, a number of innovations are available. Such panels may be held together by simple supports (page 202), by connectors (page 190), or by groove-and-bolt links (page 200) which can also be used for three-dimensional assemblies.

At the end of this line are two exhibition systems based on the use of collapsible cubes. In one case, these consist of metal rods with appropriate connectors (page 194), in the other of wooden frames held together by hinges and pins (page 192). In either case, the cubes can be used for the mounting of panels which may consist of the most variegated materials, and for the assembly of extensive three-dimensional display supports.

The examples comprised in this collection range from the large to the small. In selecting them, the attempt has been made to expose certain fairly general trends which are linked –

by no means accidentally – with developments in other fields of design work. This kinship is not confined to the fine arts. Pop Art gags are obviously suited for certain exhibition themes only so long as they remain comparatively rare – for, who has the courage of self-irony? Whilst pure Op Art might be too delicate for the loud publicity of exhibition design, the influence of the kinetic art is more frequently apparent in the various efforts to apply motion features even to exhibitions.

More closely associated with exhibition design are the spheres of agency art, permanent architecture, industrial design. As in these spheres, the beginnings of a completely new conception date back to the 1920s. Post-war development was marked by the break-through and consolidation of new ideas, already discussed in earlier investigations into this subject – a process which was not entirely free from the risk of dogmatisation as witnessed by the excessively schematic module structures in multi-storey construction and exhibition design. Recent years may not have brought any drastic innovations; but they were marked by consistent progress in differentiation and intensification. An important aid, not only in exhibition design, has proved to be the introduction, in many different forms, of dynamic features which lend life and motion to the form (fig. 19–22). Yet there is no lack of excesses which should be regarded as a warning lest the introduction of dynamics should lead to cheap effects which would tend to reduce the exhibition to the level of a show.

11. Aerial view of the Swiss National Exhibition, Lausanne, 1964.

11. Luftaufnahme der Schweizerischen Landes-ausstellung 1964 in Lausanne.

Einleitung

12. Swiss National Exhibition, Lausanne, 1964. Harbour zone with the multi-coloured tent roofs of the restaurants at night (Architect: M.-J. Saugey).

12. Schweizerische Landesausstellung 1964, Lausanne: Hafenzone mit den verschiedenfarbigen Zeltdächern der Restaurants bei Nacht (Architekt: M.-J. Saugey).

Eine Architekturdokumentation erweist sich dann als besonders wichtig, wenn sie ein Thema behandelt, dessen Beispiele nicht für die Dauer geschaffen wurden (Abb. 1). Die meisten Ausstellungen, auch Schaufenster- oder Vitrinendekorationen, gehören zu dieser Kategorie. Unsere Materialsammlung wurde allerdings nach zwei Seiten hin begrenzt: Einmal sind alle Arten von Schaufenstergestaltungen ausgeklammert, denn ihnen fehlt die Beziehung zur Architektur; sie bleiben rein dekorativ. Und zum anderen werden keine inhaltsneutralen Ausstellungsbauten behandelt, soweit sie – wie etwa ständige Messe- oder Versammlungshallen – lediglich zur Unterbringung beliebiger Schauen dienen. Dagegen ist eine Reihe von pavillonartigen Bauten einbezogen, die bestimmte Auftraggeber (Behörden, Verbände, Firmen) für einen längeren Zeitraum errichten ließen (Seite 44, 48, 60). Was darin an Ausstellungen gezeigt wird, umkreist zwar – wie beispielsweise der Messepavillon – immer wieder das gleiche Grundthema, doch wechselt die Ausgestaltung, das heißt die Präsentation des im Prinzip gleichbleibenden Ausstellungsgutes.

In dem Zeitabschnitt, den dieses Buch erfaßt – etwa von 1961 an –, hat sich das Niveau der Ausstellungsgestaltung wesentlich gehoben. Bestimmte grundsätzliche Erkenntnisse, technische Vorbedingungen und Gestaltungselemente, die vor einem Jahrzehnt noch als beinahe revolutionär angesehen wurden, gehören heute zu den Selbstverständlichkeiten wie zum Beispiel die Rastergitter des üblichen Messestandes (Abb. 2) oder die demontable und auf kleinstem Raum transportable Konstruktion einer Wanderausstellung (Abb. 3). Klaus Franck hatte recht, wenn er 1961 in seiner Arbeit zum gleichen Thema von den technischen Voraussetzungen, von Systemen, Konstruktionen, Elementen ausging und daraus im Verlauf seiner Untersuchung gewissermaßen die Ausstellung als Ganzes zusammenbaute (Klaus Franck: »Ausstellungen«, London – New York – Stuttgart, 1961). Heute zeichnen sich neue Möglichkeiten ab, erheben sich neue Probleme und Fragen, die es angebracht erscheinen lassen, den umgekehrten Weg zu gehen und die Reihe der Beispiele mit den großen Ausstellungen zu beginnen.

Damit ist bereits das Prinzip angedeutet, nach dem hier das Material geordnet wurde. Es fehlt in der bisherigen Literatur nicht an theoretischen Erörterungen des Ausstellungswesens, an Versuchen einer Systematisierung. So hat man Ausstellungen gerne nach ihren Aufgaben in repräsentative, informative und kommerzielle Veranstaltungen unterteilt. Welche repräsentative Schau käme jedoch ohne Information und ohne Verkaufsabsichten aus, selbst wenn ausschließlich Kultur angeboten wird, welche Lehrschau ohne repräsentative Aufmachung, welche Verkaufsausstellung ohne Information und Herausstellen des Firmenimages?

Aus einer derartigen Schematisierung ergibt sich vor allem keinerlei Hinweis auf gestalterische Möglichkeiten und Notwendigkeiten. Eine sinnvolle Einteilung wird man nur nach ganz einfachen, von der Praxis bestimmten Gesichtspunkten vornehmen können. Mit den umfangreichsten Beispielen beginnend stehen daher am Anfang dieses Buches Gesamtausstellungen, das heißt Ausstellungen, bei denen die raumumschließende Architektur und der Inhalt zusammengehören und die als Einheit konzipiert sind. Daran schließen sich Pavillons für Wechselausstellungen gleichen oder ähnlichen Inhalts an. Es folgen Ausstellungen in neutralen Ausstellungsbauten und Hallen, zunächst die großen, vorwiegend von offiziellen Auftraggebern als einmalige Ereignisse veranstaltet, dann kleinere, vielfach von Firmen und als Wanderausstellungen organisiert, ferner die großen und kleinen Messestände und schließlich neue Systeme und Elemente.

Drei Weltausstellungen gab es in dem hier zu behandelnden Zeitabschnitt: 1962 eine kleinere in Seattle, Washington; 1964–1965 eine umfangreiche, aber nicht offiziell anerkannte in New York, und schließlich 1967 zur Hundertjahrfeier Kanadas die große und offizielle in Montreal, alle drei also in Nordamerika. Bei ihrer Beurteilung bezog sich die Kritik immer wieder auf die 1958 in Brüssel veranstaltete Weltausstellung. Sie diente sozusagen als Ausgangspunkt und Maßstab. Rückblickend ist anzuerkennen, daß in Brüssel tatsächlich eine recht glückliche Synthese gefunden wurde zwischen dem auf Weltausstellungen schon zur Tradition gewordenen Jahrmarkt der nationalen Eitelkeiten und einer gestalterischen Bewältigung des Ganzen (durch geschickte Zueinanderordnung der Bauten in viel Landschaft und Freiraum) ebenso wie der wichtigsten Einzelbeiträge. Diese Wirkung ging zweifellos von der Architektur aus; sie beherrschte den Eindruck. Verstieg man sich auch mit dem Atomium bis zum abbildenden Baudenkmal, so führte doch im allgemeinen der Zwang des Wettbewerbs zur Harmonie der Qualität.

Von Brüssel her boten sich verschiedene Wege an, einer wurde in Seattle beschritten. Er führte zur Straffung und Konzentration – räumlich, thematisch und nicht zuletzt gestalterisch. Gegenüber dem Gesamtthema des technischen und wissenschaftlichen Fortschritts trat Nationales zum Beispiel ganz in den Hintergrund. Die Architektur, die heute noch als Civic Center von Seattle weiterbesteht, strebte allerdings etwas zu offensichtlich nach künstlerischer Bedeutsamkeit (Abb. 4) und geriet in jenen artifiziellen Trend, der in den letzten Jahren bei einer ganzen Gruppe von kulturellen Bauten Amerikas zur Formensprache eines bestenfalls den Architekten befriedigenden, technoiden Kunstgewerbes geführt hat.

In New York dagegen ließ man dem Schaugeschäft des Jahrmarktes freie Hand (Abb. 5). Hier waren es vor allem die großen Industrieunternehmen, die die Gelegenheit zu üppigster Werbung aufgriffen. So begegnete man monumentalisierten Straßenkreuzerformen, riesigen, mondoberflächenartig verzierten Kuppeln (Abb. 6), Bedachungen, die Luftballontrauben ähnelten, und selbst ein so bedeutender Architekt wie Saarinen ließ es sich nicht nehmen, den IBM-Pavillon mit einer ins Überdimensionale vergrößerten Schreibmaschinen-Typenkugel dieses Unternehmens zu krönen. Als architektonisch wesentlichstes Gebilde hat die Kritik nicht zu unrecht den spanischen Pavillon herausgestellt (Seite 32), der, darin ganz dem Vorbild von Brüssel folgend, moderne konstruktive und gestalterische Möglichkeiten mit einer durchaus nationalen Atmosphäre verband und bei dem man sich im Inneren auf die zwanglose Darbietung kostbarer Einzelstücke beschränkte.

Das widersprach völlig der allgemeinen Tendenz, die sich sonst in New York und in anderer Form auch in Seattle abzeichnete, nämlich die Ausstellung zu intensivieren, zu dramatisieren, zu dynamisieren und dadurch den Besucher zur aktiveren Teilnahme zu bewegen. So bildete in Seattle den Mittelpunkt des Wissenschaftspavillons ein ovaler Raum mit einer Simultanfilmprojektion auf sechs Flächen, so wurden im großen Coliseum die Besucher im Bubbleator, in großen Plastikkugeln, auf einem schräg geführten Aufzug in »Die Welt von morgen« gebracht (Abb. 7). Entsprechend dem Konzept einer völlig freien Entfaltung suchten die Aussteller in New York einander durch sensationelle Attraktionen zu überbieten, bauten Panoptiken der Welt von gestern bis übermorgen auf, durch die man im Auto gleiten, sich auf Sesseln oder Förderbändern tragen lassen konnte, vervollkommneten die Technik der Simultanprojektion, zu der Charles und Ray Eames – wie schon im Wissenschaftspavillon in Seattle – mit dem IBM-Pavillon einen wesentlichen Beitrag leisteten (Seite 62).

Denkt man in diesem Zusammenhang noch einmal an Brüssel zurück, so hatte sich zwar dort schon eine Abkehr von der allgemein ausgebreiteten Gesamtinformation vollzogen (nur die Russen hielten an der bazarartigen Messehalle fest) zugunsten der pointierten Akzentuierung des Interessanten und Wesentlichen. Extremere Möglichkeiten kündigten sich aber nur in bescheidenem Umfang an: jene Wegspirale des brasilianischen Pavillons, die sinnigerweise an einer Bar endete, die Modeschau im Zentrum des amerikanischen Rundbaues sowie die Rundumprojektion in einem Nebengebäude und nicht zuletzt Le Corbusiers kühnes Zelt aus Spannbeton, in dessen Innerem sich Bild, Licht und Raumton zu einer neuen Gesamtwirkung verbanden (Abb. 8).

Inzwischen hat sich ganz allgemein die Erkenntnis durchgesetzt, daß der Ausstellungsbesucher nicht überfordert werden darf, daß er gelenkt werden sollte, ohne einen Zwang zu verspüren, daß ihm aber auch komplizierteste Vorgänge sinnfällig demonstriert werden können. Diese Erkenntnis gilt für die große Gesamtausstellung (Seite 24–43), ebenso wie für den kleinen Messestand. Die Lenkung der Besucher erfolgt durch eine entsprechende Plazierung von Ausstellungswänden und durch die Wegführung, die sich aus der Abfolge einzelner Räume oder Gänge ergibt. Sie wird verstärkt durch besondere Schwerpunkte, die die Aufmerksamkeit auf sich ziehen, wie Vorführungen, bewegliche Schaubilder und Modelle und nicht zuletzt Projektionen, von der einfachen Dia- und Filmprojektion bis zu den von Jahr zu Jahr immer raffinierter werdenden Simultanprojektionen.

Es ist durchaus möglich, ganze Ausstellungen oder zum mindesten Ausstellungsabteilungen auf eine derartige Großprojektion zu konzentrieren, wie es die auf den Seiten 62 bis 75 zusammengestellten Beispiele zeigen. Dabei gibt es schon in der Art und Verteilung der Projektionsflächen die verschiedensten Möglichkeiten: die bereits in Brüssel gezeigte Rundumprojektion im 360°-Theater; die Vorführung verschiedener, inhaltlich miteinander verbundener Bilder und Szenen auf Teilen einer großen Fläche (Eames in New York, Seite 62, oder das tschechoslowakische System des Diapolyecran, Seite 70); Projektionen auf Haupt- und Nebenflächen, die im Raum verteilt sind (die Holländer auf der IVA, Seite 64); ein umfangreiches, synchronisiertes Programm auf mehreren Projektionsstreifen hintereinander (die Deutsche Bundesbahn auf der IVA, Seite 66) und schließlich Bild- und Filmprojektionen auf Flächen, die in verschiedenen Winkeln und Höhenstellungen im Raum verteilt sind (»Alarm« in Stockholm, Seite 68).

13. Electric 'Minirail' at the Expo '67 Montreal.

13. Elektrische Minirail auf der Expo '67 in Montreal.

14. Classification of recommended ways of viewing the "Art of Living" sector of the Lausanne Exhibition, 1964: (1) Rapid general orientation (monorail). (2) Synoptic walk. (3) Perambulation for detailed studies.

14. Rundganghierarchie durch den Sektor »L'Art de vivre« auf der Lausanner Expo 1964: 1. Rundgang für rasche Allgemeinübersicht (Monorail), 2. Zusammenfassender Rundgang, 3. Rundgang für eingehende Betrachtung.

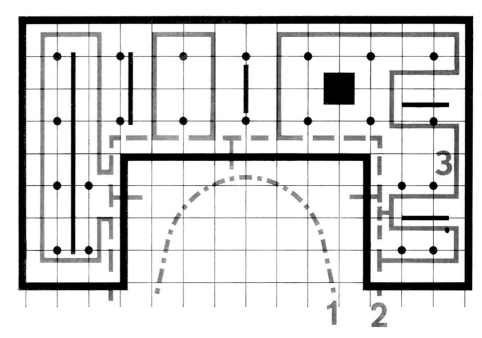

183 Tage lang hätte man sich in Montreal nur Filme anschauen können; mit anderen Worten: kaum ein Aussteller und kaum eine Ausstellung kamen hier ohne Filme oder filmähnliche Projektionen aus. Dabei galten nicht nur gewöhnliche Filme, sondern auch die bisher bekannten Simultanprojektionsverfahren als konventionell, wenn nicht veraltet. Man fand neue Möglichkeiten, gesteigert bis zum multi-media Happening, in krassester Form erlebbar im »Gyrotron« als Weltraumflug, der in einem Vulkankrater endet. Allerdings gehörte dieses Erlebnis in das Vergnügungsviertel der Expo. Sein Gestalter, der als Bühnenbildner bekannt gewordene Ire Sean Kenny, baute aber den Briten ähnlich vielfarbig, wabernd, grollend, leuchtend in den Keller ihres Turmes eine Entstehungsgeschichte Großbritanniens. In Grotten ließ für die Italiener Vedova sein »percorso-plurimo-luce«-Lichthappening aus einem Dutzend Projektoren in einem elektronisch gesteuerten Rhythmus von rotierenden Farbmustern über die Wände kreisen. Der »Polytope« von Xenakis vollführte im Treppenhaus des französischen Pavillons eine akustisch-visuelle Elektroschau mit wissenschaftlichem Anstrich. Bei den Russen drehten sich und hämmerten sachliche und zweckgebundene Modelle von Kraftwerken und Fabriken mit der Faszination der Spielzeugeisenbahn. Eine wirkliche Spielzeugeisenbahn rollte, von Stoeckl skurril verkitscht, durch die deutsche Seelenlandschaft, einer der wenigen humorvollen Lichtblicke in der deutschen Ausstellung.

Auch mit rein filmischen Mitteln wurde Neues gezeigt. Der National Film Board of Canada bot in fünf Stockwerken übereinander in fortlaufenden und zum Schluß verfünffachten Filmprojektionen wahrhaft labyrinthisch die Geschichte des Menschen. Die Tschechen brachten einen Film, bei dem die Zuschauer durch Knopfabstimmung den weiteren Handlungsablauf bestimmen konnten, wobei in der Regel der Trend zum Happy-End obsiegte.

Das alles könnte den Anschein erwecken, als sei man in Montreal den Weg der Dynamisierung weitergegangen, wenn auch sicherlich qualifizierter als seinerzeit im Showgeschäft von New York. Allerdings waren selbst die kühnsten Happenings in Bauten untergebracht, die vor allem als Bauwerk die Szene bestimmten (Abb. 1). Im Grunde hat man sich bei der Weltausstellung des Jahres 1967 – in der Weite eines jungen Landes kühner und großzügiger – also doch eher der guten Tradition von Brüssel angeschlossen, jenem Wettstreit der Nationen, für den hier Saint Exupérys »La Terre des Hommes« das Leitmotiv abgab (das übrigens nur die Kirchen nicht rein optimistisch auslegten).

Diese Tradition ging bis ins Detail. Wieder standen sich, wenn auch durch einen breiten Kanal getrennt, aber immerhin durch eine Friedensbrücke verbunden, die USA und die UdSSR gegenüber. Wieder boten, wenn auch geschmackvoller, die Russen eine Supermessehalle, deren Entwurf und Errichtung sie allerdings den Italienern überließen. Wieder wählten die Amerikaner den Kreis, diesmal vollkommener und konsequenter in der genialen Kugelkonstruktion Fullers (Seite 24). Und wieder herrschte im Inneren große und durchschaubare Weite, selbst in der beherrschenden Darstellung der Weltraumfahrt, frei von propagandistischer Schwere und ansonsten in der Ironie so funkelnd, daß konservative amerikanische Volksvertreter sich zu härtester Kritik provoziert sahen. Auch die Engländer haben ihren Trutzbunker mit Turm aus angestrichenem Gips heftig kritisiert, zumal die Ironie der Selbstdarstellung im Inneren tatsächlich etwas schwerfällig geraten schien. Die Franzosen füllten wieder, wenn auch architektonisch elegant verkleidet, ein Warenhaus mit Industrieerzeugnissen und Gloire, nur in der Kunstgalerie wirklich von erlesener Qualität. Das Museum ohne Muff bildete auch den wohltuenden Mittelpunkt der deutschen Ausstellung (Seite 28), die wieder allzu sehr durch Ideologie, Schulmeisterei und widersprüchliche Gruppeninteressen belastet war, während ihre Hülle, das eigenwillige Zelt von Frei Otto und Rolf Gutbrod, nicht nur von den eigenen Landsleuten bewundert wurde. Immerhin gewährten die Deutschen den Besuchern Bewegungsfreiheit, während in manchen Pavillons der in den letzten Jahren allgemein zu verzeichnende Trend zur Lenkung des Besuchers unangenehme Stauungen mit sich brachte. Nicht vergessen werden dürfen als reine Architekturidee, kühn in der Konstruktion und doch nicht steril, die Themenbauten der Kanadier selbst, Pagodentürme aus Holz (Abb. 9), Gitter aus Stahl (Abb. 10). Aufs Ganze gesehen geht man nicht fehl, wenn man die Qualität der Architektur als den bleibenden Wert dieser Weltausstellung hervorhebt.

Wenn es auch oder gerade weil es in den letzten Jahren an Experimenten fehlte, wird man die 1964 in Lausanne veranstaltete Schweizerische Landesausstellung als das wichtigste europäische Ereignis auf dem Gebiet der Großausstellungen bewerten dürfen – jene umfassende Selbstdarstellung der Schweiz, die ja schon interessante Vorgänger hatte. Was an dieser »Expo'64« bestach, war die sorgfältige und ausgewogene Planung des Ganzen (Abb. 11), die Aufteilung in die einzelnen ausstellenswerten Gebiete, die Sektoren, die jeweils besonderen Gestalterteams überlassen wurden. Schon dadurch ließ sich jeglicher Schematismus vermeiden, wie er leicht bei allzu intensiver Planung entstehen kann. Auch in den einzelnen Sektoren sorgten sinnvolle Unterteilung und qualitätvolle Gestaltung für Eindrücke, die nicht nur Schweizer mit dem Begriff Schweiz verbinden.
Vor allem überzeugte das Zusammenwirken der technisch und konstruktiv bewußt einfach und provisorisch gehaltenen Architektur – vorwiegend Holz, Plastikfolien, Zeltdächer (Abb. 12) – mit dem Ausstellungsinhalt. »Der Weg der Schweiz« (Seite 36) blieb frei von den Versuchungen eines nationalistischen Lokalpatriotismus; »L'Art de Vivre« (Seite 38) war liebenswürdig und attraktiv; die technischen und wirtschaftlichen Sektoren vermieden Langeweile durch aufgelockerte und gezielte Information.
Man hatte insbesondere ein komplettes System von Transportmöglichkeiten und Besucherwegen vorbereitet. Das »Telekanapee« trug den Ausstellungsgast vom Eingang zum Zentrum und gewährte einen ersten Einblick. Die »Monorail«, eine durch Stützen vom Boden abgehobene Einschienenbahn, verband die verschiedenen Sektoren miteinander und gestattete einen schnellen Gesamtüberblick, ohne die Fußgänger zu behindern – ein Vorteil, der dazu führte, daß dieses System in Montreal wiederverwendet wurde (Abb. 13). Durch die Ausstellungen selbst war jeweils ein schneller, zusammenfassender Rundgang und ein ausführlicher Weg zur genauen Betrachtung auch der Einzelheiten angelegt (Abb. 14).

In der Gruppe kleinerer integrierter Ausstellungen (Seite 41–64) wurden weitere Beispiele zusammengefaßt, die sich in ihrer Gestaltung ähnlich stark voneinander unterscheiden wie die Großausstellungen, obwohl die Bauten selbst vorwiegend aus vorgefertigten Montageteilen bestehen, meist Gerüstkonstruktionen aus Metall oder Holz, in die als Flächenelemente Tafeln aus Metall, Kunststoff, Holz, Glas oder auch Stoffbahnen gespannt sind. Selbst das Dach des IRI-Pavillons (Seite 48) setzt sich aus Montageteilen zusammen. Dieses Bauwerk hat mit dem Aluminiumpavillon in Hannover (Seite 44) nicht nur die Kühnheit der konstruktiven Form gemeinsam, sondern auch den Anspruch auf dauerhafte Repräsentation. Bei anderen Beispielen, auch bei der deutschen Industrieausstellung in Khartum (Seite 40) und selbstverständlich bei den Zelten von Kuhn (Seite 52), werden die Vorteile der Montagekonstruktion genutzt, die sich gerade für Wanderausstellungen anbietet, da sie schnellen Auf- und Abbau und außerdem formale Variationen erlaubt. Derartige Konstruktionen bewähren sich dann am meisten, wenn es gelingt, den Ausstellungsinhalt auf die umgebende Architektur abzustimmen. Das kann schon allein durch die Lichtführung geschehen. Mitunter bauen sich auch die inneren Ausstellungselemente nach ähnlichen Prinzipien auf wie die Außenkonstruktion (Seite 44, 52) oder die den Gerüstkonstruktionen eingefügten Tafelelemente werden zugleich zu Wänden und Ausstellungsträgern (Seite 56, 58). Selbstverständlich ist auch bei diesen Bauwerken an eine Lenkung der Besucher gedacht, am offensichtlichsten vielleicht bei Ionel Scheins kleinem französischen Holzpavillon in Paris (Seite 60).

Ausstellungen ohne eigenen außenarchitektonischen Rahmen (Seite 76–133) müssen sich in irgendeiner Weise mit der Architektur auseinandersetzen, in die sie hineingestellt werden. Nur in den seltensten Fällen läßt sich das Ausstellungsgebäude unmittelbar gestalterisch verwerten; häufig wird man sogar die vorgegebene Raumhülle zu

15. Demonstration with electric measuring instruments at the travelling exhibition "Medicine in USA", 1959–1960.

15. Demonstration einer Patientenuntersuchung mit elektrischen Meßgeräten auf der Wanderausstellung »Medizin in USA«, 1959 bis 1960.

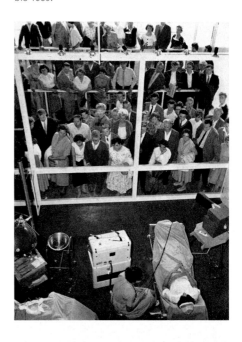

verbergen suchen, damit die Ausstellung eine in sich geschlossene Form erhält. An technischen Möglichkeiten zur Abschirmung gibt es Beleuchtungseffekte, die nur die Ausstellungselemente und -objekte anstrahlen und die umgebende Architektur nahezu zum Verschwinden bringen (Seite 98, 108, 110); Gerüstkonstruktionen und -systeme, die sich zu selbständigen Raumfolgen zusammenfügen (Seite 104, 122), wie Segel ausgespannte Zeltdecken (Seite 106) und schließlich umfangreiche Ein- und Umbauten. Die zuerst genannten Möglichkeiten haben den Vorteil des leichten Auf- und Abbaues, und da sie sich ohne Schwierigkeiten den verschiedensten räumlichen Gegebenheiten anpassen lassen, eignen sie sich besonders gut für Wanderausstellungen.

Mit aufwendigen eigenen Gehäusebauten arbeitet man hauptsächlich bei großen Ausstellungen internationalen Charakters, die in vorhandenen Messe- oder Ausstellungshallen untergebracht werden müssen, so bei den Mailänder Triennalen (Seite 76), bei der »Italia 61« in Turin (Seite 88) oder bei der Internationalen Verkehrsausstellung 1965 in München (Seite 64). Ausstellungen dieser Art sind in der Regel in Abteilungen aufgegliedert, als deren Träger meist die verschiedenen Nationen oder doch nationale Verbände und Organisationen fungieren. So ergibt sich hier – ähnlich wie bei den Länderpavillons der Weltausstellungen – die Möglichkeit, gewisse nationale Eigenarten zu entdecken. Beispielsweise verstehen sich die Italiener vortrefflich auf dynamisch-dramatische Effekte (Seite 72, 84, 114), Frankreich dagegen spielt im internationalen Ausstellungswesen kaum eine Rolle. Die Engländer wiederum haben eine Reihe von recht interessanten und praktikablen Systemen entwickelt (Seite 104, 108, 118) und neben den Skandinaviern (Seite 134) am ehesten zeitgenössische künstlerische Tendenzen wie Pop Art mit einbezogen (Seite 130). Einige finnische Beispiele (Seite 80, 82, 98) vereinen Einfachheit der Mittel mit phantasievoller Konzeption; interessant der Vergleich zweier finnischer Beiträge zum Thema Freizeit (Seite 80, 82) und eines gleichlautenden englischen Beispiels (Seite 76).
Die Gestalter der deutschen Lösungen, besonders die der Münchner Verkehrsausstellung (Seite 90, 94, 96), verwenden durchaus dynamische Akzente, ohne indessen allzu dramatische Effekte auszuspielen. Sie vergessen über dem Reiz der Schau nicht die Aufgabe der instruktiven Information, ohne langatmig oder ermüdend zu werden (Seite 86, 102, 112). Der Anteil, mit dem sich die USA an ausländischen Ausstellungen kulturpolitischer Themenstellung beteiligen, ist in den letzten Jahren stark zurückgegangen. Die wenigen Beispiele (Seite 124, 128) überzeugen jedoch immer noch durch die Perfektion des Programms wie der technischen und formalen Ausführung.
Die gestalterischen Mittel, die bei diesen größeren Ausstellungen in vorgegebenen Architekturgehäusen eingesetzt werden, gleichen weitgehend denen, die sich schon bei den integrierten Gesamtausstellungen beobachten ließen: auch hier der Zug zur Intensivierung des Dargebotenen und zur Aktivierung des Betrachters. Kaum eine größere Ausstellung verzichtet darauf, den Besucher scheinbar zwanglos von Raum zu Raum, von Akzent zu Akzent, von Objekt zu Objekt zu führen. Als Akzente dienen Projektionen, Vorführungen, bewegliche Modelle, Schaubilder und Spiegelungen.
Am einfallreichsten sind dabei die Italiener. Der Eingang zur 13. Triennale (Seite 72) ist eine ganze Komposition von Projektionen, Spiegelungen und Klangbildern. Bei einem anderen Beispiel, dem Olivetti-Beitrag zur »Italia 61« (Seite 84), läßt man das Ausstellungsmaterial am Besucher vorbeiziehen. Die Verwendung bestimmter, auch einfachster Materialien faßt selbst eine umfangreiche Ausstellung wie die Mailänder Schau »Vie d'acqua« (Seite 114) optisch zusammen. Große Sorgfalt wird ganz allgemein auf die Beleuchtung und Lichtführung gelegt. Dem Licht verdanken zu einem wesentlichen Teil die deutschen Beiträge zur Münchner Verkehrsausstellung ihre Wirkung. Die Finnen haben selbstleuchtende Tafelelemente entwickelt (Seite 98). Die Angelsachsen benutzen gerne Punktleuchten, die sich auf kostbare oder besonders diffizile und beachtenswerte Objekte konzentrieren (Seite 104, 108). Der gleichmäßig ausgeleuchtete Ausstellungsraum wird immer seltener (Seite 80, 102), aber auch hier sorgt die Anordnung der Ausstellungselemente für die notwendige, den Besucher anziehende Schwerpunktbildung. Hinsichtlich der Wegführung sei auf einige deutsche Beispiele hingewiesen (Seite 86, 112, 116). Hier galt es, besonders spröde und eigentlich nur grafisch darstellbare Inhalte in einem bestimmten Ablauf an den Besucher heranzutragen. Eine plastische Durchdringung und Auflockerung der Wandelemente, eine geschickte räumliche Disposition führte zum Erfolg. Praktische Vorführungen, sei es in einem Theaterraum, sei es in einem offenen Ausstellungsteil (Abb. 15), gehören zu den wichtigsten Charakteristika der amerikanischen Beispiele (Seite 124, 128).

Die folgende Gruppe von Ausstellungen (Seite 134–155) in gegebenen Räumen unterscheidet sich von der vorangegangenen einmal durch die geringeren Ausmaße der Beispiele, vor allem aber durch die Tatsache, daß sie von Industrieunternehmen und Firmenverbänden, nicht von öffentlichen Organisationen getragen werden. Alle diese

Ausstellungen bringen vorwiegend sachliche Information, verbinden sie aber geschickt mit der werbenden Repräsentation. Die eigenen Firmenprodukte werden jedoch nirgends plump in den Vordergrund geschoben. Gestalterisch gibt es gegenüber Ausstellungen mit »neutraler« Thematik kaum Unterschiede. Gewisse nationale Eigenheiten lassen sich auch hier beobachten, so die Vorliebe der Italiener für die dramatische Inszenierung (Seite 146, 148, 150), die einfallsreich die Geschichte des Erdöls erzählt oder durch eigenwillig gestaltete, leuchtende Schaukästen und Vitrinen den Besucher zur Aufmerksamkeit zwingt. Ein eindrucksvolles Firmenimage spiegeln Burtins Kugelkonstruktionen wider (Seite 140), während seine faszinierenden wissenschaftlichen Großmodelle (Seite 138) gerade durch den Verzicht auf die besondere Betonung des Auftraggebers eine starke propagandistische Wirkung erreichen. Sie können als besonders kühne und erschöpfende Synthese gegenwärtiger Erkenntnisse und Möglichkeiten der Wissenschaft, der Ausstellungstechnik und der bildenden Kunst (Op Art, Kinetik) gelten. Sehr bewußt bestimmen Elemente der Pop Art eine skandinavische Ausstellung (Seite 134), die auf diese Weise trockene Firmenhistorie witzig anschaulich macht. Sachlichere, doch keineswegs phantasielose Ausstellungen in bekannter Schweizer Qualität (Seite 142, 156) und die holländische Präsentation grafischer Kostbarkeiten (Seite 154) runden das Bild ab.

Was die Gestaltung angeht, so unterscheiden sich Messestände (Seite 156–187) größeren Ausmaßes kaum von kleineren Firmenausstellungen. Bei den Ausstellungen überwiegt vielleicht die informatorisch-repräsentative Absicht gegenüber der kommerziell-repräsentativen, außerdem sind sie selbständigere Gebilde, während Messestände sich zu Blöcken und Ketten aneinanderreihen. Im vergangenen Jahrzehnt erwiesen sich die auf Moduleinheiten basierenden Montagesysteme – wie sie von fortschrittlichen Unternehmen, etwa der Braun AG (Abb. 16), eingeführt worden waren – als so erfolgreich, daß derartige Rasterstände heute allgemein üblich sind. Natürlich entsteht dadurch die Gefahr einer gewissen Eintönigkeit, der man im einzelnen nur durch akzentuierende und qualitative Nuancierungen entgehen kann, es sei denn, man hat den Mut und die Möglichkeit, sich freizumachen von der allerdings so vorteilhaften und raumausnutzenden Rasterkonstruktion. Manche Messen wie die Kölner Möbelmesse 1966 sind bereits zu festen Einheitsständen übergegangen; andere wie die Automobilausstellungen können auf eine betonte Standgestaltung so gut wie ganz verzichten, da ihre Ausstellungsobjekte selbst genügend Attraktivität besitzen. Es läßt sich überhaupt feststellen, daß Messestände um so einfacher und zurückhaltender bleiben können, je ausgeprägter die Exponate an sich sind.

Das Programm eines normalen Messestandes liegt fest (Abb. 17). Seine Außenseiten, seine Randzonen werden für werbende Ausstellungen benutzt; sie umgeben einen Kern, der der intensiveren Information vorbehalten bleibt und häufig auch abgeschlossene Räume für interne Verhandlungen enthält. Situation und Proportion der einzelnen Standteile hängen von Größe und Lage des Gesamtstandes ab, der zum Beispiel nach einer oder nach mehreren oder gar nach allen Seiten offen sein kann beziehungsweise auf einer oder mehreren Seiten an Nachbarstände anschließt. Je größer der Stand, desto deutlicher lassen sich die Funktionen »Ausstellung – Information – Verhandlung« voneinander trennen, und desto leichter können durch zentral herausgestellte neue Erzeugnisse Schwerpunkte gesetzt werden (Seite 162). Ferner beeinflußt auch die Art der Messe die Standkonzeption: Fachmessen benötigen mehr Verhandlungs- und weniger Ausstellungsraum; Messen, die auch einem allgemeinen Publikum zugänglich sind, betonen stärker Ausstellungs- und Vorführungsmöglichkeiten. Schon aus diesen grundsätzlichen Erwägungen ergibt sich eine Fülle von Variationsmöglichkeiten, auch wenn man die gebräuchliche Rasterkonzeption beibehält und modische Übertreibungen vermeidet.

Bei Messeständen stellt sich ebenfalls recht häufig das Problem, den Stand gegen die Hallenarchitektur abzuschirmen. Neben den üblichen horizontalen Bespannungen mit Textilbahnen oder Kunststoffolien, die allerdings lüftungstechnisch nicht ideal sind, werden am häufigsten Gitterdecken aus hochkant gestellten Brettern (Seite 162) oder Metallkonstruktionen verwendet. Oft bleiben alle oder auch nur einzelne Gitterfelder nach oben offen, man begnügt sich um des Vorteils ausreichender Belüftung willen mit einer lediglich optischen Begrenzung. Doch gibt es auch Zwischenlösungen, die eine verhältnismäßig geschlossene Deckenzone bei günstigeren Lüftungsverhältnissen bieten. Das sind einmal die Stab-Zelt-Konstruktionen (Seite 170), bei denen zwischen sattelförmig gespannten Bahnen Lüftungsschlitze freibleiben, oder Beispiele mit rhythmisch wechselnden Deckenfeldern und originell gestalteten Beleuchtungselementen (Seite 164), die dem ganzen Stand ein unverwechselbares Gepräge geben. Man hat ferner eine Reihe von Verfahren entwickelt, mit deren Hilfe – unter Verwendung vorgefertigter Teile und bei verhältnismäßig geringem technischem Aufwand – ganze Deckengewölbe eingezogen (Seite 160) oder von oben beleuchtete Deckenprismen (Seite 168) montiert werden können. Weitere Möglichkeiten in dieser Richtung eröffnet das Kokonspritzverfahren (Seite 204).

Wenn man sich vom Rechteckraster freimacht und, unter Umständen auf ein Mehr an Grundfläche verzichtend, dem Stand einen runden, ovalen oder übereck gestellten Grundriß gibt (Seite 176, 182, 184), hebt er sich, selbst ein Akzent, von den umgebenden Standreihen ab. Die sinnvolle Präsentation des Ausstellungsmaterials mag allerdings bei solchen freieren Grundrissen auf gewisse Schwierigkeiten stoßen, wenn der verhältnismäßig große Standkern – als Raum für Verhandlungen oder für eine besonders effektvolle Repräsentation – die sachliche Information etwas an den Rand rückt.

Bei Rechteckständen auch kleineren Ausmaßes kommt es darauf an, über einer zweckmäßigen Grundrißdisposition den konstruktiven Elementen eine individuelle Wirkung abzugewinnen. Diese Konstruktionsglieder sind, von technischen Details abgesehen, einander in den meisten Fällen recht ähnlich: Sie bestehen normalerweise aus einem Gerüst, in oder auf das Platten als Ausstellungsträger und Wandstücke montiert werden (Abb. 18). Metallgerüste wirken besonders leicht und transparent und betonen die technische Präzision. Viele Entwerfer bevorzugen aber auch für Standgerüste das kompaktere und wärmere Holz, genauso wie sie auf die massive Wandplatte verzichten, wenn es darum geht, Raumtrennungen zwar anzudeuten, aber doch den Durchblick über die ganze Ausstellungsfläche zu erhalten. Lockere Textilien, Holzstabgewebe, Metallgitter oder Lattenwände eignen sich dafür besser. Im einzelnen bleibt es der Phantasie des Gestalters überlassen, durch besondere Einfälle den werbenden Effekt eines Messestandes noch zu steigern – durch ein grafisches Signum (Seite 184), eine Gläserwand (Seite 180) oder Ausstellungsgestelle, die in ihrer Form die Erzeugnisse des Ausstellers symbolisieren (Seite 166).

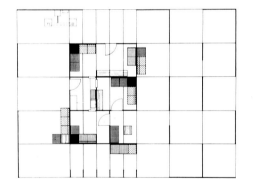

17. Plan of a Fair Stand of the Wiggins Teape Group, London, 1961, based on a square module system.
18. View of the Wiggins Teape exhibition stand, which is open on all sides. Central core with interview booths, roofed by fabric. Design: Glahé Design Group. Construction: Glahé Workshops, Cologne.

17. Grundriß des Messestandes für The Wiggins Teape Group, London 1961, auf einem quadratischen Rastersystem.
18. Ansicht des sich nach allen Seiten öffnenden Ausstellungsstandes der Wiggings Teape Group. Geschlossener Standkern mit Besprechungsräumen, durch eine Deckenbespannung überdacht. Entwurf: Glahé Design Group; Ausführung: Glahé Kölner Werkstätten.

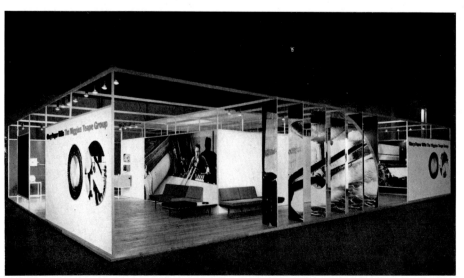

Demontable Konstruktionen und leicht zu transportierende Exponatträger für Wanderausstellungen bilden die letzte Gruppe (Seite 188–205). Einige vielseitig verwendbare Konstruktionsprinzipien und Ausstellungssysteme sind bereits genannt worden, so die Raumkonstruktionen von Kuhn und die im Kokonspritzverfahren hergestellten Deckenelemente von Zerning. Für kleinere Ausstellungsobjekte und Dokumente beliebiger Art erweisen sich Kuppelvitrinen als gute Lösung (Seite 188). Zerlegbare Elemente, die sich zu Vitrinengestellen und Flächenfolgen zusammenbauen lassen, ermöglichen insbesondere für Wanderausstellungen räumlich interessante Konzeptionen (Seite 196, 198). Die Beleuchtungsanlagen gehören bei den meisten dieser Systeme mit zu den Aufbauteilen. Auch für reine Tafelsysteme gibt es eine Reihe von neuen Beispielen. Sie werden zusammengehalten durch einfache Ständer (Seite 202), durch Verbindungsstücke (Seite 190) oder durch Nuten-Bolzenverbindungen (Seite 200), mit denen sie auch zu Raumkörpern zusammengefügt werden können.

Am Ende dieser Reihe stehen zwei Ausstellungssysteme, die sich aus Kuben aufbauen. Die Kuben sind jeweils zusammenfaltbar und bestehen einmal aus Metallgestängen mit entsprechenden Verbindungsstücken (Seite 194) und zum anderen aus einer durch Scharniere und Steckbolzen zusammengehaltenen Holzleistenkonstruktion (Seite 192). In beiden Fällen können an den Gestellen Platten aus den verschiedensten Materialien befestigt und aus den Kuben auch umfangreiche räumliche Ausstellungsaufbauten entwickelt werden.

Die Beispiele dieser Materialsammlung reichen vom Großen zum Kleinen. Bei ihrer Auswahl wurde auch der Versuch unternommen, gewisse allgemeinere Tendenzen sichtbar werden zu lassen, die keineswegs zufällig mit der Entwicklung auf anderen Gestaltungsgebieten zusammenhängen. Man braucht dabei nicht nur an Beziehungen zur bildenden Kunst zu denken. Pop-Art-Gags eignen sich offensichtlich nur für bestimmte Ausstellungsthemen und bleiben deshalb verhältnismäßig selten – denn wer hat schon Mut zur Selbstironie? Während die reine Op Art wohl zu diffizil für die werbende Lautstärke der Ausstellungsgestaltung ist, spürt man häufiger den Einfluß der kinetischen Kunst in den verschiedenartigen Bestrebungen, auch Ausstellungen Bewegungsimpulse zu geben.

Enger sind die Verbindungen zu den Bereichen der angewandten Formgebung, zur permanenten Architektur, zum Industrial Design. Wie auf diesen Gebieten reichen auch im Ausstellungsbau die Anfänge einer völlig neuen Auffassung in die zwanziger Jahre zurück. Nach 1945 erfolgte der in älteren Untersuchungen zu diesem Thema festgehaltene Durchbruch und die Konsolidierung der neuen Ideen – ein Prozeß, der nicht ganz frei von der Gefahr der Dogmatisierung verlief, wie die allzu schematischen Rasterstrukturen im Hochbau und in den Ausstellungsbauten beweisen. In den letzten Jahren mag es keine entscheidenden revolutionären Taten mehr gegeben haben, dafür aber ein ständiges Differenzieren und Intensivieren. Als wesentliches Mittel nicht nur in der Ausstellungsgestaltung hat sich dabei die Dynamisierung (Abb. 19–22) erwiesen, die der Form Leben und Bewegung verleiht, ganz gleich, welche Wege man im einzelnen beschreitet. Es fehlt aber auch nicht an Übertreibungen, die warnend wirken, wenn etwa die Dynamisierung zum billigen Effekt führt und aus der Ausstellung eine Show wird.

19. 'Dynamizing' the exhibits. The "Anti-Machine" by Jean Tinguely which solely produces a pattern of motions (Swiss National Exhibition, Lausanne, 1964).
20. 'Dynamizing' by audio-visual means: Subdivision of a film screen into zones, with simultaneous displays of coloured and black/white projections, underlined by music or spoken words (Czechoslovak Pavilion at the Expo '67, Montreal; design: Josef Svoboda).
21. 'Dynamizing' the display: Display panels fastened to diagonally placed sliding rails move past the visitors in continuous sequence (Olivetti Exhibition at the "Italia 61", Turin. Design: Franco Albini and Egidio Bonfante).

19. Dynamisierung des Ausstellungsobjektes: Die »Anti-Maschine« von Jean Tinguely, die nichts als reines Bewegungsspiel produziert (Schweizerische Landesausstellung 1964, Lausanne).
20. Dynamisierung durch audio-visuelle Mittel: Auflösung einer Filmfläche in Teilbereiche, auf der, untermalt durch Musik oder gesprochene Worte, gleichzeitig farbige und schwarzweiße Projektionen stattfinden (Tschechoslowakischer Pavillon auf der Expo '67, Montreal; Entwurf: Josef Svoboda).
21. Dynamisierung der Ausstellungsgestaltung: Schautafeln, an diagonal verlaufenden Gleitschienen befestigt, ziehen in endloser Folge an den Besuchern vorbei (Olivetti-Ausstellung auf der »Italia 61« in Turin; Gestaltung: Franco Albini und Egidio Bonfante).

22. 'Dynamizing' effects obtained by blurring the spatial boundaries; by escalators carrying a steady stream of visitors; by the 'to-and-fro' of the public inside and outside the enclosed zones (U.S. Pavilion, Expo '67, Montreal).

22. Dynamisierung durch Verwischen der Raumgrenzen, durch das stete Fließen der Besucherkette auf den Rolltreppen, durch das Hin- und Herfluten des Ausstellungspublikums innerhalb und außerhalb der geschlossenen Zonen (US-Pavillon auf der Expo '67 in Montreal).

United States Pavilion at the Expo '67

World Exhibition, Montreal, 1967
Architects: R. Buckminster Fuller,
Fuller & Sadao, Inc., Geometrics Inc.,
Cambridge Seven Associates, Inc.,
Cambridge, Mass.

The space frame of the transparent, seemingly weightless "three-quarter sphere" dome of the United States Pavilion, a geodesic dome structure of 250 ft. diameter, covered a vast space. The impression of grandeur was not impaired by the indoor equipment which included exhibit platforms, staircase towers and escalators. The light-weight structure consisted of a double-layer frame composed of welded steel pipes whose thickness varied with the loads in the structure. The structure was enclosed by 1900 transparent moulded and framed acrylic panels which, for glare and sun protection purposes, were given a green bronze tint gradually intensified from bottom to top. On seven levels, the achievements of the United States in the spheres of folk art, contemporary painting, film and space travel were displayed informatively and with witty self-criticism.

US-Pavillon der Expo '67

Weltausstellung Montreal, 1967
Architekten: R. Buckminster Fuller,
Fuller & Sadao, Inc., Geometrics Inc.,
Cambridge Seven Associates, Inc.,
Cambridge, Mass.

Die transparente, scheinbar schwerelose Dreiviertelkugel, eine geodätische Kuppelkonstruktion von 76 m Durchmesser, umhüllte mit ihrem Stabwerk einen riesenhaften Innenraum, der auch durch die hineingestellten Ausstellungs-Plattformen, Treppentürme und Rolltreppen nicht an großzügiger Wirkung verlor. Die Leichtgewicht-Konstruktion bestand aus einem doppelschichtigen Tragwerk aus verschweißten Stahlrohren. In das Stabwerk waren als Raumabschluß 1900 Kugelkappen aus durchsichtigem Kunststoff eingesetzt, die als Blend- und Sonnenschutz eine nach oben hin stärker werdende bronzegrüne Tönung erhielten. Auf sieben Ebenen wurden Amerikas Leistungen auf den Gebieten der Volkskunst, der zeitgenössischen Malerei, des Films und der Raumfahrt in ebenso informativer wie witzig-ironischer Weise demonstriert.

1. At night, the filigree pattern of the space
frame of the 200 ft. high dome was clearly apparent. The triangular system of the outer layer
members and the hexagons of the inner layer
frame members were inter-penetrating. The
platforms, placed on different levels, as well as
the staircase and lift towers gave the appearance of large sculptures within the dome. The
brighter hexagons were obtained by the provision of triangular sunshades made of alumini-
um-coated fabrics. The opening and closing of
these sunshades was controlled by a program
tape, governed by the position of the sun.
2. The gradually intensified green bronze tint
of the transparent acrylic panels reduced the
light transmission from 93 per cent at the bottom to 45 per cent at the top.
3, 4. Tabs are inserted into the triangular frame
of the outer layer. The hexagons of the inner
layer are linked with the triangles of the outer
layer by inclined web members. The hubs are
of cast steel. Total weight of the structure is 720
tons.

1. Bei Nacht trat die filigrane Stabkonstruktion
der 61 m hohen Kugel deutlich in Erscheinung:
Das Dreiecksystem der äußeren Gitterstruktur
und die Hexagone der innenliegenden Stäbe
durchdrangen sich. Die verschieden hohen
Plattformen und Treppen- bzw. Fahrstuhltürme
wirkten wie eine Großplastik im Innern der
Hülle. Die helleren Sechsecke entstanden durch
das Ausspannen von dreieckigen Sonnen-
schutzsegeln aus aluminiumbeschichtetem
Stoff. Sie öffneten und schlossen sich lochband-
gesteuert je nach dem Sonnenstand.
2. Die zunehmende bronzegrüne Färbung der
durchsichtigen Kunststoff-Kugelschalen redu-
zierte die Lichtdurchlässigkeit von 93% am Boden auf 45% am Scheitel.
3, 4. Schwenktore, in das äußere Dreiecksgitter
eingepaßt; die innenliegenden Sechsecke
durch schräge Verbindungsstäbe mit den
außenliegenden Dreiecken verbunden. Knoten-
punkte aus Gußstahl. Gewicht der Gesamtkonstruktion 720 tons.

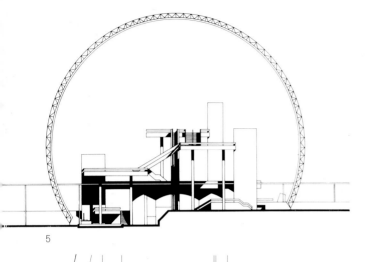

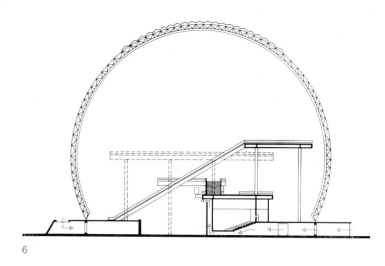

5

6

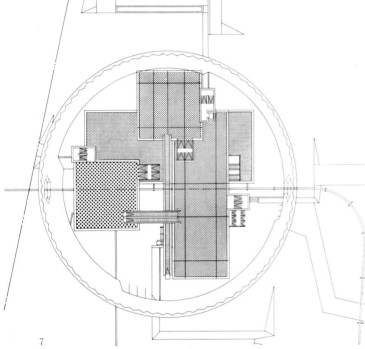

7

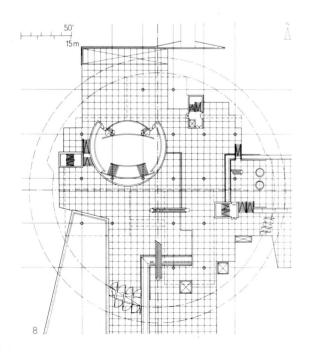

8

5. Indoor equipment, seen from the south.

6. Cross-section in the north-south direction, with the 123 ft. long escalator leading to the highest platform.

7. Plan with the four upper platform levels.

8. Plan with the three lower platform levels.

9. In spite of the manifold spatial interpenetrations and intersections of platforms, ramps and display boards (this photograph shows a view from the historic section upwards to the exhibition of contemporary paintings displayed on high, narrow wall panels), the dome was impressive from every vantage point. The dynamic effect was reinforced by the escalators and the 'Minirail' system which provided local transportation through the Pavilion.

10. Almost playfully, space travel was displayed on the highest platform. The dominant feature under the spacious dome was provided by the three orange-white striped parachutes of the Apollo capsule.

11. Instead of pedagogic pedantry, wit and self-deprecation were the dominating features. The section entitled "The American Spirit" contained selected samples of folk art: branding irons of cowboys, sprouting like flowers; guitars of pop singers, and a tower of home-made dolls.

12. In the "Film" section, Hollywood is gaily debunked: Among film stills Ben Hur's Roman chariot of 1925, Charlie Chaplin's garbage bin, and Greta Garbo's golden bed.

5. Ansicht der Pavilloneinbauten von Süden.

6. Schnitt in Nord-Süd-Richtung mit der 37,5 m langen Rolltreppe zur obersten Plattform.

7. Grundriß mit den vier oberen Plattformebenen.

8. Grundriß mit den drei unteren Ebenen.

9. Trotz vielfältiger räumlicher Durchdringungen und Überschneidungen von Plattformen, Schrägrampen und Ausstellungstafeln (hier ein Blick aus der historischen Abteilung hinauf zur Ausstellung zeitgenössischer Malerei, auf hohen schmalen Wänden) war die Kugelhülle von jedem Standpunkt aus erlebbar. Rolltreppen und die quer durch den Pavillon fahrende Minirail-Einschienenbahn verstärkten den dynamischen Effekt.

10. Fast spielerisch präsentierte sich die Raumfahrtschau auf der obersten Plattform. Stärkster Akzent unter der weiträumigen Kuppel waren die drei orange-weiß gestreiften Fallschirme der Apollokapsel.

11. Statt lehrhaften Ernstes dominierten Witz und Selbstironie. Die Abteilung »Der amerikanische Geist« operierte mit ausgesuchten Volkskunst-Beispielen: Brenneisen von Cowboys, wie Blumen sprießend, Gitarren der Volkssänger und ein Turm aus selbstgemachten Puppen.

12. Im Sektor »Film« heitere Entmythologisierung Hollywoods: zwischen Filmbildern Greta Garbos goldenes Bett, Ben Hurs römischer Wagen von 1925 und Charlie Chaplins Mülltonne.

9

10

11

12

German Pavilion at the Expo '67

World Exhibition, Montreal, 1967
Architects: Rolf Gutbrod and Frei Otto,
Stuttgart

A tract of approximately 86,000 sq.ft. was converted by freely developed terraces and platforms into an "exhibition landscape" in which the visitors followed a spiral path. The whole tract was covered by a gigantic irregularly shaped tent, consisting of a pre-stressed inversely curved cable net spanned over eight tubular steel masts and three low-level restraint points. The tensile forces were transmitted to the concrete anchor blocks by means of 30 edge cables. Suspended from this cable net was a translucent membrane of PVC-coated polyester fabric. Inside, the combination of the tent system with the built-in platforms (free-standing steel structures supported by steel columns) was not regarded as wholly felicitous. The exhibition seemed liable to fall apart, and the space inside the tent did not seem to be sufficiently activated.

Deutscher Pavillon der Expo '67

Weltausstellung Montreal, 1967
Architekten: Rolf Gutbrod und Frei Otto,
Stuttgart

Rund 8000 m² Grundfläche, die durch muldenförmige Vertiefungen und unterschiedlich hohe Plattformen in eine spiralförmig zu durchwandernde »Ausstellungslandschaft« verwandelt waren, wurden von einem riesigen, frei geformten Zeltdach überspannt. Es bestand aus einem sattelförmig gekrümmten, vorgespannten Seilnetz, das über acht Stahlrohrmaste und drei tiefliegende Abspannpunkte geführt war. Dreißig Randseile leiteten die Zugkräfte in Betonanker ab. Unter das Netztragwerk war mit etwa 50 cm Abstand eine Dachhaut aus PVC-beschichtetem Polyestergewebe gehängt. Im Inneren wurde die Kombination von Zeltkonstruktion und eingebauten Plattformen (Raumfachwerke aus Stahlblechprofilen auf Stahlstützen) nicht überall als glücklich empfunden: Die Ausstellung drohte zu zerfließen und konnte den Zeltraum nicht genügend aktivieren.

1. View from the west, with the bridge leading to the main entrance and the projection of the tent above the small island in the lagoon. Eight steel masts, ranging in height from 46 to 125 ft.; greatest width of the tent roof 426×328 ft. The structure was designed, computed, manufactured and erected within no more than 14 months. Below the part of the tent in the foreground is the auditorium which is covered by wood lattice shells.

2. Close-up. The $1/2''$ thick steel cables of the load-bearing net formed a mesh of 1'8'' side length. On the right, a $2^1/_8''$ thick edge cable which served to transmit the tensile forces to one of the anchor points. In the cable net, the transoms with the turnbuckles on which the roof skin was attached.

3. Aerial photograph of the building site. At the masts and low-level restraint points are the "eyes", covered for lighting purposes with transparent PVC foil, at which cable loops served to transmit the tensile forces. The narrow projection of the tent, seen on top, covered the entrance to the exhibition island which was added later.

4. View at night.

1. Ansicht von Westen mit der Brücke zum Haupteingang und der Zeltzunge über der kleinen Laguneninsel. Acht Stahlmasten von 14 bis 38 m Höhe; größte Ausdehnung des Zeltdachs 130×100 m. Entwurf, Berechnung, Herstellung und Montage in nur 14 Monaten. Unter dem Zeltteil im Vordergrund das mit Lattenkuppeln überwölbte Auditorium.

2. Detailansicht. Die 12 mm starken Stahlseile des tragenden Seilnetzes bildeten rautenförmige Maschen von etwa 50 cm Seitenlänge. Rechts ein 54 mm starkes Randseil, das die Zugkräfte auf einen der Ankerblöcke ableitete. Im Seilnetz die Traversen mit den Spannschlössern zum Befestigen der Dachhaut.

3. Luftansicht des Bauplatzes. An den Masten und tiefliegenden Abspannpunkten die zur Belichtung mit glasklarer PVC-Folie abgedeckten »Augen«, an denen schlaufenförmige Seile die Zugkräfte ableiteten. Die schmale Zeltzunge oben überspannte den Zugang zur späteren Ausstellungsinsel.

4. Nachtansicht.

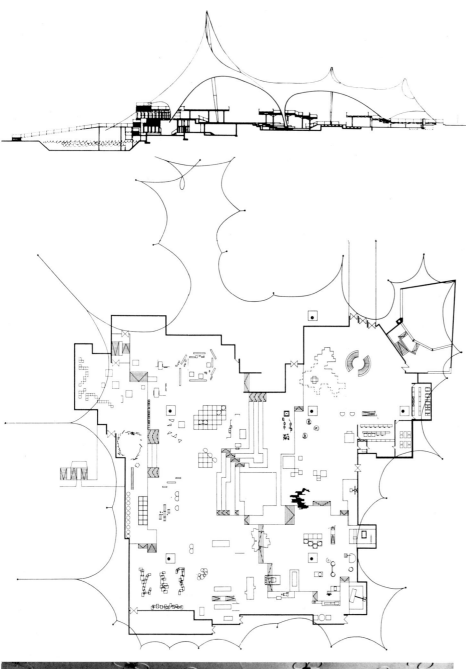

5, 6. Section and plan. The terrace-shaped platforms of the "exhibition landscape" were arranged in steps of 2 ft. or so. In the centre, the library and a pool of water.

7. The roof membrane was suspended, in portions ranging from 30 to 50 sq. ft., from the open cable net by means of spring steel cloverleaves. In this way, the wind and snow loads were transmitted to the cable net.

8. One of the masts with the transparent "eye" which was tensioned by a steel cable loop.

5, 6. Schnitt und Grundriß. Die terrassenartigen Plattformen der »Ausstellungslandschaft« waren in Höhensprüngen von 60 cm gestuft. Im Zentrum die Bibliothek und das Wasserbecken.

7. Jeweils 3 bis 5 m² der untergehängten Dachhaut waren mit kleeblattförmigen Federtellern am freiliegenden Seilnetz befestigt. Dadurch wurden aus Wind- und Schneebelastung resultierende Kräfte auf die Seilkonstruktion abgeleitet.

8. Einer der Masten mit dem durchsichtigen »Auge«, das durch ein schlaufenförmiges Stahlseil abgespannt war.

9. Interior. View of the centre with the terraced library. In the pool of water the concrete block for one of the three low-level anchor points to which the roof was lowered. However, the built-in platforms tended to impair the integral space effect and to break up the area horizontally so that the impression of a somewhat exaggerated fragmentation of the exhibition was strengthened.

9. Innenansicht. Blick auf das Zentrum mit der stufenweise ansteigenden Bibliothek. Im Wasserbecken der betonierte Zuganker für einen der drei tiefliegenden Abspannpunkte, zu dem das Zeltdach heruntergezogen war. Die eingebauten Plattformen schmälerten allerdings die großzügige räumliche Wirkung und verstärkten noch als horizontale Zäsur den etwas kleinteiligen Eindruck des Ausstellungsarrangements.

Spanish Pavilion

World's Fair, New York, 1965
Architect: Javier Carvajal, Madrid

The critics were united in regarding this pavilion as one of the outstanding architectural features of the entire World's Fair. Amid the ballyhoo of the World's Fair, this pavilion was almost alone in reflecting the pursuit of architectural quality which had also been predominant at the Brussels Exhibition of 1958. The design was the result of a competition. Shortage of time and the program requirement of easy demountability called for a simple basic structure so that it was decided to adopt a steel structure from which prefabricated light-weight concrete panels were suspended. Other materials included floors of ceramic tiles, smoked glass windows, wooden ceilings, and plenty of aluminium for light fittings, claddings and showcases. Although, in regard to materials and design, the architect made the most of the possibilities offered by contemporary building construction, he succeeded in creating a specifically Spanish atmosphere.

Spanischer Pavillon

World's Fair, New York, 1965
Architekt: Javier Carvajal, Madrid

Die Kritik war sich in der Beurteilung dieses Pavillons als der wesentlichsten architektonischen Leistung auf der ganzen Weltausstellung einig. Im lauten Schaugeschäft der World's Fair vertrat er beinahe einsam das Bemühen um die baukünstlerische und auch nationale Repräsentation, wie sie 1958 in Brüssel noch vorgeherrscht hatte. Der Bau war das Ergebnis eines Wettbewerbs. Zeitmangel und die Forderung nach Demontierbarkeit bedingten eine einfache Grundkonstruktion, so daß man sich für ein Stahlgerüst mit vorgehängten Leichtbetonplatten entschloß, dazu Plattenböden, farbige Glaswände, Holzdecken und viel Aluminium. Obwohl der Architekt die Möglichkeiten des modernen Bauens nutzte, gelang es ihm, eine spezifisch spanische Atmosphäre zu schaffen.

1. Arts and Crafts section on the upper floor. Daylight access to the exhibition rooms was through glass panels around the patios whilst artificial lighting was provided by spotlights mounted in the square-shaped aluminium tubes suspended from the ceiling. The flooring consisted of conventional ceramic tiles, the ceiling of wooden blocks, combined in sets of four.
2. The light-weight concrete panels suspended from the load-bearing steel structure formed a sculptured texture for the windowless upper floor.
3. View across one of the patios. Above the aluminium-clad ground floor (right) is the glazed metal grill of the top floor exhibition hall.
4, 5. Plans of ground floor and upper floor. Key: 1 Entrance, 2 Patio, 3 Modern Arts, 4 Old Masters, 5 Manager, 6 Information, 7 Technical premises with electric switchboard and air conditioning plant, 8 Restaurant, 9 Kitchen, 10 Bazaar, 11 Lecture room, 12 Stage, 13 Bar, 14 Model house, 15 Industrial museum, 16 Books, 17 Arts and crafts.

1. Kunsthandwerkliche Abteilung im Obergeschoß. In den Ausstellungsräumen erfolgte die natürliche Beleuchtung durch Glaswände von den Innenhöfen her, die künstliche durch Punktstrahler in den von der Decke hängenden Blöcken aus Aluminium-Vierkantrohren. Der Boden bestand aus traditionellen Keramikplatten, die Decke aus in Vierergruppen zusammengefaßten Kiefernholzblöcken.
2. Der geschlossene Block des Obergeschosses, an dem die vor die tragende Stahlkonstruktion gehängten Leichtbetonplatten eine plastische Textur bildeten.
3. Blick aus einem Innenhof. Über dem rechts mit Aluminiumplatten verkleideten Erdgeschoß die verglaste Metallgitterwand der Ausstellungshalle im Obergeschoß
4, 5. Grundriß Erdgeschoß und Obergeschoß. Legende: 1 Eingang, 2 Patio, 3 Moderne Kunst, 4 Alte Meister, 5 Direktion, 6 Information, 7 Technische Räume (Elektrozentrale und Klimaanlage), 8 Restaurants, 9 Küche, 10 Bazar, 11 Auditorium, 12 Bühne, 13 Bar, 14 Musterhaus, 15 Industriemuseum, 16 Bücher, 17 Kunsthandwerk.

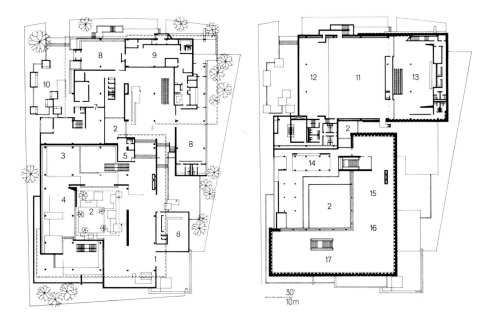

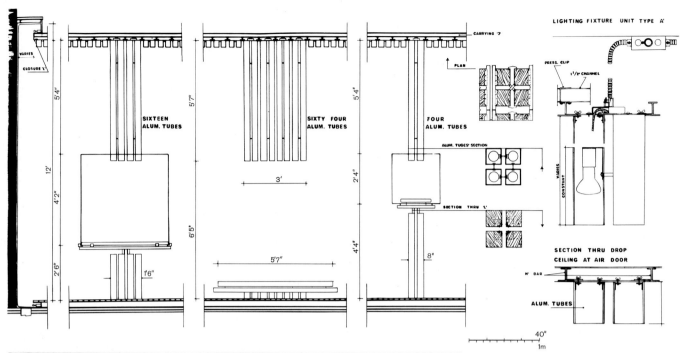

SIXTEEN ALUM. TUBES

SIXTY FOUR ALUM. TUBES

FOUR ALUM. TUBES

LIGHTING FIXTURE UNIT TYPE 'A'

PLAN

ALUM. TUBES' SECTION

SECTION THRU 'L'

PRESS. CLIP

1 1/2" CHANNEL

SECTION THRU DROP CEILING AT AIR DOOR

H' BAR

ALUM. TUBES

40"
1m

6. Sections and structural details of ceiling, showcases and light fittings.
7. Interior of upper floor. In the industrial section, too, the showcases were placed on sets of aluminium tubes, of a size matching that of the fittings. In the background, an inside view of the 'celosia' grill.
8. The wooden block ceiling above the Arts and Crafts section was reminiscent of the carved ceilings in the sitting rooms of many Spanish houses. Light fittings and showcase supports were organically developed from the design of the ceiling.
9. Showcase in a ground floor exhibition room where even the ceiling consisted of suspended square-shaped aluminium tubes.

6. Schnitte und Konstruktionsdetails von Decke, Vitrinen und Beleuchtung.
7. Die Gitterwand von innen. Auch in der Industrieabteilung ruhten die Vitrinen auf Blöcken aus Aluminiumrohren, die in ihren Dimensionen den Beleuchtungskörpern entsprachen.
8. Die Holzblockdecke über der kunsthandwerklichen Abteilung erinnert an die geschnitzten Zimmerdecken in manchen spanischen Wohnhäusern. Beleuchtungskörper und Vitrinensockel entwickelten sich organisch aus der Deckenkonstruktion.
9. Vitrine in einem Ausstellungsraum des Erdgeschosses, in dem auch die Decke aus abgehängten Aluminium-Vierkantrohren bestand.

1

The Swiss Way

Swiss National Exhibition,
Lausanne, 1964
Architectural Bureau of the Lausanne
Exposition; Chief Architect:
Alberto Camenzind, Lausanne
Associates: G. Cocchi and B. Meuwly

Weg der Schweiz

Schweizerische Landesausstellung,
Lausanne, 1964
Architekturbüro der Expo; Chefarchitekt:
Alberto Camenzind, Lausanne
Mitarbeiter: G. Cocchi and B. Meuwly

Thematically, architecturally and topographically, this sector represented the core of the exhibition. In its six sub-sections, it dealt with specifically Helvetian themes of the past, continuing with themes from present-day life, and concluding with indications of the problems with which Switzerland will be confronted tomorrow. Among the display aids were concrete and stylised presentations, short films, wood and stone, light and water, colours and shapes. The wooden structure of the tent-like groups of pavilions, intersected at two points by covered walkways, rested on concrete foundations and consisted of a system of joists of up to nearly 100 ft. length, spaced at 4 ft. centres. The roofing, which also served as a wall and partly even as a load-bearing structure for the exhibits, consisted of a polyester-reinforced PVC foil.

Dieser Teil war thematisch, architektonisch und topografisch das Kernstück der Schweizerischen Landesausstellung. Er befaßte sich in insgesamt sechs Abteilungen zunächst mit speziell helvetischen Themen der Vergangenheit, dann mit dem täglichen Leben des Landes von heute und schließlich mit dem Aufzeigen der Zukunftsprobleme für die Schweiz. Gestaltungsmittel waren konkrete und stilisierte Darstellungen, Kurzfilme, Holz und Stein, Licht und Wasser, Farben und Formen. Die auf Betonfundamenten ruhende Holzkonstruktion der zeltartigen Pavillongruppen, zweimal durch Verkehrswege kreuzende, überdachte Stege unterbrochen, bestand aus einem System bis zu 30 m langer Binder mit einem Achsabstand von 1,20 m. Als Dachhaut, die darüber hinaus Wandfunktion hatte und teilweise auch tragendes Element für die Ausstellungsobjekte war, diente eine mit Polyestergewebe verstärkte PVC-Folie.

2

3

1. Nocturnal view of the group of pavilions at the north end of the exhibition.
2. Within the Maladière Roundabout in the foreground of this picture is the north entrance to the exhibition. In the top central part of the picture is the monorail which visitors can use after leaving the open-air exhibition entitled "A day in Switzerland".
3. One of the groups of pavilions. The photograph clearly shows the load-bearing joists which have a web varying in height between 40 and 120 cm (1′4″ to 4′). Buckling was prevented by metal wind bracing, the lateral wind forces were absorbed by box girders at the gable ends which were additionally secured by steel cables in the roofs.
4. Interior of one of the tent pavilions. Wooden display troughs suspended from the ceiling showed typically Swiss industrial products.
5. From pedestrian bridges, visitors were able to study problems of traffic and transport.
6. A section of the parallelogram of tubular steel which, with its display of 500 ensigns showing the coats of arms of Swiss cantons and towns, was the symbolic centre of Sector 1 of the exhibition.

1. Nachtaufnahme der am Nordende gelegenen Pavillongruppe.
2. Im Vordergrund des Luftbildes der Nordeingang zur Ausstellung innerhalb des Verkehrskreisels Maladière, in der oberen Bildmitte das Monorail nach Verlassen des Ausstellungsfreigeländes »Ein Tag in der Schweiz«.

3. Eine der Pavillongruppen. Deutlich erkennbar sind die tragenden Binder, deren Steghöhe zwischen 40 und 120 cm variierte. Metallene Windverbände bewahrten vor dem Ausknicken, die seitlichen Windkräfte wurden durch Kastenträger in den Giebelfronten aufgenommen, die durch Stahlkabel in den Dachflächen zusätzlich gesichert waren.
4. Blick in einen Zeltpavillon. Von der Decke hingen hölzerne Ausstellungsträger mit typisch schweizerischen Industrieerzeugnissen.
5. Von Fußgängerbrücken aus orientierten sich hier die Besucher über Fragen des Verkehrs.
6. Ausschnitt aus dem Stahlrohrparallelogramm, das mit seinen fünfhundert Wappenfähnchen das Wahrzeichen des »Platzes der Kantone und Gemeinden« war.

4

5

6

Clothing and Jewellery

Swiss National Exhibition,
Lausanne, 1964
Architect: Tito Carloni, Lugano

The "Clothing and Jewellery" section was part of the larger section under the heading "Joie de vivre" to which it was attuned also architecturally. A central piazza permitted easy orientation, offering the choice of a brief visit or a more thorough study of the different subsections. The "Clothing and Jewellery" section was entered through an alley with audio-visual displays, reminding the visitor of the meaning and necessity of clothing and adorning oneself. A partly roofed patio was the core of an informally arranged 'foyer' where products such as textiles, shoes, watches, jewellery, etc. were displayed in spherical showcases made of acrylic plastics. On the upper floor was the "Tea Room de la Mode", reached via a flight of stairs bridging a water basin. Next to the foyer is a domed rotunda of 105 ft. diameter, freely spanning a second water basin.

Kleid und Schmuck

Schweizerische Landesausstellung,
Lausanne, 1964
Architekt: Tito Carloni, Lugano

Die Abteilung »Kleid und Schmuck« war ein Teil des Expo-Sektors »Froh und sinnvoll leben«, in den sie sich auch architektonisch einordnete. Von einem zentralen Platz aus bot sich hier die Möglichkeit des schnellen Überblicks, der Kurzbesichtigung oder des eingehenden Studiums der einzelnen Unterabteilungen. Zu »Kleid und Schmuck« führte eine Eingangsgasse mit grafischen und akustischen Hinweisen auf Sinn und Notwendigkeit des Kleidens und Schmückens. Um einen zum Teil überdachten Innenhof verteilte sich locker die Produktausstellung, wo Textilien, Schuhe, Uhren, Schmuck und so weiter in Kugelvitrinen aus Acrylglas ausgestellt waren. Im Obergeschoß lag der »Tea-Room de la Mode«. An das »Foyer« schloß sich eine Kuppelrotunde an, die sich mit einem Durchmesser von 32 m über einem Wasserbassin stützenlos wölbte.

1. Showcases made of acrylic plastics contained the precious exhibits. Together with the coloured spheres bubbling out, as it were, from ceiling and floor, these displays struck a gay note.
2. Spatial centre of the exhibition was a patio with lawn and shrubs. In the background the rotunda roofing the water basin, in the foreground the foyer with the display of products.
3. Inside the "Cupola of fashion", the model dummies displayed on "floating dishes" were floodlit by fairy-lights.
4. A flight of stairs (on the right), bridging a water basin in which the entire scenery was mirrored, led from the 'foyer' to the entire upper floor.

1. Acrylglasvitrinen dienten zur Aufnahme der zum Teil recht kostbaren Exponate. Zusammen mit den aus Decke und Fußboden wachsenden farbigen Kugeln waren sie heiter belebende Ausstellungselemente.
2. Räumlicher Mittelpunkt der Ausstellung war ein mit Rasen und Sträuchern bepflanzter Innenhof. Im Hintergrund der Kuppelbau mit Wasserbassin, vorne die Produktausstellung, das sogenannte Foyer.
3. Im Inneren der »Kuppel der Mode« wurden die auf »schwimmenden Tellern« ausgestellten Mannequinpuppen verschiedenfarbig angestrahlt.
4. Eine Freitreppe (rechts) führte über einem Wasserbecken, in dem sich die ganze Szenerie spiegelte, vom Foyer zum Obergeschoß.

1, 4. The side view clearly shows the lattice work structure composed of tubular bars as well as, behind it, the light-metal slat blinds which served for ventilation and lighting purposes. On the approach of sand storms, these blinds could be closed rapidly. The lateral wall panels consisted of heavily profiled aluminium sheeting. The hall shown in Fig. 4 faces an artificial pool of water. All the buildings were designed in accordance with the same principle.

1, 4. In der Seitenansicht ist nicht nur die Fachwerkkonstruktion aus Rohrstäben, sondern auch die dahinterliegende Leichtmetall-Jalousette für Belichtung und Belüftung deutlich zu erkennen. Sie konnte bei Sandstürmen durch einen Schnellverschluß geschlossen werden. Seitliche Wandfelder aus stark profiliertem Aluminiumblech. Die in Bild 4 gezeigte Halle stand am Rande eines künstlichen Wasserbeckens. Alle Gebäude waren nach demselben Prinzip konstruiert.

German Industrial Exhibition

Khartoum/Sudan, 1961
Architects: Georg Lippsmeier,
Düsseldorf–Munich, and Franz Reiser
Associates: Franckson, Reicher,
Hasselmann, Rothe

Deutsche Industrieausstellung

Khartum/Sudan, 1961
Architekten: Georg Lippsmeier,
Düsseldorf–München, und Franz Reiser
Mitarbeiter: Franckson, Reicher,
Hasselmann, Rothe

This exhibition, consisting of four halls and a number of ancillary buildings, was sponsored by the German Federal Republic and the West German industry for prestige and information purposes. No more than 12 months were available for planning and prefabrication, transport and erection of the halls, including the extensive development works at the desert site available. The structure of the halls consisted of a system of external lattice frames of "Mero" standard components from which, on the inside, the profiled light-metal sheets of walls and ceiling were suspended. Daylight access was through corrugated polyester toplight panels which could also be covered by awnings, and through light-metal slat blinds extending over the whole height of the wall. Together with air conditioning plants, these blinds also served for ventilation purposes.

Die aus vier Hallen und verschiedenen Nebengebäuden bestehende Anlage vereinte Repräsentations- und Informationsausstellungen der Bundesrepublik und der westdeutschen Industrie. Für Planung und Vorfabrikation, Transport und Aufbau der Hallen einschließlich der umfangreichen Erschließungsarbeiten des Wüstengeländes standen nur zwölf Monate zur Verfügung. Die Hallenkonstruktion mit dem Vorteil eines stützenfreien Innenraumes war ein System von außenumlaufenden Fachwerkrahmen aus Mero-Normteilen, innerhalb derer Wand- und Deckenelemente aus Leichtmetallprofilblechen aufgehängt wurden. Die Belichtung übernahmen Polyesterwellplatten als Oberlichter, die zusätzlich durch Sonnensegel abgedeckt werden konnten, und wandhohe Leichtmetalljalousetten, die neben Klimaanlagen der Belüftung dienten.

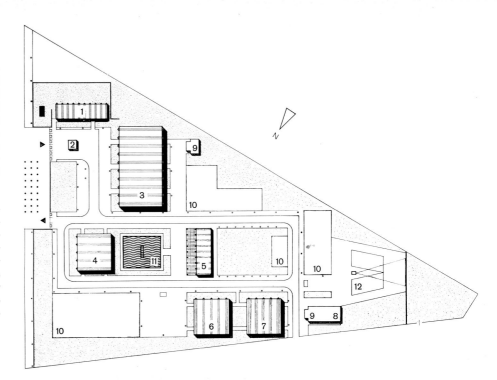

2, 3. Site plan and model photograph of the entire exhibition. Key: 1 Administration, 2 General information and post office, 3 Exhibition hall (32 300 sq. ft.), 4 Exhibition hall with industrial information office (10 760 sq. ft.), 5 Exhibition restaurant, 6, 7 Exhibition halls (10760 sq. ft. each), 8 Special building (police, fire brigade, etc.), 9 Sanitary installations, 10 Outdoor exhibition grounds, 11 Large pool of water with fountains, 12 Open-air-cinema.

2, 3. Lageplan und Modellaufnahme der Gesamtanlage. Legende: 1 Verwaltung, 2 Allgemeine Information und Postamt, 3 Ausstellungshalle (3000 m²), 4 Ausstellungshalle mit Wirtschaftsinformation (1000 m²), 5 Ausstellungsrestaurant, 6, 7 Ausstellungshallen (je 1000 m²), 8 Sonderstation (Polizei, Feuerwehr usw.), 9 Sanitäre Anlagen, 10 Ausstellungsfreiflächen, 11 Großes Wasserbecken mit Wasserspielen, 12 Freilichtkino.

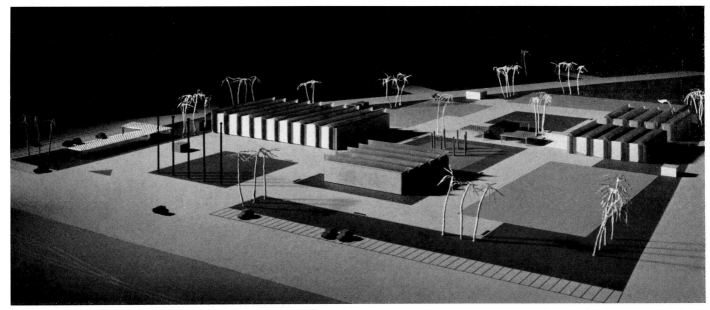

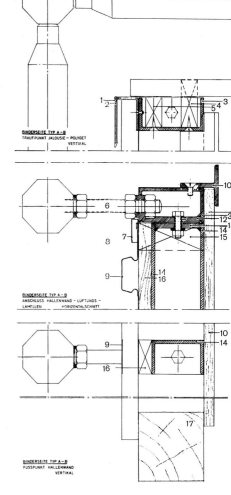

5. Corner of a hall with one of the load-bearing lattice work frames composed of "Mero" standard components.
6. Details of the wall structure. Key: 1 Aluminium gutter, 2 Gutter holders, 3 Channel section, 4 Rack, 5 Filling batten, 6 Threaded pin, 7 Angular fish plate, 8 Tee section keyed to standard strip, 9 Standard section keyed to each corrugation, 10 Tee section, 11 Novopan, $^5/_8$ in., 12, 13 welded flat section, 14 Channel section, 15 Vertically braced lattice work, 16 Wooden batten bolted to channel section, 17 Timber joists, supported by foundation piles.
7. Cross-section of type B hall of approx. 130 ft. width.

5. Hallenecke mit einem der tragenden Fachwerkrahmen aus Mero-Normteilen.
6. Details der Wandausbildung. Legende: 1 Traufblech Al, 2 Traufblechhalterung, 3 U-Profil, 4 Zahnleiste, 5 Futterleiste, 6 Gewindestift, 7 abgewinkeltes Flachmaterial, 8 auf Normalbahn geklemmtes T-Profil, 9 mit Profilband (jede Welle) aufgeklemmtes Normalprofil, 10 T-Profil, 11 Novopan 16 mm, 12, 13 eingeschweißte Flacheisen, 14 U-Profil, 15 senkrecht eingestrebte Lattenkonstruktion, 16 Holzleiste mit U-Profil verschraubt, 17 Lagerholz auf Setzpfählen.
7. Querschnitt durch den Hallentyp B mit rund 40 m Breite.

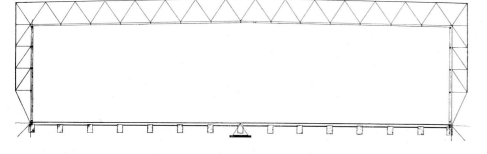

8–10. The interiors convey an impression of the spatial effect of the structure and of the alternation between the wide light-metal panels and the narrow daylight strips which, in the roof, consisted of polyester ribbons and, in the walls, of aluminium slat blinds. In the part of the exhibition shown here (industrial design), the enlarged photographs on the walls matched the actual shapes of the exhibits, some of which were displayed in plastic spheres.

8–10. Die Innenansichten geben einen Begriff von der räumlichen Wirkung der Konstruktion und des Wechsels zwischen breiten Leichtmetallplatten und schmalen Belichtungsstreifen, die beim Dach aus Polyesterbändern, in den Wänden aus Aluminiumjalousetten bestanden. In dem hier gezeigten Ausstellungsteil (industrielle Formgebung) korrespondierten die Großfotos an den Wänden mit den realen Formen der Exponate, die zum Teil in Plastikkugeln untergebracht waren.

Permanent Exhibition Pavilion of the Aluminium Centre

German Industrial Fair, Hanover, 1962
Architect: Hans Maurer, Munich
Associate: Ernst Denk
Civil Engineer: Friedrich Zöschinger

This pavilion has been designed for annually changing exhibitions of the aluminium industry so that it seemed appropriate to use aluminium even for the structure. The architects designed a three-dimensional structure, covering an equilateral triangle of 89 ft. side length and suspended by steel cables from a 66 ft. high central pylon, stayed on three sides. The glass walls, merely sub-divided by narrow bars, reinforce the impression of weightlessness. They stand in water, thus incidentally demonstrating the corrosion resistance of aluminium. Within the load-bearing frame, the ceiling is formed by tetrahedrons, the tops of which are stayed by aluminium bars. Apart from the concrete foundations for the floor slab, the glass walls and the steel cables, aluminium was the only building material.

Ständiger Ausstellungspavillon der Aluminium-Zentrale

Deutsche Industrie-Messe, Hannover, 1962
Architekt: Hans Maurer, München
Mitarbeiter: Ernst Denk
Statik: Friedrich Zöschinger

Dieser Pavillon nimmt jährlich wechselnde Ausstellungen der Aluminiumindustrie auf, so daß es nahelag, den Werkstoff Aluminium bereits in der Konstruktion herauszustellen. Die Architekten errichteten über einem gleichseitigen Dreieck von 27 m Seitenlänge ein Raumtragwerk, das mit Stahlseilen an einem 20 m hohen, nach drei Seiten verspannten Zentralmast aufgehängt ist. Die nur von schmalen Sprossen gegliederten Glaswände, die den Eindruck der Schwerelosigkeit verstärken, tauchen ins Wasser ein und beweisen damit auch die Korrosionsbeständigkeit des Aluminiums. Die Decke wird innerhalb des tragenden Rahmens von Tetraedern gebildet, deren Spitzen durch Zugstangen aus Aluminium verspannt sind. Abgesehen von den Betonfundamenten für die Bodenplatte, den Glasfronten und den Stahlseilen wurde nur Aluminium für den Bau verwendet.

1. Side view of the pavilion which appears to float on a lake in the exhibition ground.
2. This bird's eye view demonstrates the structural principle: the aluminium pylon, standing in water, rises in the centre of a triangular opening of 17 ft. 9 in. side length. Suspended from this pylon by the three main cables and another six steel cables is the roof frame from which the glass walls – sub-divided by narrow bars – are suspended in their turn.

1. Seitenansicht des Pavillons, der auf einem Teich im Messegelände zu schwimmen scheint.
2. Der Blick aus der Vogelperspektive gibt Aufschluß über die Konstruktion: Der im Wasser stehende Aluminiummast erhebt sich in der Mitte einer dreieckigen Öffnung von 5,40 m Seitenlänge. Über seine drei Hauptverspannungen und sechs weitere Stahlseile trägt er den Dachrahmen, an dem wiederum die von Sprossen unterteilten Glaswände aufgehängt sind.

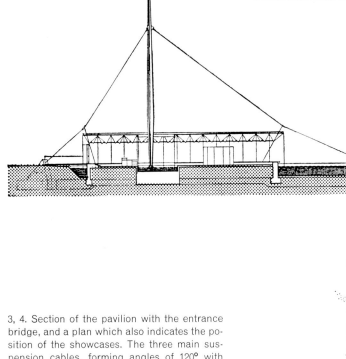

3, 4. Section of the pavilion with the entrance bridge, and a plan which also indicates the position of the showcases. The three main suspension cables, forming angles of 120° with each other, are anchored in concrete abutments which are placed at 82 ft. from the foot of the pylon.

3, 4. Schnitt in der Ebene der Eingangsbrücke und Grundriß mit eingezeichneten Ausstellungsvitrinen. Die drei Hauptseile sind in Beton-Widerlagern verankert, die 25 m vom Mastfuß entfernt in einem Winkel von 120° zueinander stehen.

Verpackung

5

6

5. The basic shapes of the pavilion structure – triangles and tetrahedrons – are repeated in the exhibition elements.

6. The deeply sculptured ceiling is in contrast to the smoothness of the suspended glass panels which dip into the water at some distance from the floor slab.

7. Technical details. On top, pyramid at outer edge with cornice cover above the fittings from which the glass panels are suspended; below, standard window bar and outer corner bar.

8, 9. The bolted aluminium hexagons forming the roof are matched by the stayed tetrahedrons of the three-dimensional load-bearing structure.

10. A hemisphere forms the articulated base of the central aluminium pylon.

11. The roof is suspended from three anchored main cables (Z) and six intermediate cables (H), converging at the top of the central pylon which is designed as a hinged support. The lateral bracing is provided by six internal bars (S).

5. Die Grundformen der Pavillonkonstruktion, Dreiecke und Tetraeder, kehren in den Ausstellungselementen wieder.

6. Die tief strukturierte Decke kontrastiert zu der Glätte der hängenden Verglasung, die in einiger Entfernung von der Bodenplatte ins Wasser taucht.

7. Technische Details. Oben äußere Randpyramide mit Gesimsabdeckung über den Befestigungselementen der hängenden Verglasung; darunter Normsprosse und äußere Ecksprosse.

8, 9. Den verschraubten Aluminiumsechsecken, aus denen sich der Dachbelag zusammensetzt, entsprechen die verspannten Tetraeder des Raumtragwerks.

10. Eine Halbkugel bildet den gelenkigen Fußpunkt des zentralen Aluminiummastes.

11. Das Dach hängt an drei verankerten Seilen (Z) und sechs Zwischenhängern (H), die in der Spitze des als Pendelstütze ausgebildeten Pylons zusammenlaufen. Sechs Innenstangen (S) bilden die Seitenversteifung.

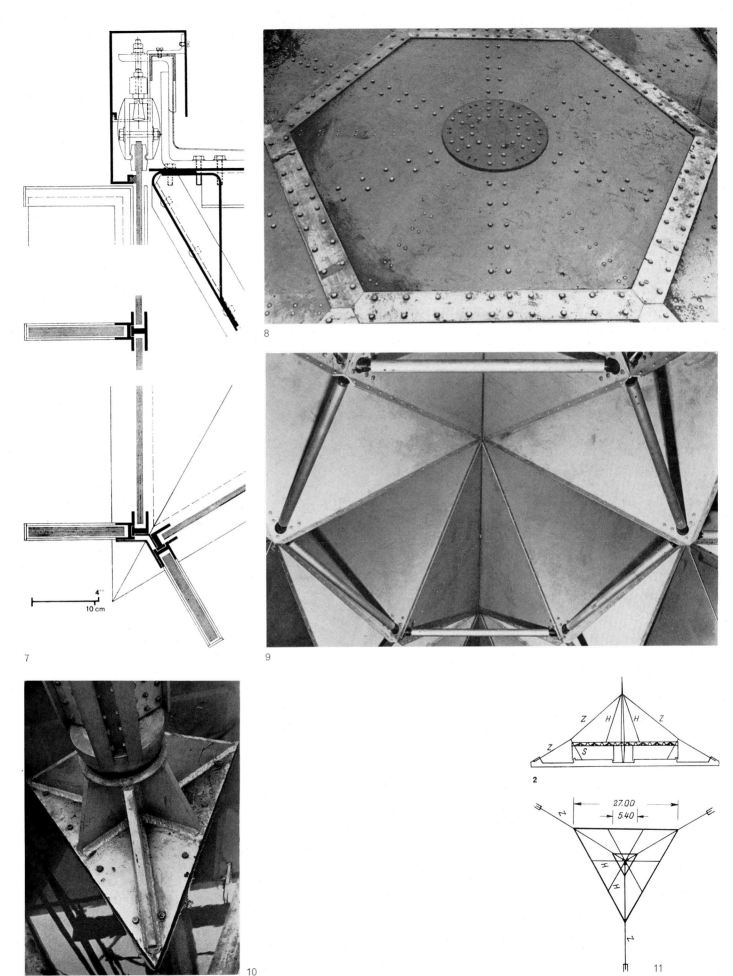

7

8

9

47

10

2

27.00
5.40

11

Pavilion of the IRI Corporation

Fiera del Mare, Genoa, 1964
Architect: Angelo Mangiarotti, Milan

This pavilion was designed for periodically changing displays of products of the IRI Industrial Combine, comprising all stages of shipbuilding. For a unique situation, completely isolated from other buildings on a site close to the seashore, the architect designed a structure reminiscent of ancient temples in similar positions, e.g. at Cape Sunion. Here again, contemporary architectural means were applied to a monument in splendid isolation. Above a concrete platform floats the comparatively light steel structure of the roof, scantily supported by four slender, tapered steel columns, and covered – top and bottom – by 3 ft. 4 in. wide and no more than $1/_{12}$ in. thick steel sheeting. The vaulted shape of the intrados is repeated in the six concave twin showcases placed on the platform. The exhibition premises proper are in the basement.

Pavillon des Industriekonzerns IRI

Fiera del Mare, Genua, 1964
Architekt: Angelo Mangiarotti, Mailand

Der Industriekonzern IRI zeigt in diesem Pavillon mit Wechselausstellungen Ausschnitte aus seiner Produktion, die alle Stadien des Schiffsbaues umfaßt. Für eine einzigartige Grundstückssituation dicht am Meer entwarf der Architekt ein Gebilde, das an klassische Tempel in ähnlicher Lage, etwa an Kap Sunion, denken läßt. Auch hier wurde, mit den architektonischen Mitteln der Gegenwart, ein Monument in den Raum gestellt. Über einer Betonplattform schwebt auf vier schlanken, sich nach oben verjüngenden Stahlsäulen die verhältnismäßig leichte Stahlkonstruktion des Daches, das oben und unten durch sich herauswölbende, 1 m breite und nur 2 mm starke Stahlblechstreifen abgedeckt ist. Die Kurve des Daches kehrt wieder in den sechs konkaven Doppelvitrinen, die allein auf der Plattform stehen. Die eigentlichen Ausstellungsräume liegen im Untergeschoß.

1. The Pavilion seen from the exhibition ground entrance, with the sea as backcloth. In the foreground left are the stairs leading down to the basement.
2, 3. Longitudinal section and plan of the exhibition platform.
4. Side view with the six twin showcases which are placed slightly off-centre. In the background, part of the Port of Genoa.

1. Der Pavillon vor dem Hintergrund des Meeres, vom Ausstellungszugang her gesehen. Vorne links die Treppe zu den Räumen im Untergeschoß.
2, 3. Längsschnitt und Grundriß der Ausstellungsplattform.
4. Seitenansicht mit den sechs etwas aus der Mittelachse gerückten Doppelvitrinen. Im Hintergrund ein Teil des Hafens von Genua.

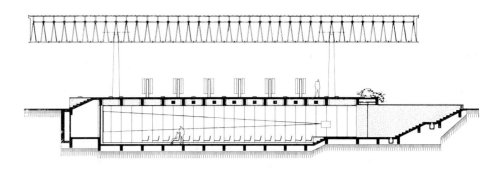

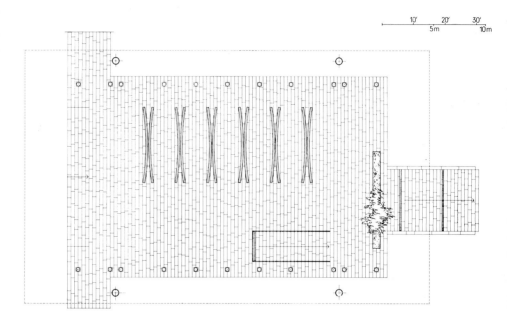

5. Floodlights embedded in the concrete platform illuminate the showcases at night, bathing the metal intrados of the roof in a flood of glittering light.
6, 7. The curved shapes, especially of the roof, are akin to those of modern shipbuilding.
8, 9. The platform itself is solely occupied by the six concave twin showcases which contain photographs and texts illustrating the production program of the sixteen companies affiliated to IRI.
10. The stairs, consisting of exposed concrete like the entire substructure of the pavilion, lead to the exhibition rooms and auditorium in the basement.

5. In den Beton der Plattform eingelassene Scheinwerfer illuminieren nachts die Schaukästen und tauchen die metallene Untersicht des Daches in gleißendes Licht.
6, 7. Die gekurvten Konstruktionsformen insbesondere des Daches sind denjenigen des modernen Schiffsbaues verwandt.
8, 9. Auf der Plattform selbst stehen nur die sechs konkaven Doppelvitrinen, in denen Fotos und Texte über die Produktion der 16 IRI-Gesellschaften Auskunft geben.
10. Die Treppe, Sichtbeton wie der ganze Unterbau des Pavillontempels, führt zu den Ausstellungsräumen und zum Auditorium im Untergeschoß.

**Afro-Asian
Sales and Information Show**

Industrial Exhibition, Berlin, 1964
Architect: Walter Kuhn, Hanover
Associate: Hans-Joachim Steiner

For the special show entitled "Partners in Progress", the architect designed a domed structure composed of 208 steel tubes of $2^3/_8$ in. diameter which were held together by tubular steel globes with tube sockets and cap screws. The canvas tent roof was fastened to the joints by means of shaped metal discs and tensioning chains. In the plan, the three tent domes were arranged in the form of a right-angled triangle. The space between the tents was designed as a covered entrance yard which, near the tent entrances, also served as wind protection. The domes themselves were developed from concatenations of cubes; they had a diameter of approx. 82 ft., an area of 5300 sq.ft., and were nearly 22 ft. high. Inside, the reticular structure of the tent was matched by the tetrahedral-cum-octahedral structure of the display tables.

**Afro-Asien-
Verkaufs- und Informationsschau**

Industrieausstellung, Berlin, 1964
Architekt: Walter Kuhn, Hannover
Mitarbeiter: Hans-Joachim Steiner

Für die Sonderschau »Partner des Fortschritts« entwickelte der Architekt eine Kuppelkonstruktion aus 208 Stahlrohren von 60 mm Durchmesser, die durch Stahlrohrkugeln mit Rohrstutzen und Überwurfmuttern zusammengehalten wurde. Die Bespannung wurde an den Verbindungskugeln mit Hilfe verformter Blechscheiben und Spannketten befestigt. Im Grundriß waren die drei Zeltkuppeln in die Form eines rechtwinkligen Dreiecks eingeordnet. Der Freiraum zwischen den Hallen wurde als überdachter Eingangshof ausgebildet, der im Bereich der Zeltzugänge zugleich als Windschutz diente. Die Kuppeln selbst sind aus Kubusreihungen entwickelt; bei rund 25 m Durchmesser haben sie eine Grundfläche von 493 m² und eine Höhe von 6,60 m. Im Innern nahmen die Tetraeder-Oktaeder-Gefüge der Ausstellungsstände die Stabkonstruktion des Außenbaues auf.

1, 2. The canvas tent was suspended on the inside of the bearing structure.
3. Additional triangular awnings protected the tent entrances from the yard.
4, 5. Site plan and elevations.
6. Structure joint.
7. Plan of dome structure.
8. Interior of one of the tent domes. The canvas sheets were sewn together in such a way that they adapted themselves to the rhythm of the structure. The suspension points were additionally protected by metal discs.

1, 2. Die Textilbespannung wurde von innen unter das Traggerüst gespannt.
3. Zusätzliche Dreieckssegel überspannen die Zugänge am Eingangshof.
4, 5. Lageplan und Aufrisse.
6. Knotenverbindung des Tragwerks.
7. Grundriß der Kuppelkonstruktion.
8. Innenansicht einer Kuppelhalle. Die Stoffbahnen der Bespannung sind so zusammengenäht, daß sie sich dem Rhythmus der Konstruktion anpassen. An den Befestigungspunkten ist die Bespannung durch Blechscheiben verstärkt.

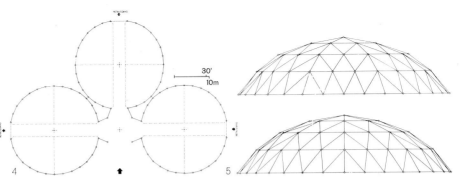

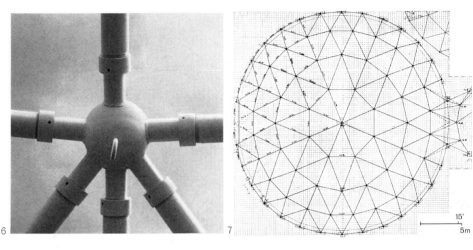

9. The display units inside the tents were composed of "Mero" standard components, forming octahedrons and tetrahedrons. In the foreground, a combination of table and glass pyramids; in the background, a number of larger units.

10. The same system was used for the signposting outside the exhibition.

9. Die Ausstellungselemente im Innern sind nach dem Oktaeder- und Tetraederprinzip aus Mero-Normstäben zusammengesetzt. Im Vordergrund eine Tisch- und Glaspyramidenkombination, dahinter größere Elemente.

10. Nach demselben System wurden auch die Hinweistafeln vor der Ausstellung konstruiert.

11. Joint connecting four glass pyramids.
12. Components of the pyramid structure. Bottom, right: the metal points for the glass showcases which also contained the light fittings.
13, 14. Display units with vertical display panels. The stands of the six African countries were housed in one tent whilst those of the eight Asian countries occupied the two other tents. The exhibits included semi-finished, craft, agricultural and industrial products. Each country was given a basic set of equipment with display panels, shelves, tables, showcases, supports, fitted units and chairs. Within this system, the exhibitors were free to vary the number and arrangement of these units at will. The wooden block flooring was covered with close carpeting.

11. Knotenpunkt zwischen vier Glaspyramiden.
12. Einzelelemente der Pyramidenkonstruktion. Rechts unten die Blechspitzen für die Glasvitrinen, in denen auch die Beleuchtung untergebracht war.
13, 14. Ausstellungselemente mit vertikalen Schautafeln. Die Stände der sechs afrikanischen Länder waren in einer Kuppel untergebracht, während sich die Stände der acht asiatischen Länder auf die beiden anderen Kuppeln verteilten. Ausgestellt wurden Rohprodukte, handwerkliche, landwirtschaftliche und industrielle Erzeugnisse. Jedes Land erhielt eine Grundausstattung an Tafeln, Regalen, Tischen, Vitrinen, Dekorationsständern, eingebauten Schränken und Sitzgruppen. Anzahl und Ordnung dieser Elemente konnte von den Ausstellern innerhalb des Systems beliebig variiert werden. Der aus Platten bestehende Holzfußboden war mit einem Spannteppich ausgelegt.

Swissair Information Stand

Swiss Industries Fair, Basle, 1961
Design: Andreas Christen, Zürich

Since 1959, the Swissair Pavilion has been an integral part of the Basle Industries Fair. But, although the structural components have remained the same all the time, not only the exhibits – mainly enlarged photographs dealing with varying themes from among the activities of the airline company – but also the layout were varied each year. Christen's unit construction system is composed of cubes of 10×10×10 ft. side length, placed on rolled steel uprights with adjustable feet. The flooring consists of bonded tiles, the ceiling in each cube of four polyester units of $1/_{12}$ in. thickness with a circular centre. The different parts of the structure are bolted to each other in the same way as the cubes themselves. All the constituent parts of the pavilion can be assembled by five men within a day and can be accommodated in a furniture van.

Informationsstand der Swissair

Schweizer Mustermesse, Basel, 1961
Entwurf: Andreas Christen, Zürich

Seit 1959 gehört der Swissair-Pavillon zum Bestand der Basler Mustermesse. Von Jahr zu Jahr änderte sich indessen nicht nur der Inhalt der Ausstellung – vorwiegend Groß-fotos zu wechselnden Themen aus dem Wirkungsbereich der Luftfahrtgesellschaft –, sondern auch der Grundriß, obwohl die Bauelemente immer dieselben blieben. Christens Baukastensystem setzt sich aus Kuben von 3×3×3 m Kantenlänge zusammen, deren senkrechte Profileisenstützen verstellbare Füße haben. Der Boden besteht aus Verbund-platten, die Decke je Kubus aus vier Polyester-Einheiten von 2 mm Stärke mit einem kreisförmigen Mittelstück. Die einzelnen Konstruktionsteile werden ebenso miteinander verschraubt wie das Kubengerüst. Alle Pavillonelemente, die von fünf Mann innerhalb eines Tages montiert werden können, haben in einem Möbelwagen Platz.

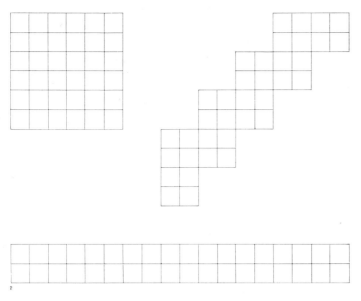

1. The freely adjustable display panels also serve as partitions. Depending on the plan, the steps leading to the raised pavilion can be bolted to one side of a cube.
2. Some variants of the layout plan, all covering the same aggregate floor area. Size and shape of the plan can be varied at will. Moreover, it is possible to add an upper floor.
3. The configuration of nine units in zig-zag arrangement, used for the 1961 Fair, provided interesting vistas and lively space effects.
4. Structural details, showing the fastening of the floor and ceiling units.
5. The pavilion, this time arranged on a square layout plan, before insertion of the walls. The disc-shaped feet, adjustable in height, are placed on square concrete slabs.

1. Frei einstellbare Tafeln für das Ausstellungsgut dienen gleichzeitig als raumabschließende Wände. Die Zugangstreppen zu dem erhöht stehenden Pavillon können dem jeweiligen Grundriß entsprechend an eine Kubusseite angeschraubt werden.
2. Grundrißvarianten bei gleichbleibender Grundfläche. Der Grundriß kann in Größe und Form beliebig variiert werden. Ferner ist es möglich, dem Pavillon ein zweites Geschoß aufzusetzen.
3. Aus dem Aufbau von neun Einheiten über einem abgetreppten Grundriß, wie er dem Pavillon des Jahres 1961 zugrunde lag, ergeben sich interessante Durchblicke und lebendige Raumwirkungen.
4. Konstruktionsdetails mit den Anschlüssen von Fußboden- und Deckenelementen.
5. Der noch wandlose Pavillon auf quadratischem Grundriß. Die höhenverstellbaren Tellerfüße stehen auf quadratischen Betonplatten.

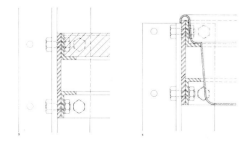

Pavilion "Aid from Open Space"

Federal Garden Show, Stuttgart, 1961
Architect: Werner Luz, Stuttgart

Despite restricted funds, the architect of this pavilion, which was designed to provide full information about the tasks of the landscape gardener, attempted to gain as much display space as possible. He therefore adopted a square plan of 82×82 ft., evenly subdivided into squares of 20×20 ft. where the four squares in the centre were left open to form a kind of patio. Openings were also left in some of the edge panels below the roof and above the floor slab which, to compensate for the unevenness of the ground, was placed on 2 ft. high concrete supports. The superstructure consisted of simple wooden beams and flat built-up roof. Instead of walls, the space between the uprights was taken up by informally arranged display panels leaving between them everchanging views into the park.

Pavillon »Hilfe durch Grün«

Bundesgartenschau, Stuttgart, 1961
Architekt: Werner Luz, Stuttgart

Trotz knapper finanzieller Mittel versuchte der Architekt mit diesem Pavillon, der über die Aufgaben des Landschaftsgärtners informieren sollte, möglichst viel Ausstellungsraum zu gewinnen. So wurde dem Interimsbau ein quadratischer Grundriß von 25×25 m zugrunde gelegt, der in 6×6 m große Rasterfelder unterteilt war und dessen vier mittlere Quadrate einen atriumartigen Freiraum bildeten. Offen blieben auch einige Randfelder unter dem Dachabschluß und über der Bodenplatte, die zum Ausgleichen der Geländeunebenheiten auf 60 cm hohen Betonsockeln auflag. Darüber erhob sich eine einfache Holzbalkenkonstruktion mit Kiesklebedach. Anstelle von Wänden waren zwischen die Pfosten in freier Ordnung verschiedene Ausstellungstafeln eingespannt, zwischen denen sich immer wieder wechselnde Ausblicke in den Park ergaben.

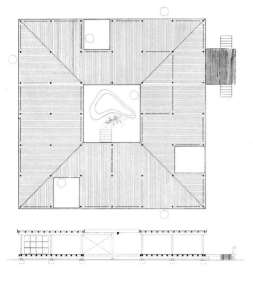

1. The metal display panels, fastened on wires tensioned between floor slab and ceiling, also served as outer walls of the pavilion.
2, 3. Section and plan.
4, 5. The views across the pavilion show the diagonally braced timber structure, which had been left in its natural state, around the patio and the informal arrangement of the display panels.
6. The pavilion, seen from south-east.

1. Die aus Blech bestehenden Ausstellungstafeln, zwischen Boden- und Deckenplatte über Halterungen an Spanndrähten befestigt, bildeten gleichzeitig die Außenwände des Pavillons.
2, 3. Schnitt und Grundriß.
4, 5. Die Blicke quer durch den Pavillon zeigen die naturbelassene Holzkonstruktion mit den Diagonalverspannungen rings um den Innenhof und die lockere Gruppierung der Ausstellungstafeln.
6. Ansicht von Südosten.

1

Pavilion of the French Ministry of Building Construction

Salon des Arts Ménagers, Paris, 1962
Architect: Ionel Schein, Paris

For the 1962 exhibition of domestic appliances, which is an annually recurring event, the French Ministry of Building Construction erected an outdoor pavilion to provide information about the tasks and activities of the Ministry. Despite its small size, the pavilion was attractive in its unorthodox design. Three corners of the square site were surrounded by three quadrants whilst the fourth corner contained the entrances and exit. The four parts of the pavilion were composed of beams, boarding and glass. Each part was surrounded by a hoop of vertical boarding which was extended upwards and downwards by octagonally arranged glass panels. The wooden roof structure of each of the three cells consisted of an 'umbrella' supported by a central post, with segments of differently coloured glass. A fourth 'umbrella' covered the inside square.

Pavillon des französischen Ministeriums für das Bauwesen

Salon des Arts Ménagers, Paris, 1962
Architekt: Ionel Schein, Paris

Auf der alljährlich stattfindenden hauswirtschaftlichen Ausstellung ließ das Bauministerium 1962 einen Freipavillon errichten, um über seine Aufgaben zu informieren. Trotz der kleinen Dimensionen entstand ein originelles Bauwerk auf quadratischem Grundriß, dessen drei Ecken jeweils drei Viertelkreise umschlossen, während die vierte Ecke Ein- und Ausgang aufnahm. Der vierteilige Pavillon war eine Konstruktion aus Balken, Brettern und Glas. Seine Wände setzten sich aus einem kreisförmig geführten Band mit vertikaler Verbretterung und einer nach oben und unten verlängernden, oktogonalen Verglasung zusammen. Die Dachkonstruktion bestand über den Grundräumen aus drei, jeweils von einer Mittelstütze getragenen Schirmen mit verschiedenfarbig verglasten Segmenten und aus einem höheren und größeren Schirm über dem Innenquadrat.

60

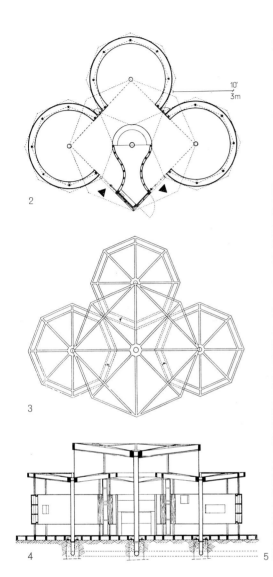

2

3

4

5

1, 6. The external views show the interplay of the different components as well as the design of the walls and 'umbrella' roofs.

2, 3, 4. Plan, underview of the ceiling, and section.

5. The centre of the inside square was taken up by the information desk (left). The displays – texts, drawings and photographs - were mounted on the inside of the panelled wall and formed a continuous sequence of exhibits.

1. 6. Die Außenansichten zeigen das Zusammenspiel der Teilkörper sowie die Konstruktion der Wände und der insgesamt vier schirmartigen Dächer.

2, 3, 4. Grundriß, Deckenuntersicht und Schnitt.

5. Im Mittelpunkt des Grundquadrates befand sich der Informationsstand (links). Die Ausstellung selbst – Beschriftungen, Grafiken und Fotos – war auf der Innenseite der holzverkleideten Wandstreifen entlanggeführt und konnte auf dem Weg vom Eingang zum Ausgang in einem Zug betrachtet werden.

6

1

"Information Machine"
at the IBM Pavilion

World's Fair, New York, 1964
Design: Charles Eames, Venice, Calif.
Eero Saarinen Ass., Hamden, Conn.

»Informationsmaschine«
im IBM-Pavillon

World's Fair, New York, 1964
Entwurf: Charles Eames, Venice, Calif.
Eero Saarinen Ass., Hamden, Conn.

Saarinen's IBM pavilion was crowned by a 115 ft. long and 90 ft. high ovoid which comprised, as a centre and main attraction, a multiple projection system with 15 screens designed by Mr. & Mrs. Eames. This projection theatre was reached by the audience of 500 people on a platform which, like a lift, was raised from the ground floor of the pavilion. The projection screens, which were of different and partly variable sizes, showed films, pictorial and textual slides which, supplemented by explanations given by a speaker, dealt with subjects ranging from simple every-day problems – a dinner table or the tactics of a football game – to difficult scientific questions. In the process, an explanation was given of the way in which these problems must be abstracted fro the operation of, or with, the computer.

Saarinens IBM-Pavillon krönte ein etwa 35 m langes und 27 m hohes Ovoid, das als Zentrum und Höhepunkt eine von dem Ehepaar Eames gestaltete, fünfzehnfache Simultanprojektion umschloß. In diesen Projektionssaal fuhren die jeweils 500 Zuschauer wie mit einem Fahrstuhl auf einer großen Tribüne, der »Zuschauerwand«, aus dem Erdgeschoß des Pavillons herauf. Auf den verschieden großen und zum Teil in ihren Abmessungen variablen Projektionsflächen wurden durch Filme, Bild- und Schriftdias und durch zusätzliche Erklärungen eines Sprechers Probleme erörtert, die vom Alltäglichen – einer Tischordnung oder der Taktik eines Fußballspieles – bis zu schwierigen wissenschaftlichen Fragen reichten. Dabei wurde der Weg der Abstraktion erläutert, wie ihn die Arbeit des Computers beziehungsweise die Arbeit mit dem Computer erfordert.

1. Interior of the ovoid projection theatre. The projection screens were arranged in arcs around the audience.
2, 6. Part of the semi-ovoid of the projection screens.
3. Schematic drawing of the entire installation which consisted of 15 projection screens.
4. Demonstration of a complicated problem by means of film slides, drawings and texts. In the centre is the speaker who, during the show, spoke from different positions.
5. The "People Wall", carrying twelve rows of seats, was raised hydraulically on an inclined ramp.

2

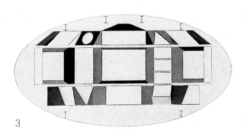

3

1. Blick in den eiförmigen Projektionsraum. Die Bildschirme sind bogenförmig an die Tribüne herangeführt.
2, 6. Ausschnitt aus dem Halboval der Projektionsflächen.
3. Schemazeichnung der aus insgesamt 15 Projektionsschirmen bestehenden Gesamtanlage.
4. Veranschaulichung eines komplizierten Problems durch Film, stehendes Bild, Zeichnung und Schrift. In der Mitte der Erklärer, der im Laufe der Vorführung von verschiedenen Stellen aus spricht.
5. Die in zwölf Sitzreihen aufsteigende, hydraulisch auf einer Schrägrampe bewegte Zuschauertribüne.

4

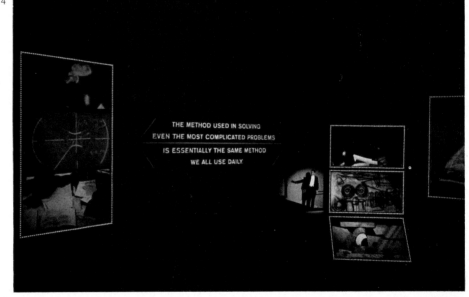

5

6

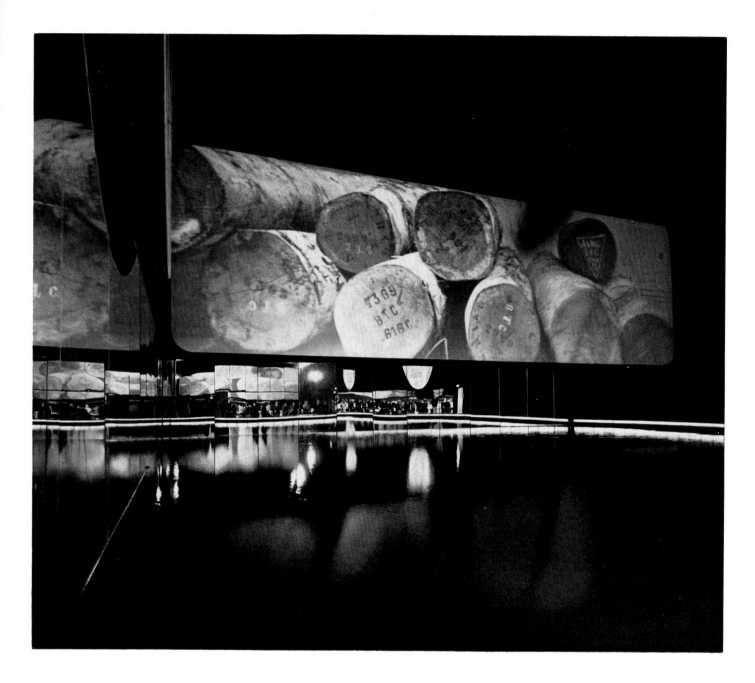

Dutch Pavilion

International Exhibition of Transport
and Communications, Munich, 1965
Design: Wim Crouwel, Total Design,
Amsterdam
Architect: Oyevaar Stolle van Gool,
Amsterdam

Niederländischer Pavillon

Internationale Verkehrsausstellung,
München, 1965
Entwurf: Wim Crouwel, Total Design,
Amsterdam
Architekt: Oyevaar Stolle van Gool,
Amsterdam

Like a gigantic wooden box, the Dutch Pavilion occupied a part of one of the halls of
the Transport Exhibition. The aim was to draw attention to the important part played by
transport in the economic life of the Netherlands. Through three entrances, the visitors
entered the dark interior of the box where they were exclusively guided by film projections. The wide screen for the main show was placed above the entrance and flanked
by two round screens on the side walls. The two corners below these round projection
screens were taken up by large, quadrantal ponds in which – as in the approx. 6½ ft.
high mirror strips immediately above them – the film projections were reflected. The
diagonal position of these ponds guided the visitors to the "causeway" in the centre of
the room which was the best position for viewing the projections.

Wie einen gewaltigen Kistenstapel hatten die Holländer ihren Pavillon in eine der IVA-
Hallen hineingebaut, um darin das Transportwesen, einen der wichtigsten Wirtschafts-
zweige des Landes, zu zeigen. Durch drei Zugänge gelangten die Besucher in das dunkle
Innere des Blocks, wo sie ausschließlich von den Filmprojektionen erfaßt und geleitet
wurden. Die Hauptvorführung fand auf der Breitleinwand auf der Stirnseite statt, begleitet von zwei Kreisprojektionen auf den Längswänden. Die beiden Raumecken unter diesen runden Projektionsschirmen nahmen große, viertelkreisförmige Wasserbecken ein,
in denen sich, ebenso wie in den etwa 2 m hohen Spiegelstreifen unmittelbar darüber,
die Filmbilder spiegelten. Die Diagonalstellung dieser Bassins lenkte die Gäste auf den
»Damm« in der Raummitte, den für die Betrachtung der Projektionen günstigsten Punkt.

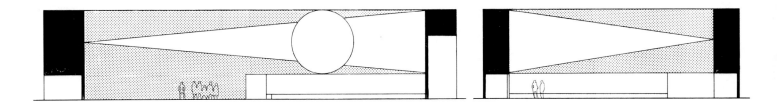

1. A view of the main film screen, measuring 20×66 ft.
2, 3. Longitudinal section and cross-section.
4. Full-length view of the room, from one end wall to the other. Due to the mirror effect below the projection screens, the quadrantal ponds appear to be round.
5. Plan. Main screen on top, complementary screens top left and bottom right.
6. Outside of end wall with the nearly circular main entrance.

1. Blick auf die 6 m hohe und 20 m breite Hauptprojektion.
2, 3. Längs- und Querschnitt.
4. Gesamtausdehnung des Raumes von einer Querwand zur anderen. Die Viertelkreise der Wasserbecken wirkten durch die Verspiegelung unterhalb der Projektionswände wie Vollkreise.
5. Grundriß. Hauptprojektion oben, Nebenprojektionen links oben und rechts unten.
6. Äußere Querwand mit dem Haupteingang.

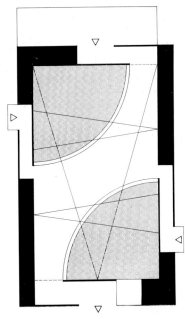

DB-Vision

International Exhibition of Transport
and Communications, Munich, 1965
Development and design: Paolo Nestler,
Edgar Reitz, Insel-Film Ltd. in co-
operation with Werner Walz
(Information and Publicity Office
of the German Federal Railway)

DB-Vision

Internationale Verkehrsausstellung,
München, 1965
Entwicklung und Gestaltung: Paolo
Nestler, Edgar Reitz, Insel-Film GmbH
& Co. in Zusammenarbeit mit Werner
Walz (Bundesbahn-Auskunfts- und
Werbeamt)

On the occasion of the Transport Exhibition the German Federal Railway ("Deutsche Bundesbahn", or "DB." for short) made use of a novel type of publicity. In Hall No. 16, the conventional presentation of objects was replaced by the projection system known as "Varia Vision" (named "DB-Vision" during the exhibition). With its scaffoldings carrying the projectors and projection screens, the hall had the appearance of a railway station. 16 film strips projected onto 16 screens arranged in four rows dealt with the general subject of "travel". The films, in the form of endless strips repeatable at will, differed in length but were, within the total program, so synchronized that the pictures were always composed and supplemented in a certain way. As each of the upright laminations of the projection screen were able to swivel around a pivot, still further possibilities of variation were available. Coloured markings on the floor guided the visitors to the focal points of acoustic and optical interest.

Die Deutsche Bundesbahn machte sich auf der IVA eine neuartige Werbemöglichkeit zunutze: sie ersetzte in Halle 16 die althergebrachte Repräsentation von Objekten durch das Projektionssystem VariaVision (während der IVA DB-Vision genannt). Der Hallenraum mutete mit seinen Gerüsten, die Projektoren und Projektionsflächen trugen, wie eine Bahnhofshalle an. Auf 16 Leinwänden in vier Reihen behandelten 16 Filmstreifen das Generalthema »Reisen«. Die Filme, als endlose Bänder beliebig wiederholbar, unterschieden sich in der Länge, waren aber im Gesamtprogramm so synchronisiert, daß sich immer wieder bestimmte Bildkompositionen und -ergänzungen ergaben. Da sich aber die hochformatigen Lamellen der Projektionsflächen um einen Drehpunkt schwenken lassen, entstanden weitere Variationsmöglichkeiten. Farbige Markierungen auf dem Boden führten die Besucher zu akustischen und optischen Schwerpunkten.

1. By turning the laminations of some of the projection screens, the size of the pictures can be reduced.
2. This composition shows the 16 projections (alternating between wide and normal screens) in a certain juxtaposition. The sound – consisting of spoken words and electronic music – was controlled through loudspeakers.
3. Plan and section.
4, 5. The hall before and during the projections. The lines and circles marked on the floor served as guides to the visitor.

1. Die Lamellen einiger Projektionsflächen sind geschwenkt; dadurch lassen sich die Bildformate verkleinern.
2. Diese Montage zeigt die 16 Projektionen (Wechsel zwischen Breit- und Normalleinwand) in einer bestimmten Simultanphase. Der Ton – Wort und elektronische Musik – wurde über 24 Lautsprechergruppen gesteuert.
3. Grundriß und Schnitt.
4, 5. Die Halle vor und während der Projektionen. Auf dem Boden die eingezeichneten Leitlinien und -kreise.

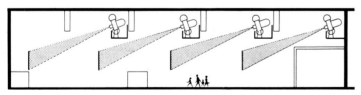

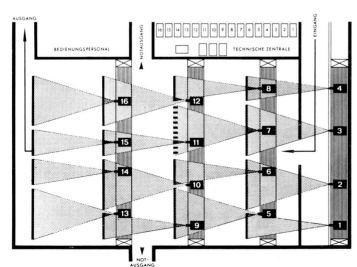

"Alarm" Architectural Exhibition

Congress of the International Union of
Architectural Students, Stockholm, 1965
Exhibition Committee: Sture Balgård,
Eva Björklund, Jöran Lindvall

Architekturausstellung »Alarm«

Kongreß der Union Internationale des
Etudiants en Architecture, Stockholm,
1965
Ausstellungskomitee: Sture Balgård,
Eva Björklund, Jöran Lindvall

Using a dynamic system of multiple projections, students tried to demonstrate the dilemma confronting the young architect of to-day: on the one hand, the Utopian city of his dreams, designed to meet ever increasing demands for comfort; on the other hand, the compelling need to cope with the population explosion in developing countries. This was demonstrated by comparing four Utopian designs with four projects for developing countries, supplemented by extracts from newspapers and journals and everyday documents. The visitors were simultaneously confronted with 25 projector screens showing 2000 pictures, accompanied by sound track music. The exhibition hall was occupied by a tubular steel scaffolding, which supported the casually arranged projection screens and the black plastic foils with which ceilings and walls were covered.

In einer dynamischen Simultanprojektion wurde das Dilemma vor Augen geführt, dem sich der junge Architekt gegenübersieht: dort die utopische Traumstadt für ständig wachsende Komfortwünsche, hier die Notwendigkeit, der Bevölkerungsexplosion in den Entwicklungsländern Herr zu werden. Das war vergleichend dargestellt durch vier utopische Entwürfe und vier Projekte für Entwicklungsländer, ergänzt durch Ausschnitte aus Zeitungen, Zeitschriften und Dokumente unseres Alltags. Fünfundzwanzig Projektoren konfrontierten die Besucher simultan mit 2000 Bildern, die von Raumtonmusik begleitet wurden. Der Ausstellungsraum war von einem Gerüst aus Stahlrohren durchzogen, wie man es von jeder Baustelle kennt. Es trug die kreuz- und quergespannten Leinwände und die schwarzen Plastikfolien, mit denen Decken und Wände verkleidet waren.

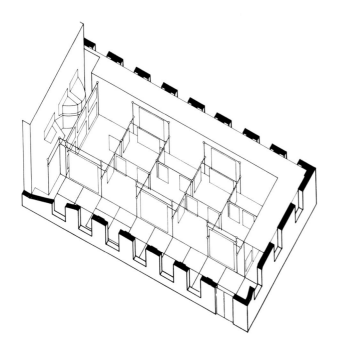

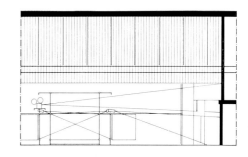

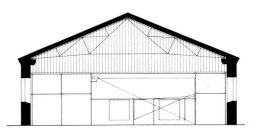

1, 2. The photographs can only convey a vague impression of the dynamic effect of the continually changing screen projections and their reflections on the tubular steel scaffolding, walls and ceiling.

3. Isometric view of the exhibition room with the scaffolding supporting the projection screens. The projections room proper was surrounded by a passage where the theme of the exhibition was varied by wall displays of film posters, advertisements and other documentary material.

4, 5. Cross section and part of longitudinal section. Slide- and film-projectors were fixed at different heights in the tubular steel scaffolding.

6. 7. Further projection screens. Against the background of black, plastic foil, the boundaries of the room were receding in the dark, only occasionally lit up by a flash of reflected light.

1, 2. Die Abbildungen vermitteln nur eine vage Andeutung von der Dynamik des ständigen Bildwechsels und dem Spiel der Reflexe auf Stahlrohrgerüst und Raumbegrenzung.

3. Isometrie des Ausstellungsraumes mit dem eingesetzten Traggerüst für die Projektionswände. Um den eigentlichen Projektionsraum führte ein Umgang, an dessen Wänden Filmplakate, Anzeigen und anderes Dokumentationsmaterial das Thema der Ausstellung variierten.

4, 5. Querschnitt und Teil des Längsschnitts. Dia- und Filmprojektoren waren in verschiedenen Höhen im Stahlrohrgerüst montiert.

6,7. Weitere Projektionsausschnitte. Die schwarze Plastikfolie ließ die Raumgrenze im Dunkel verschwinden, nur gelegentlich blitzte sie glänzend im Licht auf.

**Synchronous Projection System
''Diapolyecran''**

Czechoslovak Pavilion at the World
Exhibition, Montreal, 1967
Design: Josef Svoboda
Producer: Emil Radok

**Synchron-Projektionssystem
»Diapolyecran«**

Tschechoslowakischer Pavillon der
Weltausstellung, Montreal, 1967
Entwurf: Josef Svoboda
Regie: Emil Radok

A projection screen, measuring 20×32 ft., was constructed of 112 blocks, each two feet square. Each block was equipped with two automatic slide projectors which were electronically controlled so that in the span of 14 minutes, 15,000 slides were thrown on the screen, forming either a mosaic or continually changing picture compositions with different zones switching slowly or faster to ever new themes. Sometimes, similar pictures were shown simultaneously on several parts of the screen, or an individual slide appeared successively on different parts of the screen within the same sequence. The dynamic effect was further enhanced by the alternation of black-and-white with coloured slides and by the horizontal movement of the blocks which were shifted forward and backward in varying groupings.

Aus 112 Würfeln von etwa 60×60 cm sichtbarer Frontfläche wurde eine Projektionswand von rund 6×9,75 m aufgebaut. Jeder Würfel war im Inneren mit zwei automatischen Diaprojektoren ausgerüstet. Ein Computer steuerte die Projektoren so, daß sich aus 15000 Dias in einer 14-Minuten-Vorführung entweder mosaikartig zusammengesetzte Gesamtbilder ergaben oder aber ständig wechselnde Montagen, bei denen einzelne Teilbereiche langsamer oder rascher zu neuen Motiven überblendeten. Auch tauchten gleichartige Bilder auf mehreren Flächen zugleich auf oder nacheinander auf verschiedenen Flächen. Eine weitere Dynamisierung wurde durch den Wechsel von Schwarzweiß- und Farbdias erreicht und durch die horizontale Beweglichkeit der Würfel, die in wechselnden Gruppen vor oder hinter die normale Projektionsebene geschoben werden konnten.

1. General view. Top right, the four blocks with the picture of a flower are shifted forward, demonstrating their mobility.
2–5. Sections from an optical narration entitled "The creation of the world" and dealing with the transformation of raw materials into finished products. Top left: Pictorial transition from stone-age man to flower patterns made of gear wheels. Top right: Formal association: the small gear wheels shown in Fig. 2 have been transformed into large turbine wheels. Bottom: A composite picture with realistic sections (pictures of distribution terminals) was transformed into an abstract composition of products of the metal industry.

1. Gesamtansicht. Rechts oben die nach vorn geschobenen vier Felder mit dem Bild einer Blume als Beispiel für die Mobilität der Projektionskuben.
2–5. Ausschnitte aus einer Bildsequenz (unter dem Titel »Die Erschaffung der Welt« behandelte die Schau die Verwandlung von Rohmaterialien in Fertigprodukte). Oben links: Überblendungsphase Steinzeitmenschen/ Blumenmuster aus Zahnrädern. Oben rechts: Formale Assoziation; die kleinen Zahnräder von Abb. 2 haben sich in große Turbinenräder verwandelt. Unten: Eine mit realistischen Abschnitten (Bilder von Verteileranschlüssen) durchsetzte Montage verwandelte sich in eine abstrakte Komposition aus Werkstücken der Metallindustrie.

International Introductory Section

XIIIth Triennale, Milan, 1964
Architects: Vittorio Gregotti, Lodovico
Meneghetti, Giotto Stoppino, Milano

In the 'Introductory Section', 'Leisure Time', the general theme of the exhibition, was critically and dialectically interpreted. The display of exaltation characteristic of the publicity material of the leisure-time industry was followed by a sobering empty room and by a maze of stairs and walkway tubes all brilliant with metal effects and mirror reflections, designed by some of the boldest of Italy's young artists. In the "Corridor of Instruction", too, seeming seriousness was treated with macabre irony, and in the "Caleidoscope", forming the last part of the section, the multiple mirror reflections of projection pictures and visitors produced that perplexing profusion which threatens the leisure time of modern man. The dynamic effects of the visual design aids were supplemented by acoustic signals, spoken texts and sound track music.

Internationale Einführungsabteilung

XIII. Triennale, Mailand, 1964
Architekten: Vittorio Gregotti, Lodovico
Meneghetti, Giotto Stoppino, Mailand

Freizeit als Gesamtthema wurde in der Einführungsabteilung kritisch und dialektisch interpretiert. Der Darstellung einer euphorischen Übersteigerung, wie sie von der Freizeitindustrie in ihrer Werbung praktiziert wird, folgte ein ernüchternd leerer Raum und dann ein Labyrinth von Treppen und begehbaren Röhren, alle mit Metalleffekten und Spiegelungen glänzend und von einigen der kühnsten jüngeren Künstler Italiens gestaltet. Auch im »Korridor der Unterweisung« wurde scheinbare Seriosität makaber ironisiert, und im abschließenden »Kaleidoskop« erzeugten die vielfältigen Spiegelungen der Projektionen und der Besucher jene verwirrende Fülle, die die Freizeit des modernen Menschen bedroht. Akustische Signale, gesprochene Texte und Musik von Tonbändern ergänzten die Dynamik der visuellen Gestaltungsmittel.

1. Interior of the core of the section, known as "Maze". Walls, stairs and step-shaped ceiling were held in silvery shades and multiplied by mirrors. In the foreground, the access to one of the walkway tubes (subject: "Illusions"; design: Luciano Del Pezzo).
2. Plan. Key: 1 Entrance, 2 "Room of Exaltation", 3 "Room of Disillusionment", 4 "Maze", 5 "Corridor of Instruction", 6 "Caleidoscope".
3. The Maze with the mirror wall, reflecting the stairs and the fronts of the walkway tubes. The illuminated panels indicated the themes dealt with in the tubes.
4. Longitudinal section of the Maze where the visitor had to negotiate a difference in level of approx. 23 ft. Eight tubular containers of square cross-section, inserted between the flights of stairs, were reminiscent of an underground station. The tubes dealing with the four principal themes were combined in four circular walks.

1. Blick in das Kernstück der Abteilung, das »Labyrinth«. Wände, Treppen und Deckenstufen in Silberton, durch Spiegel vervielfacht. Vorne der Zugang zu einer der begehbaren Röhren (Thema »Illusionen«; Gestaltung Luciano Del Pezzo).
2. Grundriß. Legende: 1 Eingang, 2 Raum der Überschwenglichkeit, 3 Raum der Ernüchterung, 4 Labyrinth, 5 Korridor der Unterweisung, 6 Kaleidoskop.
3. Labyrinth mit Spiegelwand, die Treppen und Stirnseiten der begehbaren Röhren reflektierte. Die Leuchtfelder nannten die in den Röhren behandelten Themen.
4. Längsschnitt durch das Labyrinth, in dem der Besucher einen Höhenunterschied von etwa 7 m zu überwinden hatte. Acht röhrenförmige Behälter mit quadratischem Querschnitt, die sich zwischen die Treppenläufe schoben, ließen an eine U-Bahn-Station denken. Die die vier Hauptthemen behandelnden Röhren waren in vier Rundgängen zusammengefaßt.

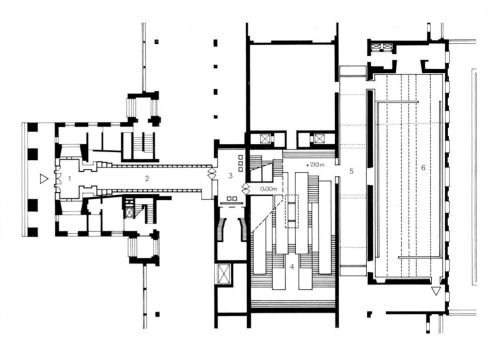

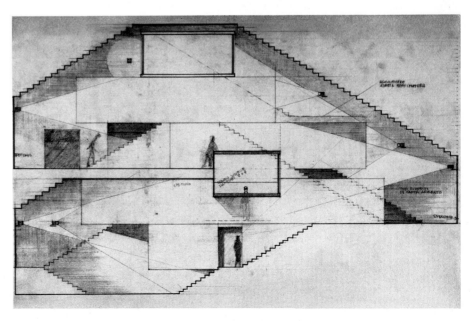

5–7. "Corridor of Instruction". The visitor took a seat on a bench in the centre of the entirely symmetric room. Each of the short sides was taken up by an illuminated panel with textual and pictorial information. Common-place slogans concerning leisure time were flashed on a screen (6), alternating with the counter slogan, warning against the industrialisation of leisure time, flashed on the opposite screen (7). Intermittent floodlights shed their light over the seated visitors and over a group of plaster dummies mounted in mirror arrangement on the ceiling – symbols of helpless victims of modern publicity.

8. Cross-section of the "Caleidoscope". The apex of the 34 ft. high equilateral triangle supported the film projector platform. The heavy lines on the outside indicate the boundary surfaces of the 59 ft. high hexagonal prism which the visitor had the illusion of seeing.

9. Interior of the 79 ft. long "Caleidoscope"; in the background on the right, adjoining the reflecting end wall, was the triangular entrance. From the projector stage, two nine-minute films were simultaneously projected on the white floor while the six-fold mirror effect gave rise to sophisticated transitions and intersections during the different phases of the films.

5–7. »Korridor der Unterweisung«. Der Besucher nahm auf einer Bank im Zentrum des völlig symmetrisch gestalteten Raumes Platz. Auf beiden Schmalseiten je ein Leuchtfeld mit Text- und Bildinformationen; abwechselnd aufflackernde banale Werbesprüche über Freizeit auf der einen Wand (6), die Gegenparole, die vor der Industrialisierung der Freizeit warnte, auf dem gegenüberliegenden Leuchtschirm (7). Aufleuchtende Scheinwerfer strahlten die sitzenden Besucher und eine spiegelbildlich an der Decke montierte Gruppe von Mannequins aus Gips an – Symbole der Hilflosigkeit gegenüber dem Ansturm der modernen Werbemittel.

8. Querschnitt durch das »Kaleidoskop«. An der Spitze des 10,30 m hohen, gleichseitigen Dreiecks die Projektionsbühne für die Filmvorführungen. Die stark ausgezogenen äußeren Linien deuten die Begrenzungsflächen des 18 m hohen, sechsseitigen Prismas an, das der Betrachter zu sehen glaubte.

9. Blick in das 24 m lange »Kaleidoskop«; rechts hinten neben der reflektierenden Stirnwand der dreieckige Zugang. Von der Filmbühne aus wurden auf den weißen Fußboden gleichzeitig zwei Neun-Minuten-Filme projiziert, wobei die sechsfache Spiegelung raffinierte Übergänge und Überschneidungen in den einzelnen Filmphasen hervorrief.

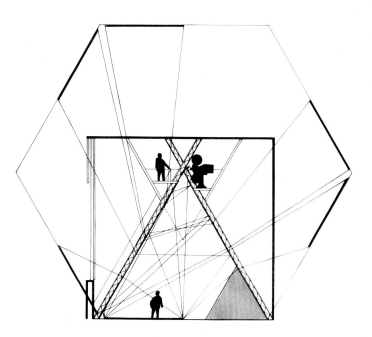

British Section

XIIIth Triennale, Milan, 1963
Architect: Theo Crosby, London

Britain's contribution to the theme of leisure-time – the leitmotif of this Triennale – was clearly influenced by Pop Art. The visitor was guided through a room of complicated shape, built with very simple materials such as raw timber boards, and displaying articles and equipment for leisure-time of all types and for all ages. The interesting arrangement of the room, which precluded the risk of any pedagogic pedantry, was further enlivened by lighting effects. Thus, provision was made for darkening the central space for simultaneous projections on five picture screens. Some products of the fine arts, especially those placed near the entrance, showed that the do-it-yourself game of Pop Art can be attractively combined with leisure-time occupations. Joe Tilson painted the ceiling of the central space with letters and symbols of the kind found on tea chests.

Britische Abteilung

XIII. Triennale, Mailand, 1963
Architekt: Theo Crosby, London

Englands Beitrag zum Thema Freizeit, dem Leitgedanken dieser Triennale, war deutlich von der Pop Art beeinflußt. Der Besucher wurde durch ein räumlich kompliziert erscheinendes Gehäuse gelenkt, das aus ganz simplen Materialien wie rohen Brettern bestand und als Exponate Freizeitgeräte jeder Art und für jedes Alter aufnahm. Die interessante Raumgliederung, durch die die Gefahr einer eintönig aufgereihten Lehrschau gebannt wurde, war durch Beleuchtungseffekte verstärkt. So konnte der Hauptraum für die gleichzeitige Projektion auf fünf Bildschirmen abgedunkelt werden. Einige Werke der bildenden Kunst, besonders am Eingang, demonstrierten, daß sich das Do-it-yourself-Spiel der Pop Art mit der Freizeitgestaltung besonders reizvoll in Verbindung bringen läßt. Joe Tilson bemalte die Decke des Hauptraumes mit Buchstaben und Symbolen, wie man sie auf Verpackungskisten findet.

1. The central space as seen from the position marked B on the plan. The leisure-time implements were casually arranged on a sloping artificial lawn.
2. The central space, darkened for the projection of slides, as seen from the position marked C on the plan. The box-shaped protrusions of the walls above the display tables served as projection screens.
3–5. Sections and plan show the polyhedral shape of the British Section. The letters on the plan indicate the points from which the photographs were taken.

1. Der Hauptraum vom Standpunkt B des Grundrisses aus. Auf der ansteigenden künstlichen Rasenlandschaft lagen wie zufällig verstreut Freizeitgeräte.
2. Der für eine Diavorführung verdunkelte Hauptraum vom Standpunkt C aus. Die kistenartig vorgezogenen Wandteile über den Ausstellungsflächen dienten als Projektionsschirme.
3–5. Schnitte und Grundriß spiegeln das polyedrische Gebilde der britischen Sektion wider. Die Buchstaben bezeichnen die Standpunkte des Fotografen für die verschiedenen Aufnahmen.

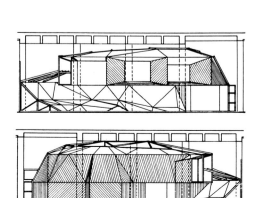

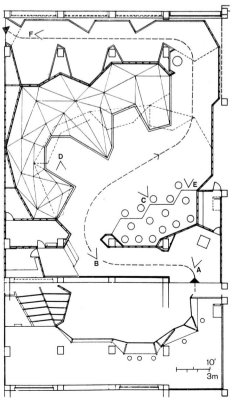

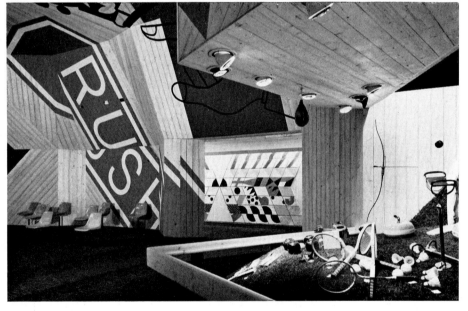

6. Entrance zone, seen from the position marked A on the plan. In front of the tapestry created by Harold Cohen is a sculpture by Eduardo Paolozzi, consisting of aluminium castings which can be combined at will and are reminiscent of machine parts and prefabricated units.

7. Entrance zone, seen from the central space (position D). In the background a mural by Joe Tilson.

8. The approach to the exit, here seen from position F, was flanked by walls on which enlarged photographs were mounted. Some of these sections were so realistic that the spectator was at pains to distinguish between photographic illusion and reality.

9. This photograph of the exit part of the central space, taken from position E, clearly shows the lively interplay of architecture, art and exhibits.

6. Eingang vom Standpunkt A aus. Vor dem Wandteppich von Harold Cohen eine Skulptur von Eduardo Paolozzi. Sie besteht aus gegossenen Aluminiumteilen, die beliebig kombiniert werden können und an Maschinenteile und vorfabrizierte Elemente erinnern.

7. Blick vom Hauptraum zum Eingangsraum (Position D). Im Hintergrund ein Wandbild von Joe Tilson.

8. Der Weg zum Ausgang, vom Standpunkt F aus gesehen, wurde von Wänden mit Großfotos begleitet. Die Ausschnitte waren zum Teil so realistisch, daß der Betrachter Mühe hatte, fotografische Illusion und Wirklichkeit auseinanderzuhalten.

9. Diese Perspektive vom Hauptraum zum Ausgang hin (Standpunkt E) verdeutlicht das lebendige Zusammenwirken von Architektur, Kunst und Ausstellungsgut.

Finnish Section

XIIIth Triennale, Milan, 1963
Design: Antti and Vuokko Nurmesniemi,
Helsinki

In contrast to the British Section with its undertones of Pop Art, the Finns had preferred a competition design which was distinguished by sophisticated simplicity. The plan of the room was rectangular, yet most of it was taken up by the differently curved arcs of two asymmetric wall panels. A ceiling of thin white fabric was stretched out at a height of 9 ft., immediately above the curved wall panels. Through this ceiling filtered the diffused light from the fluorescent light fittings mounted above it so that the room, which was deliberately left devoid of any special accents, was evenly lit. Both wall panels were covered with enlarged photographs depicting the basic elements of the Finnish landscape: water, forest, reeds, snow, sky. Exhibits such as boats, spears, skis, the model of a glider, etc. were displayed in front of these walls.

Finnische Abteilung

XIII. Triennale, Mailand, 1963
Entwurf: Antti und Vuokko Nurmesniemi,
Helsinki

Im Gegensatz zu der mit Anklängen an die Pop Art aufgemachten britischen Abteilung hatten die Finnen einem Wettbewerbsentwurf von raffinierter Einfachheit den Vorzug gegeben. Der Grundriß des Ausstellungsraumes war an sich rechteckig, doch durchzogen ihn fast in seinem ganzen Ausmaß die verschieden weit ausschwingenden Bögen zweier spiegelverkehrt symmetrischer Wandstücke. Über den gekurvten Wänden spannte sich in 2,70 m Höhe eine weiße Stoffdecke. Durch sie strömte diffus das Licht der darüber montierten Beleuchtungsanlagen, so daß der betont akzentlose Raum gleichmäßige Helligkeit erhielt. Beide Wandstücke waren überzogen von Großfotos mit den Elementen finnischer Landschaft: Wasser, Wald, Schilf, Schnee, Himmel. Davor ordneten sich die Ausstellungsgegenstände wie Boote, Speere, Skier, das Modell eines Segelflugzeugs.

1. Part of one of the two curved wall panels
which were held in position by invisible steel
frames and were placed on a floor covered with
white plastic sheets.
2, 3. Longitudinal section and plan.
4. A wooden boat and one made of plastics, displayed against the background of an enlarged
photograph of a wind-swept lake.
5. Photographic display in the entrance hall,
composed of many scenic pictures.
6. Real objects with the backcloth of an enlarged
photograph showing a snow-covered forest and
a summer sky enlivened by clouds.

1. Ausschnitt aus einer der beiden geschwunge-
nen Fotowände, die, von Stahlrahmen gehalten,
auf weißem Kunststoffboden standen.
2, 3. Längsschnitt und Grundriß.
4. Ein Holz- und ein Kunststoffboot vor dem
Großfoto einer bewegten Wasserfläche.
5. Aus vielen Szenenfotos montierte Bildwand
am Eingangsflur.
6. Reale Objekte vor den Großfotos eines ver-
schneiten Waldes und eines Sommerhimmels.

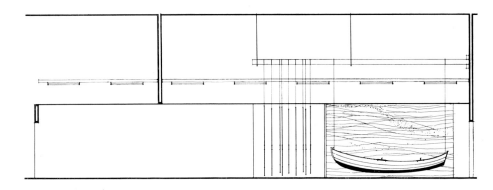

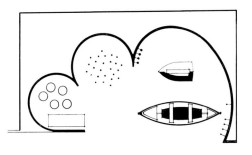

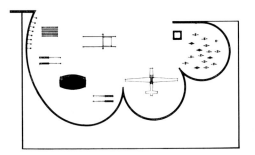

Leisure Time

Finnish Section at the ''Italia 61''
Exhibition
Palazzo del Lavoro, Turin, 1961
Design: Tapio Periänen, Helsinki

A dramatic and dynamic effect can be obtained even by the most simple means such as, in this case, the juxtaposition of display panels merely varying in height and size. The theme of 'Leisure Time' was depicted by the Finns in two large groups of photographic displays: a circular core formed by closely-spaced display panels was placed nearly into the corner of the exhibition room from which further groups of pictures radiated in several directions. Inside the inner circle, there was an audio-visual auditorium for 30 people. The panels in this part of the exhibition showed people and groups of people who faced the clusters of panels placed along the main walls of the room. These enlarged photographs illustrated the various possibilities of spending one's leisure time, offered to man in almost prodigious variety.

Freizeitgestaltung

Finnische Abteilung der Ausstellung
»Italia 61«
Palazzo del Lavoro, Turin, 1961
Entwurf: Tapio Periänen, Helsinki

Eine dramatisch-dynamische Wirkung kann selbst mit einfachsten Mitteln erreicht werden, etwa wie hier durch das Scharen von Bildtafeln, die nur in Höhe und Format variieren. Das Thema Freizeit wurde von den Finnen in zwei großen Gruppen aus Foto-tafeln dargestellt: Ein kreisförmiger Kern aus eng gestellten Tafeln war beinahe in die Ecke des Ausstellungsraumes gerückt, von wo er in mehrere Richtungen durch weitere Bildergruppen ausstrahlte. In seinem Innern umschloß er einen Aufenthalts- und Vorführraum für 30 Personen. Die Tafeln dieses Ausstellungskerns zeigten Menschen und Menschengruppen, die sich den bogenförmig an den Hauptwänden des Raumes entlanggestellten Bildtafelscharen zuwenden. Diese Großfotos illustrierten die Möglich-keiten der Freizeitgestaltung, wie sie sich dem Menschen in fast überreicher Fülle bieten.

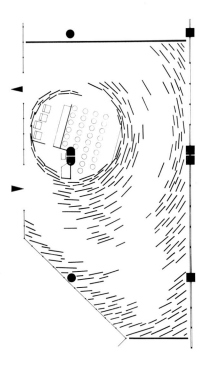

1. Cluster of display panels at the exhibition entrance: Historic prelude, showing how working conditions, and therefore also spare-time conditions, developed in the course of time. Early ways of spending one's leisure time.

2. Plan. Top left, the circular core of the exhibition with auditorium, library and storage room; on the right and below, the outer clusters of display panels.

3, 4. Further sections of the outer clusters, dealing with the various possibilities of spending one's leisure time. Each of the wooden panels displaying the enlarged photographs was placed on two tubular steel supports anchored in the marble floor.

5. The circular core of the exhibition with a composition of pictures of individual people and groups of people. The basic idea of the exhibition culminated in the problematic phrase: "Man has time to ask himself what it means to be a man".

1. Tafelgruppe am Ausstellungseingang; historischer Auftakt, Entwicklung der Arbeitszeit und damit auch der freien Zeit. Erste »Freizeitgestaltung«.

2. Grundriß. Links oben der kreisförmige Ausstellungskern mit Vortragsraum, Bibliothek und Lagerraum, rechts und unten die äußeren Bildtafelgruppen.

3, 4. Weitere Ausschnitte aus den äußeren Fotogruppen zum Thema Freizeitmöglichkeiten. Die Holztafeln mit den aufgezogenen Vergrößerungen standen auf zwei fest im Marmorfußboden verankerten Stahlrohrfüßen.

5. Der ringförmige Ausstellungskern mit den sich staffelnden Bildern von einzelnen Menschen und Menschengruppen. Die Leitidee der Ausstellung gipfelte in dem Satz »Der Mensch hat Zeit, sich zu fragen, was es bedeutet, ein Mensch zu sein«, der die Problematik der Freizeit aufzeigt.

**Industrial Organisation, Productivity,
Market**

Italian Section at the "Italia 61"
exhibition
Palazzo del Lavoro, Turin, 1961
Architects: Franco Albini,
Egidio Bonfante, Milan

**Industrielle Organisation, Produktivität,
Markt**

Italienische Abteilung der Ausstellung
»Italia 61«
Palazzo del Lavoro, Turin, 1961
Architekten: Franco Albini,
Egidio Bonfante, Mailand

The theme of "Organisation, Productivity and Market in Modern Industry" was demonstrated to the visitor by means of an ingenious contrivance. In front of three groups of seats arranged in the hall, the intensification of industrial production was demonstrated, under the headings: "Development of the Machine", "Development of Engines", and "Development in Work Organisation", by means of display panels sliding along on rails. The optical affinity to the production line and conveyor belt systems of a modern factory was obvious. By this display, the attention of the visitors was concentrated on the central part of the fairly high exhibition hall whilst further material was displayed on four of the five outer walls. This section of the exhibition was separated from the remainder of the hall by wall panels covered with dark cloth.

Das Thema »Organisation, Produktivität und Markt in der modernen Industrie« wurde dem Besucher durch einen geschickten Einfall vor Augen geführt. Auf Gleitschienen zogen an den drei im Ausstellungsraum verteilten Sitzgruppen Schautafeln vorbei, die – in die Themen »Werdegang der Maschine«, »Entwicklung der Motoren« und »Entwicklung der Arbeitsorganisation« gegliedert – die Steigerung der industriellen Produktion demonstrierten. Der optische Anklang an die Fließ- und Förderbänder einer modernen Fabrikationsstätte war offensichtlich. Diese Schau konzentrierte das Interesse der Besucher auf den mittleren Teil des recht hohen Ausstellungsraumes, an dessen vier von fünf Außenwänden weiteres Informationsmaterial dargeboten wurde. Mit dunklem Stoff bespannte Wände schlossen die Ausstellung vom übrigen Teil der Halle ab.

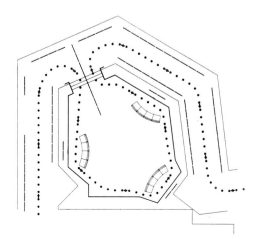

1. Three steel columns in the centre of the main room carried parts of the three lines of sliding rails, each of which was marked by a different colour. On each side of the triangle formed by these columns, the conveyor belt assigned to a given theme was lowered to eye level. The spectators were protected by railings and barriers.

2–5. Various perspectives and details of the central part of the room.

6. Plan. The core with the pictorial conveyor belts was encircled by a passageway which was, in its turn, surrounded by five outer walls. The dotted line indicates the route taken by the visitors.

1. Drei Stahlstützen im Zentrum des Hauptraumes trugen einen Teil der drei Gleitschienen, die jeweils mit einer anderen Farbe markiert waren. Auf jeder Seite des inneren Mastendreiecks senkte sich das einem bestimmten Thema zugeordnete Förderband bis auf Augenhöhe. Schutzgitter und Abschrankungen sicherten die Betrachter.

2–5. Verschiedene Perspektiven und Detailansichten des Mittelsaales.

6. Grundriß. Fünf Außenwände umschlossen einen Gang und dann den Mittelraum mit den Bild-Förderbahnen. Die gepunktete Linie kennzeichnet den Besichtigungsweg.

Careers Advice and Professional Training

German Section at the "Italia 61"
exhibition
Palazzo del Lavoro, Turin, 1961
Architect: Wolfgang Bley, Karlsruhe
Associates: Dieter Flimm, Elmar Schlote
Graphic artists: Novum, Gesellschaft für
neue Graphik mbH, Frankfurt-on-Main

Berufsberatung und Berufsausbildung

Deutsche Abteilung der Ausstellung
»Italia 61«
Palazzo del Lavoro, Turin, 1961
Architekt: Wolfgang Bley, Karlsruhe
Mitarbeiter: Dieter Flimm, Elmar Schlote
Grafik: Novum, Gesellschaft für neue
Graphik mbH, Frankfurt am Main

The entrance hall was accentuated by the "Careers Tower", built up from flat brick-shaped boxes. The front drawings wittily depicted the array of careers confronting the school-leaver; at the rear, pictures symbolizing the professions favoured by the Muses. Behind the entrance hall, the exhibition continued on two levels, with displays dealing with some typical careers on the ground floor and with academic careers on the upper floor. The displays were arranged partly on flush panels placed on a rectangular grid and supported by transverse wooden frames painted black, and partly on frames of the same size, pasted to the floor side by side and carrying either display panels or three-dimensional exhibits. Despite the somewhat dull theme of the exhibition, the treatment of the details resulted in a lively optical effect.

Den hohen Eingangsraum akzentuierte der aus flachen Rechteckkästen aufgebaute »Turm der Berufe«. Die Bildflächen der Vorderseite gaben mit grafischem Witz die verwirrende Fülle von Berufsmöglichkeiten wieder, der sich der Schulentlassene gegenübersieht; auf der Rückseite waren symbolisch die musischen Berufe angedeutet. Die Ausstellung setzte sich dann zweigeschossig fort. Sie zeigte im Erdgeschoß einige typische Berufswege und auf der Empore die Hochschulbildung. Als Ausstellungsträger kreuzten sich über einem Rechteckraster glatte Plattenwände, von quergestellten schwarzen Holzrahmen gehalten, und nebeneinanderstehende, auf dem Boden aufgeklebte Rahmen, die teils Platten, teils plastische Exponate trugen. Die einfallsreiche Behandlung der Details ergab trotz des spröden Themas eine lebendige optische Wirkung.

1. Careers Tower. Rear display, symbolizing the professions favoured by the Muses.
2. Careers Tower. Front display, symbolizing the bewildering array of careers.
3. Typical longitudinal display wall, transversed by supporting frames.
4, 5. Display panels, depicting "The forest as the patron of all timber-processing careers" and, on the opposite side, "The professional training of joiners and carpenters", with models.
6, 7. Supporting frames (measuring 9 ft. 6 in. × 3 ft. 1¹/₂ in. × 1 ft. ¹/₂ in.) with adjoining sides. Such frames were also used as supports for the longitudinal panels, as structural components for the entrance tower, and as frames for cupboards and shelves. Spherical light fittings with brackets and junction boxes. The spheres rest freely on ring supports so that they can be turned in any direction without disturbing the picture.

1. Turm der Berufe. Rückseite: Symbole der musischen Berufe.
2. Turm der Berufe. Eingangsseite: Chaos der Berufe.
3. Typische Längs-Plattenwand, durchkreuzt von Stützrahmen.
4, 5. Schautafeln »Der Wald als Basis der holzverarbeitenden Berufe« und gegenüberstehende Wand »Tischlerausbildung« mit Modellen.
6, 7. In Querrichtung nebeneinanderstehende Rahmen (292×95×32 cm), die auch als Träger für die Längswände, als Bauelemente für den Eingangsturm sowie als Schränke und Regale verwendet wurden. Kugelleuchten mit Ausleger und Anschlußkasten. Durch die auf einem Ring aufliegende Kugelform können die Strahler beliebig gedreht werden.

3

4

5

6

7

Raw Materials

Sub-section of the Italian Section at the
"Italia 61" Exhibition
Palazzo del Lavoro, Turin, 1961
Architect: Ettore Sottsass jr., Milan
Graphic artist: Heinz Waibl, Milan

Rohstoffe

Unterabteilung der italienischen Sektion
der Ausstellung »Italia 61«
Palazzo del Lavoro, Turin, 1961
Architekt: Ettore Sottsass jr., Mailand
Grafik: Heinz Waibl, Mailand

This section of the Italian centenary exhibition displayed the raw materials which are used, in modern industry, either in a traditional manner, or in finished or modified form, or as the result of recent research: steel, aluminium, plastics, synthetic fibres, etc. The entrance hall was flanked by high and slender supports, illuminated from the rear and extended to the shining black ceiling, displaying title pictures and pages from journals which provide a cross-section of our modern world. Their multi-coloured appearance in conjunction with the colour lighting was particularly attractive. The three principal groups of displays were composed of mirror-lined prismatic recesses. Through these mirrors, the exhibits were optically multiplied, which could be interpreted as an allusion to modern mass production methods.

In dieser Abteilung wurden die Rohstoffe vor Augen geführt, die von der modernen Industrie entweder in der althergebrachten Weise, in veredelter beziehungsweise abgewandelter Form oder aber als Ergebnis jüngerer Forschungsarbeiten verwendet werden: Stahl, Aluminium, Kunststoffe, synthetische Fasern usw. Um den Eingangsraum gruppierten sich hohe, schmale »Stelen«, von rückwärts erleuchtet und bis zur glänzend schwarz lackierten Decke reichend, die Titelbilder und Zeitschriftenseiten als Querschnitt durch unsere Welt trugen. Ihre Buntheit in Verbindung mit dem farbigen Licht war von besonderer Delikatesse. Die drei eigentlichen Ausstellungsgruppen setzten sich aus prismatischen Spiegelkojen zusammen. Durch die Spiegelung wurden die Ausstellungsstücke optisch vervielfältigt, als Hinweis auf die moderne Großserienproduktion deutbar.

1. Due to the reflection of the light, the entrance room ceiling, composed of narrow battens, has the appearance of a barrel vault. The flooring is of black glass mosaics.

2, 3. Mirror-lined recesses, some of them illuminated by coloured lights (blue, green, mauve).

4. Plan: Key: 1 Introductory hall, 2 Raw materials existing but only used in modern times, 3 Newly developed raw materials, 4 Existing raw materials subjected to new transformation processes.

1. Durch die Lichtreflexe wirkte die aus schmalen Leisten zusammengesetzte Decke des Eingangsraumes wie ein Tonnengewölbe. Fußboden aus schwarzem Glasmosaik.

2, 3. Spiegelkojen, zum Teil farbig beleuchtet (blau, grün, lila).

4. Grundriß. Legende: 1 Einführung, 2 Vorhandene, aber zum Teil jetzt erst verwendete Rohstoffe, 3 Neu entwickelte Rohstoffe, 4 Vorhandene und neu verarbeitete Rohstoffe.

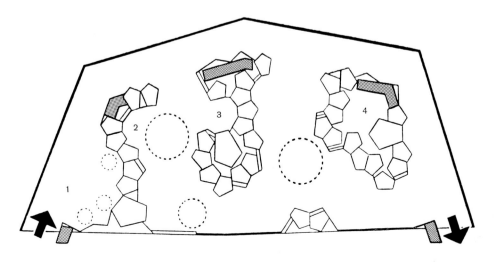

Exhibition of the German Federal Post Office

International Exhibition of Transport and Communications, Munich, 1965
Architect: Horst Döhnert, Munich

The show arranged by the German Federal Post Office was spread over two inter-linking halls. The larger hall, covering an area of 197×328 ft., was concerned with postal technology and the smaller hall, measuring 89×328 ft., with telecommunication techniques. In both halls, a skew arrangement was adopted so that several staggered sub-areas were created. The marking of a guide path for visitors was deliberately avoided. In the first hall, concerned with postal technology, the visitor was able to turn, from the representative entrance zone, either to the historic sections or to the different sections conveying an overall picture of modern postal services. In the second hall, concerned with telecommunications techniques, much of the floor area was taken up by a "sea" basin, where flashlights symbolised telecommunications over long distances.

Ausstellung der Deutschen Bundespost

Internationale Verkehrsausstellung, München, 1965
Architekt: Horst Döhnert, München

Die Deutsche Bundespost berichtete über ihre Arbeit in zwei Hallen, von denen die größere auf einer Fläche von 60×100 m die Posttechnik, die kleinere auf 27×100 m die Fernmeldetechnik zum Thema hatte. In beiden Hallen wurden die Ausstellungsgrundrisse schräg zur Hallenachse gedreht, so daß sich gegeneinander versetzte Raumgruppen ergaben. Auf eine vorgeschriebene Wegführung wurde verzichtet. In der ersten Halle konnte sich der Besucher vom repräsentativ gestalteten Eingangsbereich aus den historischen Abteilungen oder den verschiedenen Sektoren zuwenden, die einen Überblick über den modernen Postdienst gaben. In der zweiten Halle nahm ein großes »Meer«-Becken einen beträchtlichen Teil der Bodenfläche ein, über das hinweg Blinklichter die Nachrichtenübermittlung über große Entfernungen symbolisierten.

1–4. For captions, see next page.
5. Plan. Key: 1 Information centre, 2 World Postal Union, 3 Stamp printing works, 4 Postal history, 5 Automatic parcel sorting, 6 Automated post office, 7 Letter output, 8 Office, 9 Letter input, 10 Suspended monorail for mail bags, 11 Post giro office, 12 Cinema, 13 Museum, 14 Sub post office, 15 Workshop.

1–4. Bildunterschriften siehe folgende Seite.
5. Grundriß. Legende: 1 Informationszentrum, 2 Weltpostverein, 3 Briefmarkendruckerei, 4 Postgeschichte, 5 Automatische Paketsortierung, 6 Automatisches Postamt, 7 Briefabgang, 8 Büro, 9 Briefeingang, 10 Beutelhängebahn, 11 Postscheckamt, 12 Kino, 13 Museum, 14 Nebenstellenanlage, 15 Werkstatt.

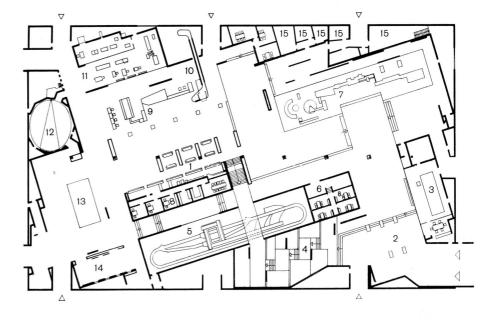

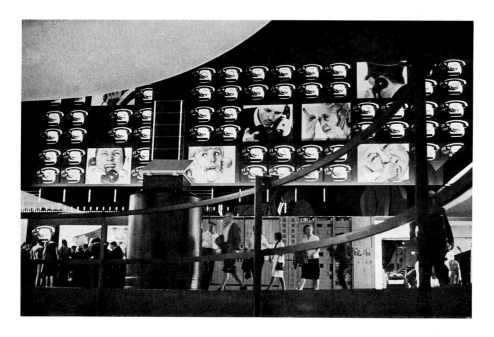

1. (Page 90) Historic-folklore section, seen from the entrance hall.
2. (Page 90) Rotary sculpture composed of interlaced cubes, symbolising the interplay of different postal services.
3. (Page 91) Philatelic section with transparent enlargements in illuminated showcases in front of informally arranged columns.
4. (Page 91) Letter sorting machine, white illuminated display panels, diagrams and black background blend into a single, integrated display.

1. (Seite 90) Blick von der Eingangshalle in die historisch-folkloristische Abteilung.
2. (Seite 90) Drehplastik aus verzahnten Kuben: Symbol des Ineinandergreifens verschiedener Dienste.
3. (Seite 91) Die Briefmarkenabteilung mit transparenten Vergrößerungen in den Leuchtkästen vor den frei gruppierten Pfeilern.
4. (Seite 91) Briefsortiermaschine, weiße Leuchtfelder, grafische Schautafeln und schwarzer Hintergrund bilden eine Einheit.

6. Part of the Telecommunications Hall. End wall of the hall, seen from the pit surrounding the radio tower (cf. Fig. 8). The wall display demonstrated the possibility of conducting several telephone conversations over the same line. The method was illustrated by photographs of different telephone subscribers and recurring pictures of telephone sets.
7. A display demonstrating the setting up of a telephone call.
8. Other highlights of this part of the exhibition were the radio tower and the technical studios (left).
9. Large abstractions at the ends of the water basin in the centre symbolised transmitter and receiver.

6. Detail aus der Halle Fernmeldetechnik: Blick von der Bodenvertiefung rings um den Funkturm (siehe Abb. 8) auf die Abschlußwand der Halle. Hier wurde eine Schaltung aufgebaut, die zeigt, wie gleichzeitig mehrere Telefongespräche auf einer Leitung geführt werden. Fotos verschiedener Fernsprechteilnehmer und Serienbilder von Telefonapparaten illustrieren den Vorgang.
7. Eine Ausstellungsgruppe, die das Zustandekommen eines Telefongesprächs demonstriert.
8. Einen weiteren Schwerpunkt dieser Halle bilden der Funkturm und die technischen Studios (links).
9. Großformige Abstraktionen an den Enden des zentralen Wasserbeckens symbolisieren Sender und Empfänger.

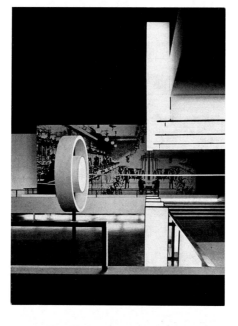

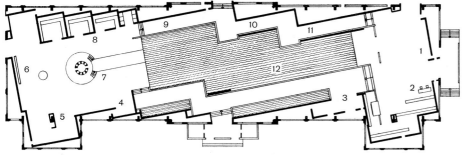

10. The commotion of the water basin, which was spanned by viewing bridges, was mirrored on large metal panels. Blue lights emerging from the water and vertical beacons flashed signals from one shore to the other. The intended effect was enhanced by models of satellites suspended from the black ceiling and by the sound track of an automatic transmitter.
11. Plan of Telecommunications Hall. Key: 1 Path of a worldwide connection set up by dialling, 2 Dialling for local, trunk and overseas telephone calls, 3 Electronic telephone exchanges, 4 Radio and television techniques, 5 Telegraphy, 6 Carrier frequency and cable techniques, 7 Radio beam techniques, 8 Advances in transmission technology, 9 Satellite techniques, 10 Radio services, 11 Cable manufacture, 12 Water basin, agitated by artificial waves, suggesting long-distance communications.

10. Die Laufstege für die Besucher führen über die von einer Wellenmaschine aufgerührte zentrale Wasserfläche, deren Bewegung sich in großen Metallflächen spiegelt. Blaue Lampen über dem Wasser und senkrechte Leuchtbalken blinken von Ufer zu Ufer. Satellitenmodelle unter der schwarzen Decke sowie die Geräuschkulisse eines Maschinensenders verstärken den beabsichtigten Effekt.
11. Grundriß der Halle Fernmeldetechnik. Legende: 1 Weg einer weltweiten Wählverbindung, 2 Wählvermittlung für Orts-, Fern- und Auslandsgespräche, 3 Elektronische Vermittlungen, 4 Hörfunk und Fernsehtechnik, 5 Telegrafie, 6 Trägerfrequenz und Kabeltechnik, 7 Richtfunktechnik, 8 Übertragungstechnische Weiterentwicklungen, 9 Satellitentechnik, 10 Funkdienste, 11 Kabelbau, 12 Wasserfläche zur Sichtbarmachung der zu bewältigenden Entfernungen.

Exhibition of the German Federal Railway

International Exhibition of Transport
and Communications, Munich, 1965
Architecture and design: Paolo Nestler,
Munich; Associates: Ludwig Steck, Hans
Krauss, Hubert Bauer, Rudolf Gehringer,
Werner März, Rudolf Werner, Simon
Butz, Reinmut Weber, Gerhard Konrad,
Rudolf Caster

Ausstellung der Deutschen Bundesbahn

Internationale Verkehrsausstellung,
München, 1965
Architektur und Gestaltung: Paolo
Nestler, München; Mitarbeiter: Ludwig
Steck, Hans Krauss, Hubert Bauer,
Rudolf Gehringer, Werner März,
Rudolf Werner, Simon Butz, Reinmut
Weber, Gerhard Konrad, Rudolf Caster

The programme of the exhibition, divided into thirteen themes, was intended to provide a picture of the activities of the German Federal Railway. The large, basically rectangular hall was entered through the transparent entrance pavilion where information was available about everything "preceding the journey". Through a tunnel, the passageway continued past displays depicting the services offered and techniques used by the Federal Railway, past the "DB-Vision" (cf. page 66), to the restaurant designed as a schematised dining car, and past a display of historic objects. The integral character of the different sections was ensured by the adoption of a uniform design principle, mainly characterized by the systematic use of light/dark contrasts and by the use of the ceiling for such exhibits as signals, illuminated panels, models, projection screens, etc.

Das umfangreiche Ausstellungsprogramm, in dreizehn Einzelthemen gegliedert, sollte die Leistungen der Bundesbahn in ihrer ganzen Breite charakterisieren. Der Besucher betrat die große, in ihrer Grundform rechteckige Halle durch den transparenten Eingangspavillon, der über alles Auskunft gab, »was vor der Reise liegt«. Durch einen Tunnel führte der Weg weiter zu Darstellungen aus dem Angebot und der Technik der Bundesbahn, zur »DB-Vision« (siehe Seite 66), zum Restaurant in Form eines stilisierten Speisewagens, durch eine Schau historischer Gegenstände. Die verschiedenen Abteilungen waren durch ein einheitliches Gestaltungsprinzip verbunden, das sich besonders auf Hell-Dunkel-Kontraste und die Ausnutzung der Decken als Ausstellungsträger für Signale, Leuchtkästen, Modelle, Projektionswände stützte.

1. Entrance room. General information, and visual extension of the "Symphony of Signals" erected outside the hall.
2. Entrance room with display panels dealing with goods traffic, seen against the background of enlarged photographs of station buildings.
3. Pyramid-shaped showcases with models of rolling stock. Illuminated boxes with photographic slides are suspended from the ceiling. In the background, a night photograph of a vast multi-track approach to a large station, covering the entire width of the wall.
4. Start of a journey. The destination boards displayed above the mock-up of the head of a diesel locomotive convey an impression of the service range of the German Federal Railway.

1. Eingangsraum. Allgemeine Informationen, Fortsetzung der vor der Halle aufgebauten »Sinfonie der Signale«.
2. Eingangsraum mit den Informationstafeln zum Thema Güterverkehr, vor Großfotos von Bahnhofshallen montiert.
3. Pyramidenschaukästen mit Modellen des Fahrzeugparks. An der Decke Dia-Leuchtkästen vor der wandbreiten Nachtaufnahme eines großstädtischen Schienengewirrs.
4. Auftakt zur Reise. Die Zuglaufschilder über der Kopfattrappe einer Diesellok verdeutlichen den Aktionsradius der Bundesbahn.

Road Traffic in Germany

International Exhibition of Transport
and Communications, Munich, 1965
Architects: G. Weber, H. Gebhard,
K. W. Boresch, Munich
Graphic design: K. Peschke and E. Strom

Straßenverkehr in Deutschland

Internationale Verkehrsausstellung,
München, 1965
Architekten: G. Weber, H. Gebhard,
K. W. Boresch, München
Grafische Gestaltung: K. Peschke und
E. Strom

For the presentation of road traffic and its problems, a hall with a floor area over 25,000 sq ft. was available. The task was to create an interesting display with exhibits mainly consisting of dry statistics and diagrams. The design was based on a three-dimensional module of 8 ft. 2 in. which governed the pattern of the ceiling, the size of the display panels suspended from it on two levels, and the dimensions of the cubes, prisms and pyramids into which further display panels were combined. The arrangement of the display material in the space available, the lively alternation of display units (enlarged photographs; canvas-mounted photographs, projections and abstract graphic designs), and effective colour scheme – black/white contrast with a few intensive colour shades – resulted in an interesting and lucid exhibition.

Für die Interpretation des Straßenverkehrs und seiner Probleme standen etwa 2500 m² Hallenfläche zur Verfügung. In diesen neutralen Raum sollte eine lebendige Ausstellung hineingebaut werden, deren Anschauungsmaterial vorwiegend aus trockenen Statistiken und schematischen Darstellungen bestand. Für den technischen Aufbau wurde ein räumlicher Raster von 2,50 m gewählt, der die Deckenausbildung, das Format der daran in zwei Höhenzonen aufgehängten Tafeln sowie der Würfel, Prismen und Pyramiden bestimmte, zu denen sich weitere Tafeln zusammenfügten. Durch geglückte räumliche Gruppierungen, abwechslungsreiche Details (Großfotos, hinterleuchtete Leinenfotos, Projektionen, freie grafische Entwürfe) und eine wirkungsvolle Farbgebung – Schwarz-Weiß-Kontrast mit wenigen Farbtönen – gelang eine anschauliche Gesamtdarbietung.

1. Entrance hall. The traffic "Moloch" was symbolised by steel guide rails and wheels suspended from the ceiling. In the background, a caricature of a piston engine.
2. Abstracted sculpture of a bus, symbolising public transport.
3. A view of the "History of the Road" exhibition in the statistical section, with statistics of road traffic densities and motor vehicle ownership in Europe.
4, 5. Parts of the "Road Documentation" section in the main exhibition hall: Counter-rotating cylinders and enlarged photographs of motorway sections; displays depicting auxiliary services for the motorist (meteorological service, road patrols).

1. Eingangshalle. Unter der Decke montierte stählerne Leitplanken und Räder symbolisierten den Moloch Verkehr. Im Hintergrund die Karikatur eines Kolbenmotors.
2. Abstrahierte Omnibusplastik als Sinnbild für Massentransportmittel.
3. Durchblick zur »Geschichte der Straße« in der statistischen Abteilung: Darstellungen der Straßenbelastung und des Kraftfahrzeugbestandes in Europa.
4, 5. »Dokumentation der Straße« im Hauptraum: sich gegeneinander drehende Walzen und Großfotos von Autobahn-Teilstrecken; Darstellung der Hilfseinrichtungen für den Autofahrer (Wetterwarndienst, Straßenwartung).

Architecture in Finland

Travelling exhibition sponsored by the
Museum of Finnish Architecture, Helsinki
Stockholm, 1960; Copenhagen, 1962;
Paris, 1964
Design: Aulis Blomstedt and Heikki
Koskelo (Stockholm),
Martti Jaatinen (Copenhagen and Paris)

Architektur in Finnland

Wanderausstellungen des Finnischen
Architekturmuseums, Helsinki
Stockholm, 1960, Kopenhagen, 1962;
Paris, 1964
Gestaltung: Aulis Blomstedt und Heikki
Koskelo (Stockholm),
Martti Jaatinen (Kopenhagen und Paris)

For its travelling exhibition, the Museum of Finnish Architecture developed a style in keeping with the character of the works displayed. The Stockholm exhibition was adapted to the oblong hall by using rhythmically arranged wall display panels, low display tables and recesses formed by display panels. A special accent was provided by a sophisticated structural composition placed near the entrance. In Copenhagen, Jaatinen arranged for the large photographic display panels to be illuminated from below, using light fittings installed in floor-mounted beams. For the Paris exhibition, he developed an interesting design of thin, two-sided display panels illuminated from inside by concealed light fittings. These panels were either suspended from the ceiling or placed on table tops with gate-legged supports.

Für seine Auslandsausstellungen hat das Finnische Architekturmuseum einen Stil entwickelt, der dem Charakter der präsentierten Arbeiten adäquat ist. Die Stockholmer Ausstellung paßte sich der langgestreckten Halle in rhythmischer Reihung an: Wandtafeln, niedrige Tische und kojenartig gestellte Tafelelemente, dazu als Eingangsbetonung eine raffinierte strukturelle Komposition. In Kopenhagen ließ Jaatinen die großen Fototafeln durch bodennahe, balkenförmige Beleuchtungskörper von unten anstrahlen. Für die Pariser Ausstellung entwickelte er eine interessante Konstruktion aus doppelseitigen, flachen Ausstellungstafeln, die von innen durch verborgene Lichtquellen erleuchtet wurden. Diese Tafeln waren hängend an der Decke angebracht oder stehend in Tischplatten auf Kreuzfußgestellen eingebaut.

1. Stockholm; lengthwise view. In the fore-ground, to the left of the entrance, the wooden structures placed on a black flooring material, rising on the side of skyscraper like clusters.
2. Stockholm; crosswise view.
3, 4. Longitudinal section and layout plan of the exhibition at the Modern Museum, Stockholm.

1. Stockholm; Längsansicht. Im Vordergrund, links vom Eingang, die aus schwarzem Grund aufwachsenden, zur Seite wolkenkratzerartig ansteigenden Holzstrukturen.
2. Stockholm; Queransicht.
3, 4. Längsschnitt und Grundriß der Ausstellung im Moderna Museet, Stockholm.

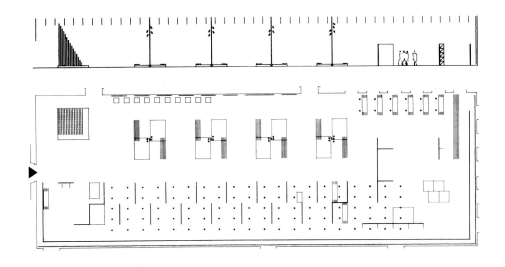

5. Copenhagen. The photographic displays are illuminated from below by light fittings installed in beams extending over the full width of the picture.
6–8. Paris. In the darkened room, the internally illuminated display panels were suspended from the ceiling or placed on robust tables. Further light fittings, radiating downwards, were installed below the wooden table tops.

5. Kopenhagen. Die Fototafeln wurden von unten durch Leuchtbalken in Bildbreite angestrahlt.
6–8. Paris. Im verdunkelten Raum hingen die von innen erleuchteten Bildtafeln von der Decke oder sie standen auf kräftigen Tischkonstruktionen. Weitere, nach unten strahlende Lichtquellen waren unter den hölzernen Tischplatten angebracht.

9. Tele-photograph of the partly echeloned table-mounted display units in the narrower of the two exhibition rooms.
10. Plan of the two exhibition rooms at the Ecole des Beaux-Arts, Paris. Within a standardised, strictly observed square module system, the units were informally arranged.

9. Teleaufnahme der zum Teil versetzt hintereinander stehenden Tisch-Tafel-Elemente im schmaleren der beiden Ausstellungsräume.
10. Grundriß der beiden Ausstellungsräume in der Ecole des Beaux-Arts, Paris. Die freie Gruppierung der Ausstellungseinheiten vollzog sich innerhalb eines einheitlich strengen, quadratischen Rasters.

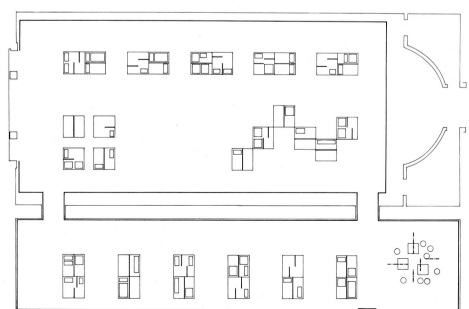

"Form and Quality" Exhibition

International Arts and Crafts Exhibition,
Munich, 1963 and 1964
Architect: Horst Döhnert, Munich

The difficulties consistently encountered with special exhibitions of this kind are due to the fact that small and precious objects must be displayed in vast, impersonal exhibition halls. In 1963, the ornamental objects were placed in showcases rhythmically arranged on brackets from a decoratively treated wall. On the floor, low tables displaying ceramic objects were placed in an artificial landscape of sand dunes intersected by flag paths. In 1964, it was decided to go in for a greater architectural effort. The objects were presented in a great number of square showcases framed by black or white boarding which carried ceiling units of robust appearance. Glassware, china and ceramics were displayed on white cubes or low podia. Some of the latter were matched by low-hung ceiling units, thus forming glassless 'super-showcases'.

Sonderschau »Form und Qualität«

Internationale Handwerksmesse,
München, 1963 und 1964
Architekt: Horst Döhnert, München

Die Schwierigkeiten, die bei diesen Sonderausstellungen immer wieder auftreten, bestehen darin, daß kleine und kostbare Dinge in großen, ungegliederten Messehallen gezeigt werden müssen. 1963 waren die Schmuckstücke in Konsolenvitrinen untergebracht, die sich rhythmisch vor einer dekorativ gestalteten Wand reihten. Davor verteilten sich, in die künstliche Landschaft eines von Plattenwegen durchzogenen Sandbodens gestellt, niedrige Tische mit keramischen Arbeiten. 1964 entschied man sich für einen größeren architektonischen Aufwand. Der Schmuck wurde in quadratischen Vitrinen dargeboten, deren Rahmenkonstruktionen kräftig wirkende Deckenelemente trugen. Glas, Porzellan und Keramik standen auf weißen Sockeln, die sich zum Teil optisch mit den tief von der Decke herabgehängten Blöcken zu glaslosen »Großvitrinen« verbanden.

1. 1963: Widely dispersed objects, showcases and suspended display panels, with emphasis on abstract forms.
2. 1964: A clearer segregation between different sections, and inclusion of objects in daily use.
3. 1964: Low podia served to combine certain exhibits in groups.
4. 1964: Free, three-dimensional structures closely associated with printed matter.

1. 1963: Weiträumig verteilte Objekte, Vitrinen und schwebende Tafeln; Schwergewicht auf abstrahierten Formen.
2. 1964: Eine deutlichere Trennung der einzelnen Raumabschnitte, Einbeziehung von Gegenständen des täglichen Bedarfs.
3. 1964: Niedrige Podeste führten zu einer Zusammenfassung einzelner Ausstellungsgruppen.
4. 1964: Freie, dreidimensionale Strukturen in enger Verbindung mit der Formensprache der angewandten Grafik.

Form and Image

Celanese House, London, 1963 and 1964
Sponsors: Hornsey College of Arts and Crafts
Design: Ronald Ingles, London

Form und Bild

Celanese House, London, 1963 und 1964
Veranstalter: Hornsey College of Arts and Crafts
Entwurf: Ronald Ingles, London

The first exhibition staged under this title in 1963 was concerned with the possibilities of using natural forms as a basis of design study. That exhibition was informally and discreetly composed of suspended display boards, three-dimensional objects, free-standing or wall-mounted showcases; individual exhibits were almost exclusively accentuated by spotlights, causing the indifferent architecture of the room to recede into the background. In 1964, the basic theme was further developed by displaying practical designs of fabrics, furniture, tools, printed matter, etc. There was no need to depart from the simplicity of the exhibition design as the exhibits themselves were sufficiently attractive and exhilarating, though a somewhat stricter architectural discipline and concentration were perceptible.

Bereits die erste Ausstellung, die 1963 unter diesem Titel veranstaltet worden war, beschäftigte sich mit den Möglichkeiten, von der Naturform zur gestalteten Form zu gelangen. Aus hängenden Tafeln, dreidimensionalen Objekten, freistehenden und in Wände eingebauten Vitrinen setzte sie sich verhältnismäßig locker und weiträumig zusammen, wobei die einzelnen Teile fast ausschließlich durch Punktstrahler akzentuiert wurden, um die belanglose Hallenarchitektur zurücktreten zu lassen. Im Jahre 1964 wurde der Grundgedanke erweitert durch die Darbietung praktisch angewandter Form bei Textilien, Möbeln, Geräten, grafischen Arbeiten usw. Die Einfachheit der Ausstellungsgestaltung konnte beibehalten werden, da die Exponate an sich anregend genug waren. Allenfalls ließ sich eine gewisse architektonische Straffung und Konzentration feststellen.

Design – Today and Tomorrow

Americana Hotel, New York, 1964
Sponsors: The Fashion Group Inc.,
New York
Design: Charles Forberg and
Donald Davidson, New York

Design – heute und morgen

Americana-Hotel, New York, 1964
Veranstalter: The Fashion Group Inc.,
New York
Entwurf: Charles Forberg und
Donald Davidson, New York

This exhibition had to be erected overnight for a one-day conference and subsequently to be dismantled within a few hours. It was to provide a distinct contrast against the modernistic banalities of the hotel ballroom setting. The exhibits were roofed by a taut, curvilinear, axially symmetric tent of Nylon fabric, which was wide open on all sides and seemed to draw the surrounding space into its sphere. This internal roof was held on the floor by concrete cones and tensioned by wires from the ceiling. The design was reminiscent of Forberg's earlier American contribution to the Milan Triennale, 1964. Concrete cones also served as supports for the informally arranged small tables and round podia on which a number of well designed utility objects were displayed.

In knapp einer Nacht mußte diese Ausstellung für eine eintägige Konferenz aufgebaut und dann innerhalb weniger Stunden wieder demontiert werden. Sie sollte sich deutlich absetzen von dem mit modernistischen Banalitäten versehenen Hotelballsaal, in dem sie unterzubringen war. So schwangen sich, in axialer Symmetrie, über dem Ausstellungsgut gekurvte Flächen aus elastischem Nylongewebe, die sich nach allen Seiten weit öffneten und den umgebenden Raum mit einbezogen. Zur Decke hin war dieses Innendach mit Drähten verspannt, während es am Boden durch Betonkegel gehalten wurde. Die Konstruktion ähnelte Forbergs amerikanischem Beitrag für die Mailänder Triennale 1964. Betonkegelstümpfe dienten auch als Füße der kleinen Tische und Rundpodeste, die in lockerer Gruppierung eine Auswahl gut geformter Gegenstände für den täglichen Gebrauch trugen.

1, 2. The dynamically shaped Nylon tent served as a roof for the exhibits which were displayed on supports of different height.
3. View along the axis of symmetry of the tent roof.
4. A diagonal view of the exhibition.

1, 2. Die bewegungsreiche Nylongewebekonstruktion überdachte die Ausstellungsstücke, die auf Trägern unterschiedlicher Höhe verteilt waren.
3. Blick auf die Symmetrieachse des Zeltdaches.
4. Schrägansicht durch die Gesamtausstellung.

1. Plan showing variable groupings of the tetrahedral showcases.
2. Exhibition booth with a silver-chiselled ornament designed by a Finnish artist.
3. Plan of the showcase base, consisting of ³/₄ in. thick laminated wood.
4. Detail of the corner of a showcase. Key: 1 Plate glass, ¹/₄ in. thick, 2 Copper angle, 3 Showcase floor made of ³/₄ in. thick wood.
5. The mirror in the background multiplies the pyramid tops of the showcases.

1. Grundriß mit variabler Gruppierung der Tetraedervitrinen.
2. Eine Nische mit dem silbergetriebenen Ornament eines finnischen Künstlers.
3. Grundriß der Vitrinensockel aus 19 mm starkem Schichtholz.
4. Detail einer Vitrinenecke. Legende: 1 Tafelglas, 6,3 mm stark, 2 Kupferwinkel, 3 Vitrinenboden aus 19 mm starkem Holz.
5. Der Spiegel im Hintergrund vervielfacht die Pyramidenspitzen der Ausstellungsvitrinen.

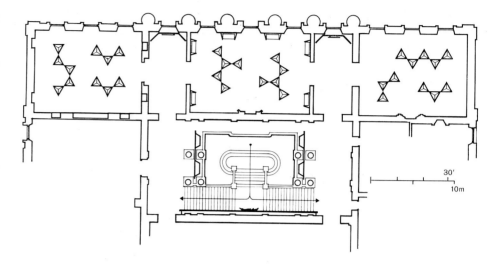

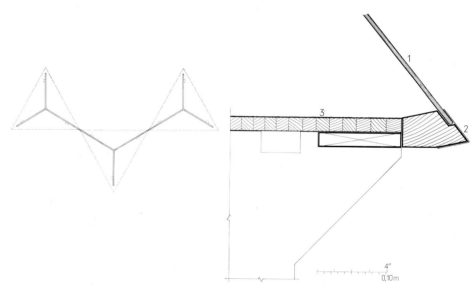

International Exhibition of Modern Jewellery

Goldsmiths Hall, London, 1961
Organiser: The Worshipful Company of Goldsmiths, in conjunction with the Victoria and Albert Museum, London
Design: Alan Irvine, London

Internationale Ausstellung modernen Schmucks

Goldsmiths Hall, London, 1961
Veranstalter: The Worshipful Company of Goldsmiths zusammen mit dem Victoria and Albert Museum, London
Entwurf: Alan Irvine, London

This exhibition, arranged chronologically in three rooms, provided a synopsis of the art of jewellery from the beginning of Art Nouveau to the present time, with contributions by well-known museums, collections, firms and artists. The jewels were displayed on the sides of triangular pyramids covered with Thai silk, and were protected by tetrahedral hoods of cemented glass. Each pyramid stood on a three-legged wooden base, painted black. Wooden bottom and glass panels of each showcase were held together by black-varnished copper sheets. The lighting was from reflector spotlights suspended above each pyramid. The concentrated light had the effect of suppressing the Victorian architecture of the building. The walls were also panelled in Thai silk, kept in different colour shades in each of the rooms.

Diese Ausstellung gab einen Überblick über die Juwelierkunst vom Beginn des Jugendstils bis zur Gegenwart mit Beiträgen bekannter Museen, Sammlungen, Firmen und Künstler. Die Schmuckstücke waren auf dreiseitigen, mit Siamseide überzogenen Pyramiden befestigt, über die mit Kittverbindungen staubdicht geschlossene Glashauben, ebenfalls in Tetraederform, gestülpt waren. Sie ruhten auf dreistrahligen Sockeln aus schwarz gestrichenem Holz. Basis und Tafelplatten waren mit schwarzlackierten Kupferplatten verbunden. Diese Vitrinen, in den drei Haupträumen nach Zeitfolgen geordnet, wurden jeweils durch Punktstrahler beleuchtet. Das konzentrierte Licht ließ die viktorianische Architektur des Ausstellungsortes zurücktreten, dessen Wände – jeder Raum in einem anderen Grundton – ebenfalls eine Bespannung aus Siamseide erhalten hatten.

"The Book of Kells"
Exhibition of Trinity College, Dublin

Royal Academy, London, 1961
Design: Alan Irvine, London

Whilst the first two exhibition rooms provided a synopsis of the importance, history and architecture of the famous Irish College, the third room prepared the visitors, by means of enlarged photographs, showcases and paintings, for the treasures of the College Library displayed in the subsequent core of the exhibition: the Celtic manuscripts. This polygon was, first of all, flanked on either side of the entrance by a series of showcases which was then continued, in a wide semi-circle, by enlarged photographs of old manuscripts and Irish landscape. In the centre of the room, the most valuable manuscripts were displayed in four showcases, among the "Book of Kells" from the eighth century. Spotlights above the photographs and stronger spotlights suspended over the showcases focussed attention on the exhibits without obscuring the architecture of the building.

Ausstellung »The Book of Kells«
des Trinity College in Dublin

Royal Academy, London, 1961
Entwurf: Alan Irvine, London

Während die beiden ersten Ausstellungsräume einen Überblick über Geschichte und Bauten des berühmten irischen College gaben, bereitete der dritte Raum mit Großfotos, Schauschränken und Gemälden auf die im Kern der Ausstellung gezeigten Schätze der Collegebibliothek vor: die keltischen Manuskripte. In diesem Polygon setzten sich zunächst beiderseits des Eingangs die Reihen der Schauschränke fort, um dann in einen weiten Halbkreis von Großreproduktionen alter Handschriften und irischer Landschaftsbilder überzugehen. Im Zentrum des Saales lagen in vier Vitrinen die wertvollsten Manuskripte aus, darunter das Book of Kells aus dem 8. Jahrhundert. Zahlreiche Punktleuchten über den Fototafeln und starke Breitstrahler über den Vitrinen hoben den Ausstellungsbereich hervor, ohne die umgebende Architektur ganz auszuschalten.

1. Main room: Semi-circular screen of enlarged photographs, forming a background for the four central showcases.
2, 4. The enlarged photograph, extending from floor to ceiling, facing the visitor on entering the anteroom to the octagon depicts the College Library. On the left, placed on hexagonal plinths, a selection of marble portrait busts of scientists associated with the College.
3. Plan.
5. The showcases in the centre of the exhibition were additionally protected by leather covered handrails round the edges.

1. Hauptraum: Halbrund der Großfotos um die vier zentral gestellten Vitrinen.
2, 4. Die Achse des vor dem Oktogon gelegenen Raumes führte auf eine wandhohe Fotoreproduktion der Dubliner Collegebibliothek. Links auf sechseckigen Sockeln die Marmorbüsten von Gelehrten, die mit dem College besonders verbunden waren.
3. Grundriß.
5. Die Vitrinen des Ausstellungskerns waren durch lederbezogene Handläufe zusätzlich geschützt.

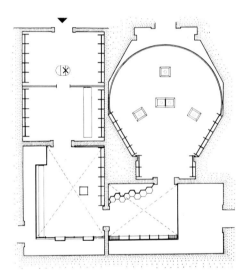

Karlsruhe, 250 Years Old

Karlsruhe, 1965
Architects: Otto and Peter Haupt,
Karlsruhe
Graphic artists: Studio Hans Lux,
Karlsruhe

250 Jahre Karlsruhe

Karlsruhe, 1965
Architekten: Otto und Peter Haupt,
Karlsruhe
Grafik: Atelier Hans Lux, Karlsruhe

This exhibition was distinguished by the quality of the displays, mainly consisting of panels with pictures and texts, by the well-planned layout, and by the variegated arrangement of the different sections. The first room was the octagonal "Foundation Hall" where documents and precious objects from the early days of the city were displayed in showcases placed in wall recesses or hexagonal columns. Walls and columns were covered with greatly enlarged silk screen prints reproduced from old engravings. These prints as well as – in other rooms depicting later epochs – other prints reproduced from photographs represented the main feature of the exhibition. A panoramic display of war damage marked the turning point from which the visitors were guided to the room containing enlarged photographs and models of present-day Karlsruhe.

Demonstrationsmaterial, das vorwiegend aus Bild- und Schrifttafeln bestand, durchdachte Raumaufteilung und die variierende Durchformung der einzelnen Abschnitte gaben dieser Ausstellung ihr Gepräge. Sie begann mit dem Oktogon des »Gründungsraumes«, in dessen Wände und Sechsecksäulen Vitrinen für Urkunden und kostbare Gegenstände aus der Frühzeit der Stadt eingelassen waren. Wände und Pfeiler waren mit Siebdrucken überdimensionaler Vergrößerungen überzogen. Diese Siebdrucke nach alten Stichen – in weiteren Räumen und damit späteren Epochen auch nach Fotos – bildeten ein Grundelement der Ausstellung. Eine Panoramawand der Kriegszerstörungen stellte zugleich den Wendepunkt des Rundganges dar, von dem aus der Besucher in den Raum mit Großfotos und Modellen aus dem Karlsruhe von heute geleitet wurde.

1. Octagonal entrance hall with eight columns combined in clusters. The forest motif, green on a golden background, was intended to symbolize the artificial foundation of the city in the landscape. The showcases placed in the columns and wall recesses display documents, tools and coins from the time around 1715. In the centre of the background is a portrait of the founder of the city, Margrave Karl Wilhelm.

2. Karlsruhe becomes a metropolitan city. With its text panels and amusing picture motifs fitted into a grid, this display wall conveyed an impression of the development of transport around 1900.

3. At the display wall showing photographs from the early days of post-war reconstruction, some panels were sculptured.

4. The large, negatively printed panorama of war-time ruins formed the background to a dramatic assembly of war-time debris.

1. Oktogonaler Eingangsraum mit den acht in Gruppen zusammengefaßten Säulen. Die Waldmotive, grün auf Goldgrund, sollen die künstliche Gründung der Stadt in der Landschaft symbolisieren. In den Vitrinen und an den Wänden Dokumente, Gebrauchsgeräte und Münzen aus der Zeit um 1715, im Hintergrund der Bildmitte ein Portrait des Stadtgründers, des Markgrafen Karl Wilhelm.

2. Karlsruhe wird Großstadt. Mit in Rasterflächen eingepaßten Schrifttafeln und amüsanten Bildakzenten gab diese Wand Einblick in die Entwicklung des Verkehrswesens um 1900.

3. Aus der Wand, die fotografische Dokumente aus der Zeit des beginnenden Wiederaufbaues nach 1945 trug, traten einzelne Blöcke plastisch hervor.

4. Vor dem großen, negativ gedruckten Ruinenpanorama eine drastische Schrottmontage.

Waterways from Milan to the Sea

Palazzo Reale, Milan, 1963
Architects: Achille and
Pier Giacomo Castiglioni, Milan

A typical Italian exhibition arrangement: With its raw jetty planks and timber walls, i.e. with wood as the only building material, and with the primitive metal reflectors above the simple bulbs, the exhibition conveyed, at first sight, an impression of primitivity until one became aware that these design aids were an emphatic means of high-lighting a theme centred on the untamed River Po. The exhibition itself, spread over numerous rooms of an old Palazzo, consisted of models, diagrams, projections and large text panels, and these optical displays and accents were intensified by recorded voices and music. A historic survey was followed by a presentation of present-day technical and economic problems, and concluded by a comparison between the River Po and other great European rivers.

Wasserstraßen von Mailand zum Meer

Palazzo Reale, Mailand, 1963
Architekten: Achille und
Pier Giacomo Castiglioni, Mailand

Eine typisch italienische Ausstellungsinszenierung: Die rohen Brückenbohlen und Bretterwände, das heißt Holz als durchweg verwendeter Werkstoff, dazu die Blechreflektoren über den einfachen Glühbirnen erweckten zunächst den Eindruck der Primitivität, wurden dann aber zum eindringlichen Gestaltungsmittel eines Themas, in dessen Mittelpunkt der ungebändigte Po stand. Die Ausstellung selbst, auf zahlreiche Räume eines alten Palazzos verteilt, konzentrierte sich mit Modellen, Schaubildern, Projektionen und großen Schriftparolen auf optische Eindrücke und Akzentuierungen, intensiviert durch Klangbilder aus Sprache und Musik. Nach einem historischen Rückblick leitete sie über zu den technischen und wirtschaftlichen Problemen der Gegenwart, um dann abschließend den Po mit anderen europäischen Strömen zu vergleichen.

1. Historic section. Folklore on old Italian canals: a boat; models, documents and illustrations, some of them displayed in showcases inserted into the rough timber walls; slide projections on a screen freely suspended from the ceiling.
2. The entrance to the exhibition was formed by old water gates.
3. The entrance to the last section, where the River Po was compared with other rivers, especially the Rhine, was flanked by high wooden walls shaped like canal banks.
4. The displays dealing with the subject of "Water and Landscape in North-Italian Art" were viewed, as it were, through the gaps of a building site fence.
5. Rough timber boarding was also used as surrounds for the models and projects of modern North-Italian canals which were illuminated by bulbs with simple metal screens.

1. Historische Abteilung. Folklore auf alten italienischen Kanälen: ein Boot, dazu Modelle, Dokumente und Abbildungen, zum Teil in Schaukästen, die in die rauhen Bretterwände eingelassen waren, sowie eine Diaprojektion auf einer in den Raum gehängten Leinwand.
2. Den Eingang zur Ausstellung bildete eine alte Wasserschleuse.
3. Hohe, wie Kanalufer abgeböschte Holzwände führten zu der letzten Abteilung, in der der Po vor allem mit dem Rhein verglichen wurde.
4. Wie durch die Öffnungen eines Bauzauns schaute man auf Darstellungen zum Thema »Wasser und Landschaft in der norditalienischen Kunst«.
5. Auch die Modelle und Projekte des modernen norditalienischen Kanalsystems umschlossen rohe Bretterwände, von Glühbirnen mit simplen Blechschirmen beleuchtet.

1. Wall projection, serving as separation between the recesses of sections B and C.
2. General view of the exhibition room. The display panels were illuminated by rotatable spherical light fittings, supported by metal brackets.
3, 4. Plan and model of the display panel wall.

1. Wandvorsprung als Trennung zwischen den Nischen der Abteilungen B und C.
2. Raumübersicht. Beleuchtung der Schauwände durch drehbare Kugelstrahler auf Metallarmen.
3, 4. Grundriß und Modell der Längswand.

New Students' Hostels in Germany

International Hostel Conference,
Dijon, 1963
Architects: Wolfgang and Margarete Bley,
Karlsruhe
Associate: Dieter Flimm
Graphic artist: Rolf Lederbogen, Karlsruhe

Neue Studentenwohnheime in Deutschland

Internationale Wohnheimkonferenz,
Dijon, 1963
Architekten: Wolfgang und Margarete
Bley, Karlsruhe
Mitarbeiter: Dieter Flimm
Grafik: Rolf Lederbogen, Karlsruhe

For a mere display of the exhibits, a simple concatenation of display panels would have been sufficient. However, the designers intended to create, as it were, an optical bridge to the theme by giving the main display front a pronounced sculptural treatment. The displays were mounted on an irregularly zigzagged wall panel, reaching nearly to the ceiling, which was placed in front of one of the sides of the long room. The projections and recesses within each section followed an imaginary triangular module system and were reminiscent of the cubes of dormitory cells. In keeping with the thematic grouping, the recesses increased in size from the entrance towards the exit and were slightly staggered so that the room appeared to widen in funnel fashion. The final accent was provided by a smaller wall unit opposite the last recess.

Um lediglich das Ausstellungsmaterial zu zeigen, hätte auch eine einfache Reihung von Tafeln genügt. Die Gestalter wollten jedoch schon durch die starke Durchformung der Hauptwand eine optische Brücke zum Thema schlagen. Sie zogen vor der einen Seitenwand des langen und schmalen Raumes eine knapp deckenhohe, plastisch gegliederte Wand als Ausstellungsträger ein, die sich über einem imaginären Dreiecksraster aufbaute und deren Vor- und Rücksprünge innerhalb der einzelnen Abschnitte an die Kuben von Wohnzellen erinnerten. Den Themengruppen entsprechend bildete diese Wand mehrere Nischen, die sich vom Eingang der Dokumentation bis zu ihrem Ende zunehmend vergrößerten und leicht zurückstaffelten, so daß sich der Raum trichterartig zu erweitern schien. Im Bereich der letzten Nische setzte ein kleineres Wandelement auf der Gegenseite den Schlußakzent.

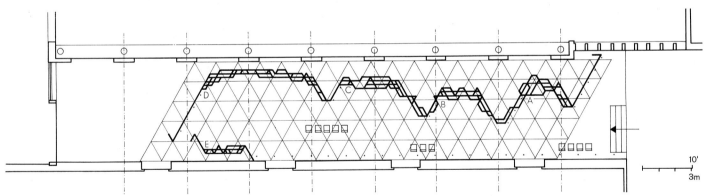

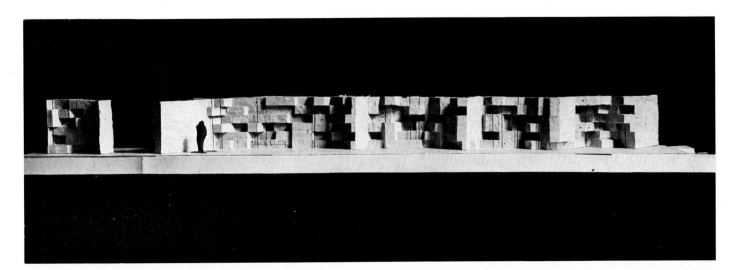

**Graphics Exhibition of the Designers
and Art Directors Association**

Reed House, London, 1964
Design: Ian Bradbery, London

**Grafik-Ausstellung der Designers
and Art Directors Association**

Reed House, London, 1964
Entwurf: Ian Bradbery, London

The sponsoring association, formed by a group of younger graphic designers, photographers and agency art directors, was founded in London in 1962 with the aim of countering the mediocrity of British commercial publicity by holding annual exhibitions of high standard. The second of these exhibitions consisted of two sections, one being exclusively concerned with posters, the other with smaller advertising media. The poster panels were fixed at different heights to pine uprights informally arranged in the room. The effect of certain individual designs was additionally accentuated by spotlights. The other, larger section contained clusters of large display panels occasionally forming recesses. Most of the panels were painted white, but some were grey, red or dark-green, in order to avoid monotony.

Die veranstaltende Gesellschaft, ein Zusammenschluß jüngerer Grafiker, Fotografen und Werbefachleute, war 1962 in London mit der Absicht gegründet worden, durch vorbildliche Jahresausstellungen der Mittelmäßigkeit englischer Gebrauchsgrafik entgegenzuwirken. Die zweite dieser Ausstellungen bestand aus zwei Abteilungen, von denen die eine ausschließlich Plakate, die andere kleinere grafische Arbeiten zeigte. Die Plakate waren in verschiedenen Höhen zwischen Vierkanthölzern eingespannt, die in freier Ordnung im Raum standen. Punktleuchten akzentuierten zusätzlich die Wirkung einzelner Entwürfe. In der anderen, mehr Raum beanspruchenden Abteilung gruppierten sich, gelegentlich kojenartige Gehäuse bildend, große Tafeln, die meist weiß, manche aber auch grau, rot oder dunkelgrün gehalten waren.

1, 2. Poster section. Together with some transoms, the wooden poster panels also served to stabilise the pine uprights.
3. Part of the section with the display of minor advertising matter. The 8×4 ft. panels, painted and edge-lipped vertically with red beech, were held in position by pine beams running below the ceiling. Some of the panels had enlarged skirting boards on which sculptured exhibits were displayed.

1, 2. Die Plakatabteilung. Die Holztafeln mit den aufgezogenen Plakaten steiften zusammen mit Querbrettern das Gerüst aus Vierkanthölzern aus.
3. Blick in die Sektion mit den kleineren grafischen Arbeiten. Die etwa 2,40×1,20 m großen und mit rot gestrichenen Kanten versehenen Tafeln waren unterhalb der Decke durch hochkant gestellte Bretter miteinander verbunden. Auf den Sockelplatten vor einigen Tafeln wurden den plastische Ausstellungsobjekte gezeigt.

German Stand at the Sydney Trade Fair

Sydney, 1961
Architect: Georg Lippsmeier, Düsseldorf

At this Australian Trade Fair, the German Federal Republic took part with a representative display entitled "German Theatre Life". The design of the stand was based on a system of hexagons. Thus, the ceiling units consisted of illuminated dark-framed hexagonal panels, supported by freestanding wall units. The theme was represented by enlarged photographs of scenes from famous German theatre performances. This display was enlivened by wall panels completely covered with textiles designed by Professor Margret Hildebrand. Minor exhibits were placed on a row of low platforms of a size matching that of the illuminated ceiling units. The interview booths and information desk also complied with this pattern. The same hexagonal scheme, with certain variants, was also adopted for the stands of the German industrial undertakings taking part in the same Fair.

Deutscher Stand auf der Sydney Trade Fair

Sydney, 1961
Architekt: Georg Lippsmeier, Düsseldorf

An dieser australischen Handelsmesse beteiligte sich die Bundesrepublik Deutschland mit einer Repräsentativschau unter dem Titel »Deutsches Theaterleben«. Der Standgestaltung lag ein System von Sechsecken zugrunde, und frei im Raum stehende Wände trugen die Deckenwaben aus hexagonalen, dunkel gerahmten Leuchtflächen. Das Thema wurde durch Großfotos von berühmten Aufführungen deutscher Bühnen dargestellt, während einige Wandflächen ganz mit Textilien nach Entwürfen von Prof. Margret Hildebrand bespannt waren. Kleinere Exponate lagen und standen auf einer Reihe niedriger Podeste, die im Format den Deckenleuchtflächen angepaßt waren. Besprechungsraum und Informationstisch ordneten sich diesem Raster ein. Die Stände der deutschen Industrieunternehmen übernahmen mit gewissen Abwandlungen das Sechsecksystem.

1, 2. Longitudinal and transverse views across the stand.
3. Plan of the exhibition stand, which was roofed by 33 hexagons.
4. One of the German industrial stands, based on the same dimensions and plan.

1, 2. Längs- und Querblick durch den Stand.
3. Grundriß des von 33 Sechsecken überdachten Ausstellungsstandes.
4. Einer der deutschen Firmenstände mit gleichen Abmessungen und Grundrißformen.

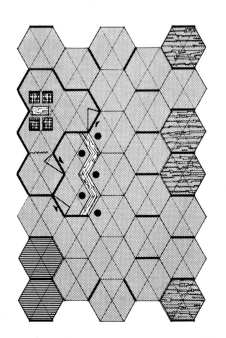

Joint Stand of the four Coastal Regions of West Germany

"Water" Exhibition, Berlin, 1963
Architect: Walter Kuhn, Hanover
Associate: Hans-Joachim Steiner

For his numerous exhibition displays, Kuhn has developed, from "Mero" standard bars and joints, an entire system of more or less complex casings and elements which are mainly composed of stereometric shapes such as tetrahedrons, octahedrons, etc. Here in Berlin, a floor area of 92 × 92 ft. was taken up by a highly sculptured three-dimensional structure, composed of geometric bodies with many – 26 or 40 – faces, or of prisms. The outer faces of this structure were filled, like shells, with the display panels proper whilst the horizontal faces were left open for the light fittings. Each "shell" dealt with a specific subject. The centre of the stand was taken up by conference and ancillary rooms, surmounted by a structure composed of three further three dimensional bodies for technical equipment such as film projectors, etc.

Gemeinschaftsstand der vier Westdeutschen Küstenländer

Ausstellung »Wasser«, Berlin, 1963
Architekt: Walter Kuhn, Hannover
Mitarbeiter: Hans-Joachim Steiner

Für seine zahlreichen Ausstellungsbauten hat Kuhn aus Mero-Normstäben und -Knoten ein ganzes System von mehr oder weniger komplizierten Gehäusen entwickelt, die sich aus stereometrischen Gebilden wie Tetraedern, Oktaedern usw. zusammensetzen. Hier in Berlin erhob sich über einer Grundfläche von 28 × 28 m ein räumliches Tragwerk, komponiert aus vielflächigen – 26flächigen, 40flächigen und prismatischen – Raumkörpern. Die Außenflächen dieses Tragwerks waren wie Schalen mit den eigentlichen Ausstellungsflächen ausgefacht, während die waagerechten Deckenflächen für die Belichtung des Innenraumes ausgespart blieben. Jede Schale behandelte ein spezielles Thema. Im Zentrum des Standes befanden sich Besprechungs- und Technikerräume, darüber erhoben sich drei weitere Raumkörper für technische Apparaturen wie Kinoprojektoren usw.

1. Interior. On the right, a wall composed of outer shells; on the left, a corner of the core.
2. Section and plan. Each component body had a circumference of 13 × 13 × 13 ft. while the inner squares measured 6¹/₂ × 6¹/₂ ft. The floor as well as the wall and ceiling panels are marked by heavy lines.
3. Elevation and plan of the three-dimensional "Mero" structure.
4. The bearing structure of the ceiling was surmounted by the structure carrying the projector equipment.
5. Interior, viewed along the centre line. The central core contained the conference rooms. In the foreground, one of the ceiling panels, left open for lighting purposes.

1. Innenansicht. Rechts eine der äußeren Schalenreihen; links eine Ecke des Standkerns.
2. Schnitt und Grundriß. Jeder Teilkörper hat einen Umfang von 4 × 4 × 4 m, die inneren Quadratflächen sind 2 × 2 m groß. Der Fußboden sowie die ausgefachten Wand- und Deckenflächen sind durch starke Striche gekennzeichnet.
3. Ansicht und Draufsicht des räumlichen Mero-Tragwerks.
4. Über dem Tragwerk der Standdecke der Aufbau für die Projektionseinrichtungen.
5. Axiale Innenansicht. Die zentrale Baugruppe enthielt die Besprechungsräume. Im Vordergrund oben eines der für Belichtungszwecke offen gelassenen Deckenfelder.

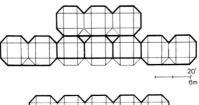

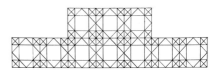

20'
6m

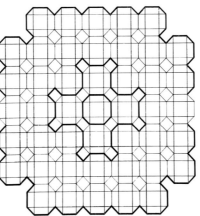

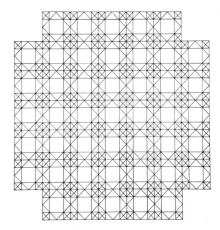

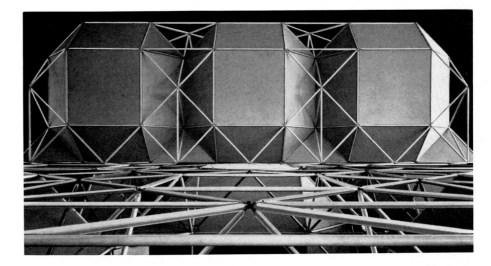

United States Food and Agriculture Exhibition

R. A. I. Building, Amsterdam, 1963
Design: Peter G. Harnden and
Lanfranco Bombelli, Barcelona

In this ambitious exhibition, the U.S. Department of Agriculture provided a synopsis of the present state of U.S. Food and Agriculture. For this purpose, it was necessary to adapt to an existing architectural framework a number of different specialised exhibitions of partly official and partly commercial character, combining the purpose of representation, information and – by means of films and displays – demonstrations. The difficult and challenging task of the designers consisted in finding a suitable solution for each of these constituent tasks without impairing the integral character of the exhibition. This was achieved by the intelligent architectural and graphic treatment of the individual ideas, some of which were highly original. This was already apparent from the information desk at the entrance.

Amerikanische Ernährungs- und Landwirtschaftsausstellung

RAI-Gebäude, Amsterdam, 1963
Entwurf: Peter G. Harnden und
Lanfranco Bombelli, Barcelona

Das Landwirtschaftsministerium der USA gab in dieser großen Ausstellung einen Überblick über den Stand der amerikanischen Ernährungs- und Landwirtschaft. Dabei mußte einem vorhandenen architektonischen Rahmen eine ganze Anzahl verschiedener Einzelausstellungen eingegliedert werden, die teils offiziellen, teils kommerziellen Charakter hatten, in denen repräsentiert, informiert und – mit Filmen und Vorführungen – demonstriert wurde. Schwierigkeit und Reiz der Gestaltung bestanden darin, für jede dieser Teilaufgaben eine angemessene Lösung zu finden und doch einen geschlossenen Gesamteindruck zu erzielen. Diese Wirkung wurde durch die klare architektonische und grafische Umsetzung der einzelnen, mitunter recht originellen Einfälle erreicht. Schon der Informationsstand am Eingang sprach in diesem Sinne für die ganze Ausstellung.

1, 3. The information booth was framed by two hoops of different size with advertising displays. The cubes in the background, showing faces of American people, were constantly revolving. The passage past this stand led to the entrance of the theatre where an introductory colour film was shown.

2. Model of the entire exhibition. Key: A Entrance hall and information centre, B Introductory Theatre, C Official display of a specialized character, D Western Barbecue, E Leather style show, "Kiddie Kitchen", cigarette machine, F Large self-service food store, G Commercial displays, H-L Conference rooms, M Restaurant, N Offices.

1, 3. Der Informationsstand war eingerahmt von zwei verschieden großen Reifen, die als grafische Werbeträger dienten; im Hintergrund drehten sich Kuben mit den Gesichtern amerikanischer Menschen. An diesem Stand vorbei führte der Weg zum Eingang des Theaters, in dem ein einführender Farbfilm gezeigt wurde.

2. Modell der Gesamtausstellung: Legende: A Eingangshalle und Information, B Theater, C Offizielle Fachausstellungen, D Freiluftgrill (Barbecue), E Lederausstellung, Kinderküche, Zigarettenmaschine, F Großer Selbstbedienungsladen, G Kommerzielle Ausstellungen, H–L Konferenzräume, M Restaurant, N Büros.

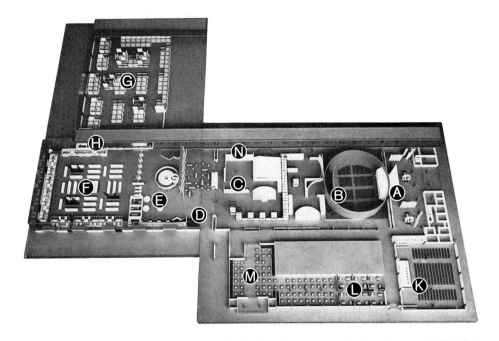

4. The visitor leaving the introductory theatre was faced with a composite wall covered with enlarged photographs showing an agricultural landscape which, as the visitor passed along, was dissolved into a series a faces of American farmers.

5. One of the stands in the special exhibits area, picturing the theme of "County Fairs" with enlarged photographs and a working model of a giant wheel.

6. The "Kiddie Kitchen" was freely available for cooking and baking.

7. European exports to the United States were symbolised by motor car components freely suspended from lightweight metal frames in front of a glass wall.

8. From a barbecue pit, American grilled specialities were served to visitors who were seated on logs at rough-hewn wooden tables. The illusion of the "Cook-out" was reinforced by a broad wall panel in the background reproducing a forest in actual size.

4. Nach Verlassen des Theaters sah man sich einer mit Großfotos überzogenen, gestaffelten Wand gegenüber, die zunächst die agrarwirtschaftlich genutzte Landschaft zeigte und sich dann im Vorbeigehen zu einer Reihe von Gesichtern amerikanischer Farmer wandelte.

5. Ein Stand im offiziellen Ausstellungsteil brachte zum Thema County Fair (Jahrmarkt) Großfotos und das sich drehende Modell eines Riesenrades.

6. In der Kinderküche durfte nach Belieben gekocht und gebacken werden.

7. Den Export europäischer Industrieerzeugnisse nach den USA symbolisierten Autoteile, die in leichten Metallrahmen frei vor einer Glaswand aufgehängt waren.

8. An einem Barbecue-Grill wurden amerikanische Spezialitäten zubereitet für die Besucher, die auf Baumstammabschnitten vor roh gezimmerten Tischen Platz fanden. Die Illusion des »Cook-out« verstärkte eine breite Fotowand im Hintergrund.

Travelling Exhibition "Medicine in USA"

Berlin-Düsseldorf-Munich, 1959 and 1960
Sponsors: United States Information
Agency
Design: Peter G. Harnden and
Lanfranco Bombelli, Barcelona

The exhibition, designed to acquaint the visitor with progress in American medical sciene, comprised various sections with greatly variegated exhibits: graphic displays and photographs, pharmaceutical products, medical instruments and equipment for practical demonstrations, including a heart-lung machine and a 9-ton cobalt bomb – but also a two-bed ward of a typical American hospital. For this travelling exhibition, which was shown in three large German cities as well as in Plovdiv, Bulgaria, the designers had developed a number of variable display units such as racks for panels and showcases made of timber and tubular steel, glass cases of various sizes and shapes, special installations for the technical displays. The result was a flexible, formally integrated system.

Wanderausstellung »Medizin in USA«

Berlin–Düsseldorf–München,
1959 und 1960
Veranstalter: US-Informationsdienst
Entwurf: Peter G. Harnden und
Lanfranco Bombelli, Barcelona

Diese Ausstellung, die mit den Fortschritten der amerikanischen Medizin bekanntmachen sollte, umfaßte Abteilungen mit sehr verschiedenartigem Ausstellungsgut: grafische Darstellungen und Fotos, pharmazeutische Erzeugnisse, medizinische Instrumente und Geräte zur praktischen Demonstration bis zur Herz-Lungen-Maschine und zur Neun-Tonnen-Kobaltbombe, aber auch das Zweibettzimmer eines typischen amerikanischen Hospitals. Für die Wanderausstellung, die in drei deutschen Großstädten sowie in Plovdiv/Bulgarien gezeigt wurde, hatten die Gestalter variable Ausstellungselemente entwickelt, so Gestelle für Tafeln und Schaukästen aus Holz und Stahlrohr, Vitrinen verschiedener Abmessungen und Formen, Spezialinstallationen für die technischen Vorführungen. Das Ergebnis war ein flexibles System von formaler Zusammengehörigkeit.

1. Pharmaceutical section at the Berlin showing. Display panels and showcases were suspended in a steel scaffold assembled from standard components; the spherical showcases were supported by square steel tubes, painted black. In the otherwise completely dark room, the exhibits were lit up by a small number of spotlights.
2. Entrance zone of the Düsseldorf exhibition. Display panels were mounted vertically and horizontally on a simple bolt-assembled timber frame.
3. Pyramid-shaped showcases, supported by a central steel tube, and prismatic showcases.
4. Panel walls, supplemented by enlarged photographs suspended from the ceiling, and textual displays placed on inclined lattice work desks served to explain the various uses of radio isotopes in modern medicine.

1. Pharmazeutische Abteilung der Berliner Ausstellung. Tafeln und Schaukästen waren in ein aus Normteilen montiertes Stahlgerüst eingehängt, die Kugelvitrinen ruhten auf schwarzem Vierkant-Stahlrohr. Nur wenige Punktstrahler beleuchteten die Objekte im sonst völlig verdunkelten Raum.
2. Eingangsbereich der Düsseldorfer Ausstellung. Senkrecht und waagerecht befestigte Demonstrationstafeln an einer einfachen, durch Schrauben verbundenen Holzkonstruktion.
3. Vitrinen in Pyramidenform, auf einem schwarzen Mittelfuß ruhend, und prismatische Schaukästen.
4. Tafelwände, ergänzt durch von der Decke hängende Großfotos, und Texttafeln auf schräggestellten Lattentischen erläuterten die Verwendungsmöglichkeiten von Radio-Isotopen in der modernen Medizin.

Anti-litter Exhibition of the Keep Britain Tidy Group

Tea Centre and Charing Cross
Underground Station, London, 1964
Design: F. H. K. Henrion, London

This exhibition, which owed its great success to its many scurrilous ideas, culminated in the imperative hidden in the pun "End of message: End the mess-age." It is questionable, however, whether the effect of the exhibition was really as deterrent and educational as was intended, or whether it was not rather regarded as an amusing and contemporary example of Pop Art – that artistic movement by which this exhibition was undoubtedly inspired. However, even Pop Art, jokingly raising the litter of civilisation to the level of an art, has a serious background, critical of its age. Such a mode of presentation is therefore eminently suited for this theme. The exhibition walls were made of fibreglass rovings, the ceiling was hardly visible, being solidly covered in a nightmare of litter cast out by the affluent society.

Anti-Müll-Ausstellung der Keep Britain Tidy Group

Tea Centre und Charing Cross
Underground Station, London, 1964
Entwurf: F. H. K. Henrion, London

Diese Ausstellung, die wegen ihrer Vielfalt skurriler Einfälle großen Erfolg hatte, gipfelte in dem in ein englisches Wortspiel gekleideten Imperativ: »Ende der Botschaft: Macht Schluß mit dem Schmutzzeitalter!« Es fragt sich nur, ob sie tatsächlich so abschreckend und erzieherisch wirkt, wie dies beabsichtigt war; ob man sie nicht vielleicht mehr als amüsante und zeitgemäße Pop Art nahm, die Kunstströmung, die diese Ausstellung zweifellos inspirierte. Jedoch: auch Pop, der Zivilisationsabfall karikierend zur Kunst erhebt, hat einen ernsten, zeitkritischen Hintergrund. Eine solche Gestaltungsweise bietet sich also für dieses Thema geradezu an. Die Wände der Ausstellung wurden von einem Geflecht aus Glasfiberstreifen gebildet, die Decke war durch einen Alptraum aus Wohlstandsmüll den Blicken des Beschauers weitgehend entzogen.

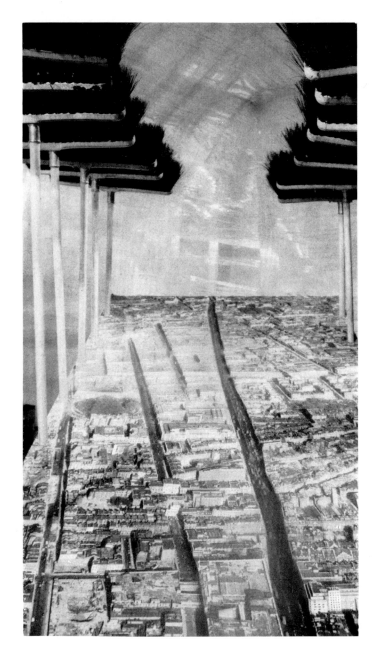

1, 2. Below a luxuriantly decorated ceiling, and by the side of towers of dirty milk bottles, the section of an aerial photograph of the London area provides an effective accent. It shows Oxford Street, flanked by the brooms of the 16 road sweepers whose sole job, by day and night, is the cleaning of this thoroughfare.
3. The enlarged photograph of car wrecks seemed to merge almost imperceptibly with the real objects in the foreground.

1, 2. Unter einer üppigen Deckendekoration, neben Türmen gebrauchter Milchflaschen bildete der Ausschnitt einer Luftaufnahme aus London einen effektvollen Akzent. Er zeigte die Oxford Street, flankiert von den Besen der 16 Straßenkehrer, die Tag und Nacht allein mit der Reinigung dieser Straße beschäftigt sind.
3. Das Großfoto der Autowracks ging im Vordergrund nahezu fugenlos in Originalobjekte über.

4, 5. The British Lion, challengingly offering his litter basket to the public, dominated one of the short sides of the exhibition. At the other end, the family assembled from the litter of the af—fluent society formed a counterpoint to the lion. Both sets of displays were placed on a relief-shaped base with the outline of the British Isles.
6. Photographic dioramas, showing many variations to a single theme, were inserted in a wall built up from old crates.
7, 8. The approach to the exhibition exit was flanked by a motley collection of litter from our daily life. A warning message stated that, during the Whitsun holiday, 20 million hikers and walkers had dumped 10,000 tons of refuse into the sea or all over the landscape. On the right, a huge dustbin lying on its side, serving as a passage and lined with creased photographs, symbolized the gigantic quantities of litter.

4, 5. Der britische Löwe, der seinen Abfallkorb dem Publikum auffordernd hinhielt, markierte eine Schmalseite der Ausstellung. Am anderen Ende bildete die aus Zivilisationsabfällen montierte Familie einen Kontrapunkt zum Löwen. Beide Bildgruppen standen auf einem reliefartigen Sockel mit den Umrissen der britischen Insel.
6. In eine aus Kisten aufgebaute Wand waren von hinten beleuchtete Dias eingespannt, die viele Variationen eines einzigen Themas zeigten.
7, 8. Der Weg zum Ende der Ausstellung wurde begleitet von den Abfalldetails unseres täglichen Lebens. Ein mahnender Text besagte, daß 20 Millionen Ausflügler und Spaziergänger während der Pfingsttage 10000 Tonnen Müll ins Meer geworfen und über die Landschaft verteilt hätten. Die begehbare Mülltonne rechts, die mit zerknitterten Luftaufnahmen ausgekleidet war, stand als Symbol für die riesigen Abfallmengen.

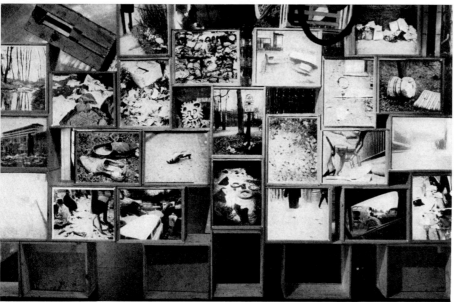

**Centenary Exhibition of the Swedish
Newspaper ''Dagens Nyheter''**

Modern Museum, Stockholm,
1964 and 1965
Design: Ulf Linde and Per Olof Ultveldt,
Stockholm

For the centenary celebrations of the Stockholm newspaper, Linde and Ultveldt contrived a witty and informative exhibition. Suspended from unpretentious racks were
enlarged front pages of historic importance (1). In between these displays were objects
which, because of their simple materials and dramatic shapes, could be regarded as
Pop Art. These were however not intended merely to symbolize our over technical
civilisation; they also provided an easily understandable picture of the production of a
newspaper. The clock face with the names of news agencies and the dangling heads
of prominent politicans indicated the channels through which the daily news is re-
ceived (2). A ''typewriter animal'' supplies the texts (3); the press photographers see
everything (4) that the printing machine must eventually print and spit out (5).

**Jubiläumsausstellung der schwedischen
Tageszeitung »Dagens Nyheter«**

Modernes Museum, Stockholm,
1964 und 1965
Entwurf: Ulf Linde und Per Olof Ultveldt,
Stockholm

Zum hundertjährigen Jubiläum der großen Stockholmer Tageszeitung hatten sich Linde
und Ultveldt eine witzig informierende Ausstellung einfallen lassen. An schlichten
Stangengerüsten hingen vergrößerte Titelseiten von journalistischer oder historischer
Bedeutsamkeit (1). Dazwischen standen Gebilde, deren simple Materialien und drasti-
sche Formen sie dem Bereich der Pop Art zuwiesen. Sie symbolisierten indessen nicht
einfach unsere übertechnisierte Zivilisation, sondern stellten recht verständlich den
Werdegang einer modernen Zeitung dar. Das Zifferblatt mit den Namen der Nachrich-
tendienste und den darunter pendelnden Politikerköpfen zeigt die Wege, auf denen die
Nachrichten täglich einströmen (2). Ein Schreibmaschinentier liefert die Texte (3), die
Pressefotocombine sieht alles (4), was die Rotationsmaschine schließlich drucken und
ausspucken muß (5).

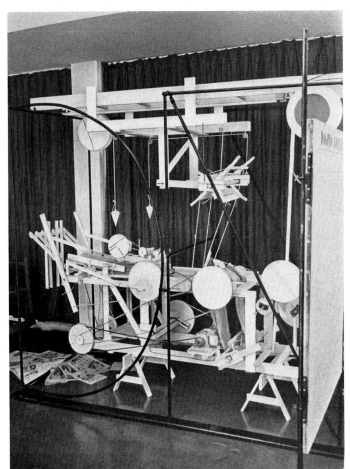

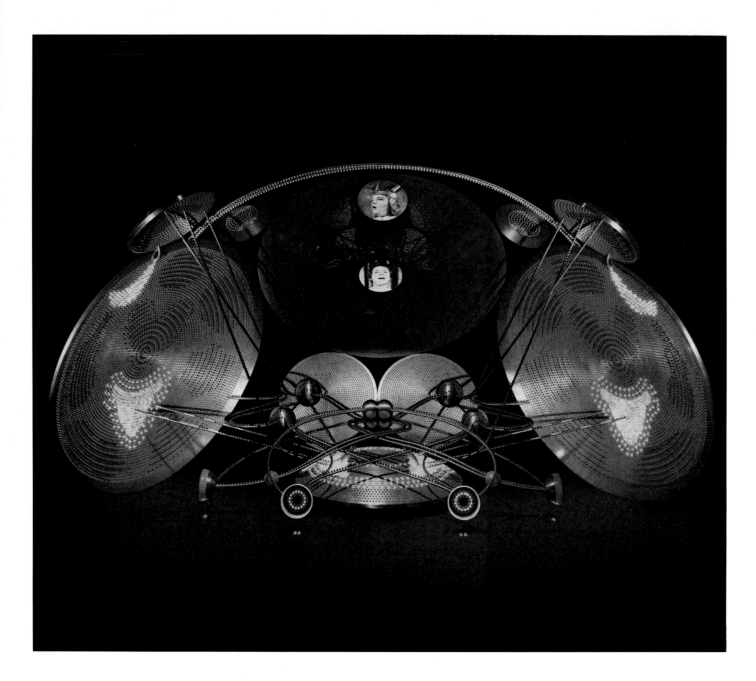

Travelling Exhibition "The Human Brain"

Sponsors: The Upjohn Company,
Kalamazoo, Michigan
Model designer: Will Burtin,
New York

**Wanderausstellung
»Das menschliche Gehirn«**

Auftraggeber: The Upjohn Company,
Kalamazoo, Michigan
Modellbauer: Will Burtin, New York

Among Burtin's works dealing with complicated physiological processes – all developed for the same manufacturers of pharmaceutical goods – is this 13×30 ft. model of the human brain. It consists of aluminium discs and tubes, about 20,000 small flashlight bulbs, and approx. 40 miles of wiring. By means of an electronic co-ordinating device, simple auditory and visual experience can be made visible on the large round disc (Fig. 1; top centre). The process is perceived by the eyes (red flashlights; bottom front) and by the ears (green flashlights; right and left); the impulses are forwarded through nerve canals (represented by tubes) to the relevant parts of the brain cortices and finally transmitted to the centre of the brain (base of the model) where they are stored in the memory cortices (large discs, right and left).

Zu Burtins Arbeiten über komplizierte physiologische Vorgänge, alle für dieselbe pharmazeutische Firma entwickelt, gehört auch das 4×9 m große Modell der menschlichen Gehirnfunktion. Es besteht aus Aluminiumscheiben und -rohren, etwa 20000 kleinen Glühbirnen und nahezu 70 km elektrischen Leitungen. Über eine elektronische Steuerung können einfache audio-visuelle Erfahrungen auf der großen, runden Scheibe in der oberen Mitte (Bild 1) sichtbar gemacht werden. Der Vorgang wird aufgenommen durch die Augen (vorne unten) und die Hörorgane (rechts und links davon), über Rohrleitungen an die zuständigen Teile der Hirnrinde (kleinere Scheiben rechts und links oben und im Hintergrund) weitergegeben und von dort zur Hirnmitte (Modellbasis) und schließlich zu den Gedächtnisspeichern (große Scheiben rechts und links) geleitet.

Travelling Exhibition "Genes in Action"

Sponsors: The Upjohn Company,
Kalamazoo, Michigan
Model designer: Will Burtin, New York

Burtin's earlier works of a similar kind are excelled in size and complexity by this 18 ft. high, 30 ft. wide model which has been exhibited, since 1966, in many cities in the United States. The model illustrates the action of the genes, i. e. the hereditary substance in a chromosome which, in its turn, merely represents a part in the nucleus of a cell. The display shows the typical pattern formed by numerous chromosomal strands in the act of expanding. At this moment, the genes become active: the DNA molecules are doubled, and RNA molecules are formed. These processes are controlled by a genetic code which determines the hereditary properties of all living organisms. Burtin's "learning machine" thus demonstrates some fundamental biological reactions. Within the model, in which people can walk, further details are displayed.

Wanderausstellung »Gene in Aktion«

Auftraggeber: The Upjohn Company,
Kalamazoo, Michigan
Modellbauer: Will Burtin, New York

Burtins frühere Arbeiten in ähnlicher Richtung übertrifft dieses Modell – das innerhalb von zwei Tagen aufgebaut werden kann und seit 1966 durch viele Städte der USA reist – an Größe (etwa 5,50 m hoch und 9 m breit) und Kompliziertheit. Dargestellt wird das Wirken der Gene, also der Erbfaktoren in einem Chromosom, das seinerseits nur Teil eines Zellkerns ist. Das Gebilde zeigt die typische gedrehte Zwiebelform, die entsteht, wenn sich die zahlreichen Fasern eines Chromosomenbandes ausdehnen. In diesem Moment werden die Gene aktiv: die DNA-Moleküle verdoppeln sich, und die RNA-Moleküle entstehen. Diese Vorgänge werden von einem Code gesteuert, der die Erbanlagen aller Lebewesen bestimmt. Burtins »Lernmaschine« demonstriert also grundlegende biologische Reaktionen. Innerhalb des begehbaren Modells sind weitere Details ausgestellt.

1. General view of the large-scale model, which can be erected in two days. The centrifugal swirling pattern of aluminium tubing represents chromosomal strands in the act of expanding.
2. Inside the model, the genetic processes are demonstrated with the aid of colour, light and motion.
3. A DNA model for display inside the large-scale structure being prepared. The plastic spheres are later marked by different colours. The aluminium tubes contain the electric wiring for the motion and lighting of the model.
4. The kinetic detail models inside the large-scale structure demonstrate different processes in the molecular zone of the chromosome.

1. Gesamtansicht des Großmodells. Die sich spiralenförmig windenden Aluminiumrohre veranschaulichen den Augenblick, in dem sich ein Chromosomenband ausdehnt.
2. Im Inneren des Gebildes werden mit Hilfe von Farbe, Licht und Bewegung die genetischen Vorgänge demonstriert.
3. Ein DNA-Modell für das Innere der Ausstellung wird zusammengesetzt. Die Plastikkugeln werden später durch verschiedene Farben gekennzeichnet. In den Aluminiumrohren verlaufen die elektrischen Leitungen für die Bewegung und Beleuchtung des Modells.
4. Die beweglichen Detailmodelle im Ausstellungsinneren machen verschiedene Vorgänge im molekularen Bereich des Chromosoms deutlich.

Representative Exhibition of the Brunswick Corporation

Entrance hall of the Brunswick Office Building, Chicago, 1963
Design: Will Burtin, New York

Repräsentationsausstellung der Brunswick Corporation

Eingangshalle des Brunswick-Verwaltungsgebäudes, Chikago, 1963
Entwurf: Will Burtin, New York

The manifold products of the company were displayed in fourteen spheres with diameters ranging from 3 to 8 ft. supported by steel tubes. One half of each sphere was made of opaque fibreglass, painted white on the outside and blue on the inside, whilst the other half was transparent, consisting of plexiglass. A motor mounted in the opaque half of each sphere served to animate the inside displays and to rotate the spheres which were turned by 180° every 30 seconds. The simultaneous rotation of all these spheres was followed by the animation of the inside exhibits through movements, slide projections and colour evolutions. In five spheres of similar design, the company displayed their activities in the fields of health, recreation, education, research and defence. Within each sphere, the shapes of the display plates were matching.

Ausstellungsträger für die vielfältigen Firmenerzeugnisse waren vierzehn Kugeln, die von verschieden hohen Stahlrohren getragen wurden. Jede dieser Kugeln – ihre Durchmesser variierten zwischen 1 m und 2,50 m – bestand aus einer undurchsichtigen Fiberglashälfte, außen weiß, innen blau, und einem durchsichtigen Teil aus Plexiglas. Ein Motor in der undurchsichtigen Hälfte bewegte sowohl die Ausstellungsstücke als auch die Kugel, die sich alle 30 Sekunden um 180° drehte. Während alle Kugeln gleichzeitig rotierten, spielten sich in ihnen Bewegungen, Projektionen und Farbveränderungen ab. In fünf ähnlich konstruierten Kugeln stellte der Konzern seine Arbeit auf dem Gebiet des Gesundheitswesens, der Erholung, der Erziehung, der Forschung und der Verteidigung dar. Die Formen der Rahmenausschnitte stimmten jeweils überein.

1. General view of the "Products" section.
2, 3. Model of the same section, showing (2) the opaque back halves of the spheres and (3) the transparent front halves after a 180° rotation.
4. The trademark of the company is displayed on the glossy white back halves of the spheres.
5, 6. The spheres of the other section of the exhibition. They merely differ by the symbolic shapes of the five consecutive plates, which become smaller in depth, and in which pictures and text messages appear in five phases.

1. Gesamtansicht der Produktausstellung.
2, 3. Modellaufnahme derselben Abteilung: einmal die geschlossenen Rückseiten der Kugeln, dann die durchsichtigen Vorderseiten.
4. Auf den schimmernd weißen Kugelrückseiten das Firmenzeichen.
5, 6. Die Kugeln der anderen Ausstellungsabteilung unterscheiden sich nur durch die Formen der fünf in der Tiefe kleiner werdenden Rahmenausschnitte, in denen in fünf Phasen Bild- und Schriftzeichen erscheinen.

Travelling Exhibition "Stile Olivetti"

Museum of Arts and Craft, Zurich, 1961
Design: Walter Ballmer, Milan
Associates: Oscar Hirs, Paolo Segotà

This travelling exhibition, based on Zurich, had the sub-title "History and design of an Italian industrial undertaking". It was meant to elucidate the typical Olivetti combination of architecture, industrial design and publicity as well as the social and cultural institutions of the company. The display structures consisted of anodized aluminium panels of 6 ft. 6 in. height and 3 ft. width which were combined in pairs and welded to each other at an obtuse angle. The panels were fitted with mouldings on which the photographic displays and striplights were mounted. In some sections, the demountable system of aluminium panels was supplemented by free-standing metal cylinders with wooden shelves, and by low tables. The publicity displays were mounted on desks.

Wanderausstellung »Stile Olivetti«

Kunstgewerbemuseum, Zürich, 1961
Entwurf: Walter Ballmer, Mailand
Mitarbeiter: Oscar Hirs, Paolo Segotà

Die Wanderausstellung mit dem Untertitel »Geschichte und Formen eines italienischen Industrieunternehmens«, die von Zürich ihren Ausgang nahm, sollte die für Olivetti bezeichnende innere Zusammengehörigkeit von Architektur, Produktform und Werbung, aber auch der sozialen und kulturellen Einrichtungen des Betriebs verdeutlichen. Technisch baute sich die Ausstellung aus paarweise zusammengestellten, eloxierten Aluminiumplatten von 200 cm Höhe und 90 cm Breite auf, die stumpfwinklig miteinander verschweißt waren. Die Platten waren mit Trägerprofilen zur Aufnahme der Bildtafeln und der Soffittenleuchten versehen. In verschiedenen Abteilungen wurde das demontable Plattensystem durch freistehende Metallzylinder mit Holzplatten und durch niedrige Tische ergänzt. Die Werbegrafik war auf pultförmigen Schautafeln ausgestellt.

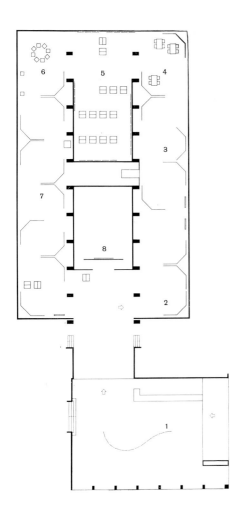

1, 3, 4. The necessary stability of the twin panels, which were arranged in units of three, was ensured by placing them at angles of 45°.
2. Plan of the exhibition at the Zurich Museum of Arts and Crafts: 1 History, 2 Architecture, 3 Industrial design, 4 Library, 5 Publicity, 6 Production, 7 Social welfare, 8 Cinema.

1, 3, 4. Die Aufstellung in Winkeln von 45° gab den zu Dreiereinheiten zusammengefaßten Tafelpaaren die nötige Standfestigkeit.
2. Grundriß der Ausstellung im Züricher Kunstgewerbemuseum. Legende: 1 Geschichte, 2 Architektur, 3 Industrieform, 4 Bibliothek, 5 Werbung, 6 Produktion, 7 Sozialfürsorge, 8 Kino.

5. In the 'Production' section, square boards of palisander wood, supported by anodised aluminium cylinders, served as tables on which different models of typewriters and calculating machines were displayed.
6. Smaller three-dimensional exhibits were – as in the 'Industrial Design' section – shown here mounted on the display panels whilst larger exhibits were shown on tables (wooden table top placed on a gate-legged support of anodised aluminium).

5. In der Abteilung Produktion trugen eloxierte Aluminiumzylinder quadratische Platten aus Palisanderholz, auf denen verschiedene Modelle von Schreib- und Rechenmaschinen präsentiert wurden.
6. Kleinere, dreidimensionale Ausstellungsobjekte waren – wie in der Abteilung Industrieform – auf den Bildtafeln montiert, während größere Exponate auf niedrigen Tischen (Holzplatte auf Kreuzfußgestell aus eloxiertem Aluminium) gezeigt wurden.

7, 8. Triangular units mounted on table tops were used, in the 'Publicity' sector of the exhibition, for a number of different purposes: for the display of printed matter inserted between the glass panels, or as a showcase with displays on one or both sides. The wooden table tops supported by the aluminium cylinders alone also served as demonstration tables.

7, 8. Auf Tischplatten montierte Dreieckselemente im Ausstellungssektor Werbung für verschiedene Verwendungsmöglichkeiten: als Träger für Drucksachen, die zwischen die Glasplatten geschoben werden, oder als ein- beziehungsweise doppelseitig beschaubare Vitrine. Die Holzplatte auf dem Aluminiumsockel allein diente auch als Demonstrationstisch.

Montecatini throughout the World

Showroom in the Montecatini Pavilion,
Milan Fair, Milan, 1961
Architect: Gio Ponti, Milan

The showroom, designed to convey an impression of the far-flung network of Montecatini factories, was given by Ponti an irregular enclosure of textile sheets placed in front of the walls proper. From the likewise cloth-covered ceiling emerged truncated cones on which the tops of the large display cylinders were fixed. The cylinders were of different sizes; they were supported on short, thin tubular supports and consisted of vertical and horizontal aluminium strips, left either in natural colour or in the blue shade of anodized aluminium. Circular showcases inserted in the cylinders at eye level contained models of factory plants. The lighting for showcases and ceiling was provided by light fittings inside the cylinders so that the display carriers – though solid – appeared to float in space.

Montecatini in der Welt

Sonderausstellung im Montecatini-
Pavillon, Fiera di Milano, Mailand, 1961
Architekt: Gio Ponti, Mailand

Dem Ausstellungsraum, der einen Eindruck von dem weitverzweigten Netz der Montecatini-Produktionsstätten vermitteln sollte, gab Ponti fließende Begrenzungen durch Stoffwände, die vor die eigentlichen Mauern gespannt waren. Lichtstreifen trennten die Wände vom Boden und von der ebenfalls stoffbespannten Decke. Aus dieser Decke wuchsen an einigen Stellen Kegelstümpfe, an denen die großen Ausstellungszylinder befestigt waren. Die unterschiedlich dimensionierten Zylinder, die auf kurzen Rohrstützen standen, setzten sich aus senkrecht und waagerecht verlaufenden Aluminiumstreifen (naturfarben und blau eloxiert) zusammen. In Sichthöhe waren Rundvitrinen ausgespart, in denen sich Modelle von Fabrikationsanlagen befanden. Beleuchtungskörper im Innern erhellten Vitrinen und Decken, so daß die an sich massiven Ausstellungselemente im Raum zu schweben schienen.

Information Stand of the Eternit Works

5th International Water Supply Congress,
Berlin, 1961
Design: Max Bill, Zurich

This stand was jointly sponsored by 34 companies which, in 31 countries of the World, produce asbestos-cement water pipes in accordance with the Mazza method. Here, the slender cylinders, rising like columns, did not constitute a design aid but were exhibits in their own right: pressure pipes of 1 ft. 4 in. diameter and 13 ft. height with polished surface. They were arranged in four rows of two around an open central space, based on a triangular grid which was apparent from the tubular steel structure linking the tops of the pipes. Each of the pipes represented one of the associated companies. The front of each pipe was marked by the flag of the country concerned and the publicity slogan in the corresponding language. The internally illuminated recesses, reminiscent of organ pipes, provided further possibilities for displays.

Informationsstand der Eternit-Werke

5. Internationaler Wasserversorgungs-
kongreß, Berlin, 1961
Entwurf: Max Bill, Zürich

Dieser Stand diente der gemeinsamen Repräsentation von 34 Industriefirmen, die in 31 Ländern der Erde Wasserdruckrohre aus Asbestzement nach dem Mazza-Verfahren herstellen. Hier waren die schlanken, wie Säulen emporsteigenden Zylinder keine gestalterischen Hilfsmittel, sondern die effektvoll ausgenutzten Ausstellungsobjekte selbst: 40 cm starke und 400 cm hohe Druckrohre mit geschliffener Oberfläche. Sie bauten sich in vier doppelreihigen Gruppen um einen freien Mittelraum über einem Dreiecksraster auf, das in der Stahlrohrkonstruktion sichtbar wurde, durch die die Rohre oben verbunden waren. Jedes Rohr symbolisierte einen Produzenten. Die Vorderseite war jeweils gekennzeichnet durch die Landesfarben und den Werbespruch in der betreffenden Sprache. Zusätzliche Ausstellungsmöglichkeiten boten die Orgelpfeifen-Ausschnitte.

Plastic Exhibition of the Montecatini Company

Montecatini Pavilion, Milan Fair,
Milan, 1961
Architects: Studio BBPR (Lodovico
Barbiano di Belgiojoso, Enrico Peressutti,
Ernesto N. Rogers), Milan

In this exhibition of elastomers, the architects deliberately kept the walls and ceilings of the room in the dark. The only source of lighting was provided by the illuminated boxes below and above the showcases which were relatively simple in design and material (wood and glass) and were informally arranged in the room. The showcases occupied squares of different sizes and were either placed on wooden supports standing on four feet or suspended from the ceiling by means of wooden parallelepipeds, reminiscent of stalagmites and stalactites. All the showcases were arranged at the same level particularly congenial to the viewer. The centre of the room was marked by a cube with lettering, illuminated from inside, which was surmounted, just below the ceiling, by a lattice frame partly covered with mirror glass.

Kunststoff-Ausstellung der Firma Montecatini

Montecatini-Pavillon, Fiera di Milano,
Mailand, 1961
Architekten: Studio BBPR (Lodovico
Barbiano di Belgiojoso, Enrico Peressutti,
Ernesto N. Rogers), Mailand

Bei dieser Ausstellung elastischer Kunststoffe hielten die Architekten die Wände und Decken des Raumes betont im Dunkel. Sie beschränkten sich als Lichtquelle auf die Leuchtkästen unter und über den Ausstellungsvitrinen, die, von Form und Material her (Holz und Glas) verhältnismäßig einfach, in freier Ordnung auf den Saal verteilt waren. Diese Schaukästen von unterschiedlich großer, durchweg quadratischer Grundfläche standen entweder auf durch vier Füße verlängerten hölzernen Sockeln oder hingen an hölzernen Vierkant-Hohlkörpern von der Decke herab, Stalagmiten und Stalaktiten vergleichbar. Alle Schaukästen befanden sich in gleicher, für den Besucher günstiger Höhe. Die Raummitte betonte ein leuchtender Schriftwürfel; über ihm war unter der Decke ein Gitterrahmen mit zum Teil spiegelverglasten Feldern montiert.

1. General view.
2. All the showcases proper, containing the exhibits, were arranged at the same level.
3. Lattice frame with some mirror-glass panels above the illuminated cube in the centre.
4. One of the suspended showcases, illuminated from above, with steel-framed windows.

1. Gesamtansicht.
2. Die eigentlichen Vitrinen mit den Ausstellungsobjekten befanden sich alle in gleicher Höhe.
3. Teilweise verspiegelter Gitterrahmen über dem zentralen Leuchtwürfel.
4. Einer der hängenden, von oben erleuchteten Schaukästen, deren verglaste Flächen in Stahlrahmen eingespannt waren.

Montecatini Pavilion

Milan Fair, Milan, 1964
Architects: Achille and Pier Giacomo
Castiglioni, Milan

An exhibition designed to illustrate the history, importance and manifold applications of petroleum might easily have become a dry catalogue or a collection of superficial rhetoric. The designers of the Milan exhibition had the knack of bringing out the salient points by interesting and variegated displays. But this variegation did not impair the integral character of the exhibition which was also emphasized by the consistent use of certain graphic elements and acoustic aids. The first exhibit was a stage setting, depicting a scene from the early history of petroleum. The historic section was continued by a gallery of projection screens. Pipelines and enlarged photographs of a refinery formed the transition to the eleven rooms in which the products of the modern petrochemical industry were displayed.

Montecatini-Pavillon

Fiera di Milano, Mailand, 1964
Architekten: Achille und Pier Giacomo
Castiglioni, Mailand

Eine Ausstellung, die die Geschichte des Erdöls und seine vielfältigen Verwendungsmöglichkeiten zu zeigen hat, gerät leicht in die Gefahr trockener Aufzählung oder allzu oberflächlicher Rhetorik. In Mailand hat man es verstanden, durch abwechslungsreiche Gestaltung das Wichtigste schwerpunktartig hervorzuheben. Diese Vielfalt führte jedoch zu einem durchaus geschlossenen Gesamteindruck, der durch immer wiederkehrende grafische Elemente oder den Einsatz akustischer Mittel unterstützt wurde. Den Auftakt der Ausstellung bildete als räumliches Schaubild eine Szene aus der antiken Frühgeschichte des Erdöls. Eine Projektorengalerie setzte den historischen Teil fort. Rohrleitungen und Großfotos einer Raffinerie leiteten über zu den elf Sälen, in denen die Erzeugnisse der modernen petrochemischen Industrie gezeigt wurden.

1. The stage setting in the entrance hall depicted the "discovery of petroleum in ancient times", dating back to the times of the Assyrians and Babylonians. The tunnel passage on the left, below the rows of floodlights, led to other exhibition rooms.
2. Layout plan of the exhibition. Principal sections: 1 Entrance hall with stage setting, 2 Gallery of projection screens, 3 Large refinery, 7 Varnishes and paints, 8 Synthetic rubber, 9 Synthetic fibres, 10 Explosives, 12 Motor-car bodies made of plastics.
3. With its simple equipment, the gallery of projection screens was reminiscent of the "Laterna Magica" stalls at Country Fairs.
4. A recurring symbol of the exhibition was provided by the chemical formulas of petrochemical products.
5. Interior of the section dealing with varnishes and paints. Walls and floors were covered with samples of paint. Diagrammatic and documentary displays were viewed through peep holes in the rear wall.

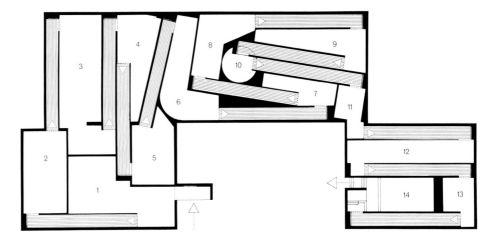

1. Eingangshalle mit dem in die Zeit der Assyrer und Babylonier zurückblendenden Schaubild »Entdeckung des Erdöls in der Antike«. Links unter den Scheinwerferreihen die tunnelartige Passage zu den weiteren Ausstellungssälen.
2. Ausstellungsgrundriß. Die wichtigsten Abteilungen: Legende: 1 Eingangsraum mit Schaubild, 2 Projektorengalerie, 3 Großraffinerie, 7 Lacke und Anstrichfarben, 8 Synthetischer Kautschuk, 9 Synthetische Fasern, 10 Sprengstoffe, 12 Kunststoffkarosserien.
3. In der Einfachheit ihrer Ausstattung erinnerte die Projektorengalerie an Jahrmarktsbuden mit der Laterna magica.
4. Als ständig wiederkehrendes Ausstellungssymbol die Strukturformeln petrochemischer Produkte.
5. Blick in die Abteilung Lacke und Anstrichfarben. An den Wänden und auf dem Boden Farbproben, in der Rückwand Gucklöcher zu den dahinter angebrachten Darstellungen und Dokumentationen.

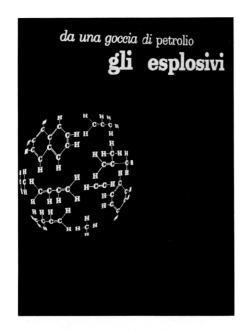

6. Fashion photographs printed on plastic foils and hung on a kind of clothes line in a gallery narrowing at the end, were designed to advertise textiles made of polypropylene.
7. Motor car bodies made of plastics, mounted on an inclined wall.
8. White walls, spotlights supported by black brackets, a silver-coloured pipeline and a composition of photographs depicting a petroleum refinery provide a further example for the seemingly spontaneous suggestiveness achieved by the architects.

6. Modeaufnahmen, auf Kunststoffolien aufgedruckt und wie an einer Wäscheleine aufgehängt, warben in einer sich nach hinten verengenden Galerie für Textilien aus Polypropylen.
7. An einer Steilwand montierte Autokarosserien aus Kunststoff.
8. Weiße Wände, von schwarzen Armen getragene Punktstrahler, eine silberne Rohrschlange und die Fotowand einer Erdölraffinerie: ein weiteres Beispiel für die spontan wirkenden Mittel der Suggestion, mit denen die Ausstellungsarchitekten hier gearbeitet haben.

Exhibitions organised by Steendrukkerij de Jong & Co.

Works canteen of the de Jong Company, Hilversum, 1961 and 1962
Design: Pieter Brattinga, Hilversum

Ausstellungen der Steendrukkerij de Jong & Co.

Firmenkantine de Jong, Hilversum, 1961 und 1962
Entwurf: Pieter Brattinga, Hilversum

Although the de Jong Printing Works are not comparable in size with companies such as Olivetti, they are none the less consistently trying to promote the artistic activities of the present time. The credit is primarily due to the young designer and critic Brattinga who, since 1954, has come to the fore with the company's own publications and has, with the assistance of prominent designers, organized various exhibitions in the works canteen. In 1957, Steendrukkerij de Jong were awarded the Pictura Prize of the Royal Academy, The Hague, for their efforts in acquainting the public and their own workers with the best examples of international art, and for showing in their non-commercial publications a wide variety of art ranging from photography to sculpture, painting and typography.

Wenn auch diese Druckerei in ihrer Größe nicht mit Unternehmen wie Olivetti verglichen werden kann, so bemüht sie sich doch nicht weniger konsequent darum, die künstlerischen Bestrebungen der Gegenwart zu fördern. Dies ist in erster Linie das Verdienst des jungen Designers und Kritikers Brattinga, der seit 1954 mit firmeneigenen Publikationen und – unter Heranziehung führender Kräfte – durch wechselnde Ausstellungen in der Betriebskantine an die Öffentlichkeit tritt. 1957 zeichnete die Königliche Akademie in Den Haag die Druckerei de Jong mit dem Pictura-Preis aus, weil sie die Begegnung mit den besten Beispielen internationaler Kunst herbeigeführt habe und weil ihre nicht-kommerziellen Veröffentlichungen die weite Vielfalt der künstlerischen Richtungen von der Fotografie über Plastik und Malerei bis zur Typografie widerspiegelten.

1, 2. The 1961 exhibition, entitled "Typography of the Architectural Review", was designed by Wim Crouwel and Benno Wissing who covered parts of the canteen wall with printed pages and displayed other, particularly noteworthy examples in a number of large hoops which were suspended in a row and, because of the mirror effect at the two ends of the room, seemed to continue into infinity.

3, 4. Gerard Wernars and Kho Liang Ie were responsible for the exhibition entitled "Japanese Toys" which was informally arranged in the room. For another exhibition, displaying book jackets designed by Dick Bruna, Wernars made use of narrow wooden boards inserted between ceiling and floor. Both exhibitions took place in 1962, representing but two out of a long series of displays which also comprise the graphic arts.

1, 2. Wim Crouwel und Benno Wissing gestalteten 1961 die Ausstellung »Typografie der Zeitschrift Architectural Review«, indem sie die Raumwände zum Teil mit Druckseiten überzogen und weitere besonders einprägsame Beispiele in einer Reihe von großen Reifen anbrachten, die hintereinander im Raum hingen und sich durch Spiegelung an beiden Raumenden ins Endlose fortzusetzen schienen.

3, 4. Gerard Wernars und Kho Liang Ie waren verantwortlich für die locker in den Raum eingefügte Ausstellung »Japanisches Spielzeug«. Für eine Ausstellung von Buchumschlägen des Entwerfers Dick Bruna benutzte Wernars schmale, zwischen Decke und Fußboden eingespannte Bretter (1962).

You and Timber

Swiss Industries Fair, Basle, 1965
Sponsors: "Lignum", Swiss Association
for Wood, Zurich
Design: A group of Swiss interior
designers, Kunz + Amrein, Lenzburg;
L. Scoob, Basle

Du und das Holz

Mustermesse Basel, 1965
Veranstalter: Lignum, Schweizer
Arbeitsgemeinschaft für das Holz, Zürich
Entwurf: Arbeitsgemeinschaft Schweizer
Innenarchitekten Kunz + Amrein,
Lenzburg; L. Scoob, Basel

The joint exhibition of the Swiss timber industry was housed in a narrow oblong hall, two-thirds of which were sub-divided into four hexagonal rooms. Cut into the walls of these rooms, through which the visitor was guided in zig-zag fashion, were seventeen niches which, with a display of a few telling attributes, indicated the relationship with wood of people in different occupations – a hunter, a businessman, a physician, a lady photographer, etc. Furniture, flooring, wall and ceiling panels consisted of the most variegated species of wood. The entrance was accentuated by a small portico with walls decorated by chunks from tree trunks, and by a 85 ft. high tower – a symbol of the exhibition – constructed of laminated beams bonded with synthetic resin.

Die Gemeinschaftsausstellung der Schweizer Holzindustrie befand sich in einem schmalen, langgestreckten Hallenbau, von dem zwei Drittel in vier sechseckige Räume unterteilt waren. Im Zickzack wurde der Besucher durch diese Räume geführt, deren Wände sich zu insgesamt 17 Ausstellungskojen öffneten. Die einzelnen Kojen stellten mit wenigen andeutenden Attributen die Beziehung zwischen Menschen verschiedener Berufe wie Jäger, Geschäftsmann, Arzt oder Fotografin und dem Holz her. Für Möbel, Fußböden, Wand- und Deckenvertäfelungen waren die unterschiedlichsten Holzarten verwendet worden. Den Halleneingang betonte ein kleiner Vorbau, dessen Wände mit Scheiben von Baumstämmen dekoriert waren, und – als Wahrzeichen dieser Ausstellung – ein 26 m hoch aufragender Turm aus vorfabrizierten, kunstharzverleimten HP-Lamellenträgern in modernster Zimmermannsbauweise.

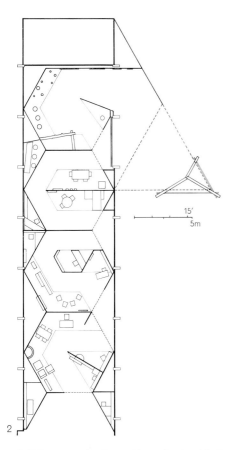

2

3

4

1. Entrance sector. Log cabin and natural timber displayed against the background of a forest photograph.
2. Layout plan of the exhibition.
3, 4, 6. Niches representing a 'hunter's lodge', a 'study belonging to a grown-up daughter', and a 'study for a young lady photographer'.
5. Entrance with wooden tower.

1. Eingangssektor. Blockhütte und Naturholz vor dem Hintergrund eines Waldfotos.
2. Grundriß.
3, 4, 6. »Jagdhütte«, »Studio der erwachsenen Tochter« und »Studio der jungen Fotografin«.
5. Eingang mit Holzturm.

5

6

WIE SITZEN SIE ?

SETZEN SIE SICH DÄNISCH

SICH DÄNISCH

1

Joint stand of the Danish Furniture Industry

International Furniture Fair, Cologne, 1966
Architects: Jesper Tøgern and
Thorkil Ebert, Copenhagen

Exhibition stands sponsored by national associations are often somewhat lacking in imagination, for the sponsors tend to display dull statistic material, or to take refuge in a non-committal neutral atmosphere in order to avoid the reproach of favouring specific firms. In contrast to such stolid solutions, this stand was completely unpretentious: ten modules wide and three modules deep, it was merely concerned with the theme "sitting". The models of armchairs and chairs, placed on small platforms in isolated positions, were backed by witty enlarged photographs, featuring the recurring slogan "Sit down the Danish way". The structure, effective through its reticence, merely consisted of wooden frames and uprights interspersed with white wall and breast panels contrasting with the dark carpeting.

Gemeinschaftsstand der dänischen Möbelindustrie

Internationale Möbelmesse, Köln, 1966
Architekten: Jesper Tøgern und
Thorkil Ebert, Kopenhagen

Nationale Repräsentationsstände auf Messen geraten gerne etwas phantasiearm, weil ihre Veranstalter sprödes statistisches Material in den Vordergrund stellen oder in eine unverbindlich-neutrale Atmosphäre ausweichen, um dem Vorwurf zu entgehen, sie bevorzugten gewisse Firmen. Gegenüber solchen mehr oder weniger steifen Lösungen gab sich dieser Stand völlig unprätentiös. Zehn Rasterfelder breit, drei Rasterfelder tief, beschäftigte er sich einfach mit dem Thema »Sitzen«. Witzige Großfotos, unterstützt von dem immer wiederkehrenden Slogan »Setzen Sie sich dänisch«, begleiteten die isoliert auf Podesten stehenden Sessel- und Stuhlmodelle. Das Standgefüge, das durch seine Zurückhaltung wirkte, bestand lediglich aus Holzrahmen und -stützen mit eingestellten weißen Wand- und Brüstungsplatten, die zu dem dunklen Teppichboden kontrastierten.

1, 3. Typical compositions of seated persons and chairs.
2. General view of the stand.
4. Layout plan of the stand.
5. Interior of the stand; in the foreground, the information and interview desk.

1, 3. Typische Zusammenstellungen von Sitzenden und Sitzmöbcln.
2. Gesamtansicht des Standes.
4. Grundriß.
5. Innenansicht des Standes; im Vordergrund der Informations- und Verhandlungstisch.

2

3

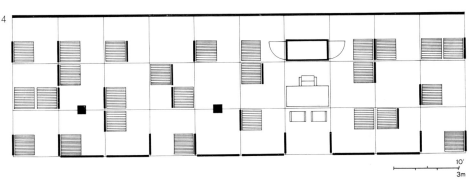

4

5

1

IBM Exhibition Stand

Business Equipment Manufacturers
Exposition, New York, 1963
Design: David Harvey, New York

The oblong area of the IBM stand was interrupted by five heavy columns and a cross-passage which separated the IBM Office Products Division from the larger and more important Data Processing Division which also included an information stand. One of the columns, bearing the initials of the company, became the symbol of the stand. The other four columns were largely concealed by the shell-shaped roof which, despite the unfortunate interruption by the public passageway, tied the two parts of the stand together. The barrel-vaulted shell sections had a rough stone-like appearance and concealed an amazingly light bearing structure, consisting of cross-reinforced wooden ribs covered with a skin made of wire mesh to which a continuous, fire-resistant coating of plastics and paints was applied.

IBM-Messestand

Business Equipment Manufacturers
Exposition, New York, 1963
Entwurf: David Harvey, New York

Der langgezogene Standgrundriß war unterbrochen durch fünf schwere Pfeiler und einen querlaufenden Hallengang, der die IBM-Büromaschinenabteilung von der größeren und wesentlicheren Abteilung für Datenverarbeitung mit vorgeschaltetem Informationsstand trennte. Einer der Pfeiler, mit den Firmeninitialen versehen, wurde zum Standsymbol. Die übrigen vier Stützen waren weitgehend von der schalenförmigen Deckenkonstruktion verdeckt, durch die der Stand trotz des ungünstigen Grundrisses auch über den Hallengang hinweg zu einer Einheit zusammengefaßt wurde. Ein breitgespanntes Tonnengewölbe mit rauher, fast steinartiger Oberfläche verbarg in seinem Inneren ein erstaunlich leichtes Traggerüst. Es bestand aus kreuzverstärkten, mit Maschendraht überzogenen Holzrippen, auf die eine feuerfeste Plastik- und Farbschicht aufgespritzt war.

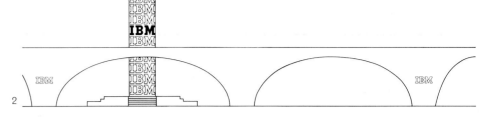

1. Viewing platform in the Data Processing Division. Light railings separated the visitors on the two-level platform from the exhibits.
2. Elevation. The shell roof, composed of 120 individual sections, was surmounted by the column bearing the initials of the company.
3. Plan. Key: 1 and 3 Data Processing Division, 2 Raised viewing platform, 4 Information desk, 5 Public passageway, 6 Office Products Section.
4. Standing on a platform in the centre of the Data Processing Division, the visitors were able to follow the demonstration of the machines.
5. The curvature motif of the ceiling was echoed by the display units, by the flower troughs in the Office Products Division, by the illuminated signs, and by the hand rails.
6. General view of the stand. On the left the Data Processing Division with the raised viewing platform; on the right, behind the second arch, the display of office products. Large, flat arcs were cut into long sides of the roof shell; at its ends, somewhat steeper quadrantal arcs formed a kind of protective roof.

1. Publikumsraum der Abteilung für Datenverarbeitung.
2. Aufriß. Das aus 120 Einzelelementen zusammengesetzte Tonnengewölbe wurde von einem Pfeiler mit den Firmenzeichen überragt.
3. Grundriß. Legende: 1 und 3 Abteilung für Datenverarbeitung, 2 Erhöhter Publikumsraum, 4 Informationsstand, 5 Öffentlicher Hallengang, 6 Büromaschinenabteilung.
4. Von der Abteilung für Datenverarbeitung aus verfolgte das Publikum, auf einem Podest stehend, die Vorführung der Geräte.
5. Bei den Ausstellungsständern, hier in der Büromaschinenabteilung, den Pflanzenwannen, Leuchtschildern und Geländern wiederholten sich die Bogen der Deckenkonstruktion.
6. Gesamtansicht des Standes. Links die Abteilung für Datenverarbeitung mit dem überhöhten Publikumsraum; rechts, hinter dem zweiten Bogen, die Büromaschinenschau. Auf den Längsseiten waren in die Tonnen große, flache Bögen eingeschnitten, an den Enden bildeten etwas steilere Viertelkreisbögen eine Art Schutzdach.

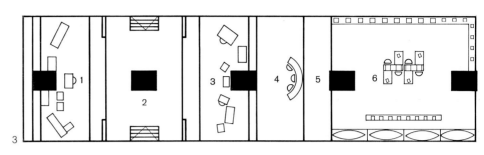

Exhibition Stand of the IBM Germany

German Industrial Fair, Hanover, 1965
Architect: Hans Köhler, Sindelfingen

The IBM display was spread over two sections, each representing one principal range of products, and separated from each other by a public passage. It was therefore necessary to re-integrate the two sections by adopting uniform design features – the red colour dominating the colour scheme; the characteristic light fittings mounted in the ceiling; the rounded shapes recurring with numerous details, etc. The larger of the two sections was reserved for the Data Processing Division. Its centre was taken up by a circular platform displaying a large computer, surrounded by display panels. The dominant feature of the other section, placed in its corner, was a gigantic typewriter matrix. The rear of the stand was taken up by several large circular booths serving as conference and show rooms.

Messestand der IBM Deutschland

Deutsche Industrie-Messe, Hannover, 1965
Architekt: Hans Köhler, Sindelfingen

Da die beiden Abteilungen des Messestandes, die je ein Hauptproduktionsgebiet repräsentierten, durch einen Hallengang getrennt waren, mußten sie durch die Art der Gestaltung – das in der Farbgebung vorherrschende Rot, die Leuchtschalen in der Decke, Rundformen bei zahlreichen Details – wieder zusammengefaßt werden. Der ausgedehntere Standteil war den Computern vorbehalten. In seinem Zentrum stand auf einem kreisförmigen Podest eine größere Anlage, von Tafelelementen umgeben. Den Blickfang des anderen Teiles bildete ein auf die Ecke gesetzter Riesenschreibkopf aus verchromtem Stahl; im Mittelpunkt nahm ein sternförmiges Gestell, dessen Strahlen als Schreib- und Schreibmaschinentische ausgebildet waren, Büromaschinen auf. Große Besprechungs- und Vorführkabinen schlossen den Ausstellungsstand nach rückwärts ab.

4

1. General view: On the left, the display of the Data Processing Division; on the right, that of the Office Products Division, both placed on charcoal-carpeted platforms. Nearly all the metal fittings of the stand consisted of chromium-plated steel.
2. The smaller section of the stand, displaying typewriters and calculating machines. Colour scheme: all display supports white; round carpets and background colour of display panels red; platform carpeting and circular flower tubs charcoal.
3. The larger section of the stand, reserved for computers.
4, 5. White-red circular booths serving as conference and show rooms, placed at the far end of the stand; in front of them, a small computer and some office machines. Each of the flat-bottomed hemispherical aluminium light fittings occupied four ceiling panels.
6. An open showroom booth with projection screens for films and slides. The lightweight chairs consisted of white-varnished wire netting.

1. Gesamtansicht: links Computer-, rechts Büromaschinenabteilung, beide auf anthrazitfarben belegten Podesten. Fast alle Metallteile der Stand-architektur bestanden aus verchromtem Stahl.
2. Der kleinere Standteil für Schreib- und Rechenmaschinen. Bestimmende Farbgebung: sämtliche Ausstellungsträger weiß, Rundteppiche und Farb-felder auf den Tafelständern rot, Podestbespannung und kreisförmige Pflanzkübel anthrazitfarbig.
3. Der den Computern vorbehaltene größere Standteil.
4, 5. Weiß-rot gehaltene Vorführ- und Besprechungstrommeln am Stand-ende, davor kleinere Computeranlage bzw. Büromaschinen. Die halbkugel-förmigen, nach unten abgeflachten Aluminiumleuchten nahmen jeweils vier Rasterfelder der Hallendecke ein.
6. Eine geöffnete Vorführtrommel mit Projektionsflächen für Filme und Diapositive, davor leichte Stühle aus weißlackiertem Drahtgeflecht mit ro-ten Sitzkissen.

5

6

Exhibition Stand of the Remington Rand Company

German Industrial Fair, Hanover, 1965
Architect: Heinz E. Bläser, Frankfurt/Main

The effect of the large stands of leading companies is primarily derived from the exhibits themselves. In this case, the most interesting design feature is the ceiling which has the function of providing uniform lighting – even if the arrangement of the exhibits should be varied – and ensuring proper ventilation in keeping with the regulations in force. These regulations generally prohibit the provision of a continuous ceiling made of materials permeable to air. In this case, the ceiling was sub-divided into panels which matched those of the flooring. Open ventilation panels, merely covered by a wire mesh, alternated with closed lighting panels. From the latter, large, intersecting circles had been cut out. The whole ceiling, including the open panels, was covered with double layers of transparent plastic foils.

Messestand der Firma Remington Rand

Deutsche Industrie-Messe, Hannover, 1965
Architekt: Heinz E. Bläser, Frankfurt/Main

Die Großstände führender Unternehmen beziehen ihre Wirkung in erster Linie aus den Ausstellungsstücken selbst. Gestalterisch interessant ist in solchen Fällen vor allem die Decke. Sie hat die Aufgabe, den Stand gleichmäßig hell auszuleuchten sowie eine einwandfreie und den Vorschriften der Messeleitung entsprechende Be- und Entlüftung zu gewährleisten. Diese Richtlinien verbieten zumeist eine durchgehende Decke aus luftdurchlässigem Material. Die Deckenfläche wurde hier in Felder aufgeteilt, die mit der Rasterung des Fußbodens übereinstimmen. Offene, nur mit Draht bespannte Belüftungsfelder wechseln mit geschlossenen Beleuchtungsfeldern ab. Diese bestehen aus Platten, aus denen sich überschneidende Kreise ausgeschnitten wurden. Alle Platten sind mit doppelter Transparent-Plastikfolie als Blendschutz überspannt.

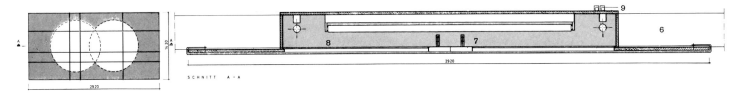

SCHNITT A-A

LICHTKASTENUNTERSICHT

1, 5. On the ceiling, which covered an area of 6200 sq. ft., 50 ventilation panels alternated with an equal number of lighting panels.
2–4. Underview, section and axonometric drawing indicate the structural details of the lighting panels which were suspended from a load-bearing steel framework. The two circles were profiled by thin steel hoops which, together with some tensioned plastic wires intersecting at right angles, gave the lighting panels an interesting pattern. Key: 1 Box cover, 2 Box ventilation, 3 Holding board, $^5/_6$ in. thick, 4 Transparent foil, 5 Plastic-coated wire, $^1/_4$ in. thick, 6 Load-bearing frame, 7 Steel hoops, 8 Fluorescent light fitting, 9 Electric accessories.

1, 5. Je 50 Belüftungs- und Beleuchtungsfelder wechseln miteinander auf der 570 qm großen Deckenfläche ab.
2–4. Unteransicht, Schnitt und Perspektive zeigen die konstruktiven Einzelheiten der Lichtkästen, die in eine tragende Stahlkonstruktion eingehängt werden. Dünne Flacheisenbögen konturieren die beiden Kreisformen und geben den Leuchtflächen, zusammen mit einigen rechtwinklig gespannten Kunststoffdrähten, eine effektvolle grafische Note. Legende: 1 Kastendecke, 2 Kastenentlüftung, 3 Tischlerplatte, 16 mm, 4 Transparentfolie, 5 Kunststoffbezogener Draht, 6 mm, 6 Tragkonstruktion, 7 Stahlblechkontur, 8 Langfeldleuchte, 9 Vorschaltgeräte.

1. The two principal sides of the stand are marked by the rows of octahedrons. The gaps in the longer row lead directly to the reception area with the information desk.

1. An den beiden Hauptseiten des Standes reihen sich die Oktaeder der Ausstellungsgestelle. Zwei Öffnungen in der Längsreihe führen direkt zum Empfangsbereich mit der Informationstheke.

Exhibition Stand of Continental-Gummi-Werke

German Industrial Fair, Hanover, 1965
Architect: Rudolf Riedel, Hanover
Graphics and showcase design:
Horst Meschke, Hanover

Messestand der Continental-Gummi-Werke

Deutsche Industrie-Messe, Hannover, 1965
Architekt: Rudolf Riedel, Hannover
Grafik und Gestaltung der Vitrinen:
Horst Meschke, Hannover

This stand – open on three sides and covering some 2800 sq.ft. of the upper floor of the "Chemistry and Plastics" Hall, but also visible from the ground floor – provides an accent in keeping with the importance of the company. The design of the stand remains the same from year to year but for certain modifications which mainly affect the display units along the two principal sides. The core, consisting of a central lounge surrounded by interview booths, utility rooms and an information desk facing the reception corner, remains essentially unchanged. Steel columns support a wooden lattice-work ceiling which contains lighting panels, covered with plexiglass. The display units – consisting of octahedrons, made of chromium-plated "Mero" bars from which open showcases are suspended – are reminiscent of chains of molecules.

Im Obergeschoß der Halle »Chemie und Kunststoffe« gelegen, aber auch vom Erdgeschoß her sichtbar, bildet dieser etwa 260 m² große, nach drei Seiten offene Stand einen der Bedeutung des Unternehmens entsprechenden Akzent. An seiner Gestaltung werden von Jahr zu Jahr nur gewisse Variationen vorgenommen, die sich hauptsächlich auf die Ausstellungselemente an den beiden Hauptschauseiten konzentrieren. Der Kern, ein zentraler Sitzbereich, umgeben von Besprechungskojen und Wirtschaftsräumen sowie der Informationstheke an der zum Empfangsbereich gelegenen Ecke, bleibt im wesentlichen unverändert. Stahlstützen tragen eine Rasterdecke aus Tischlerplatten, in die Leuchterfelder eingelassen sind. Die Ausstellungselemente, Oktaeder aus Mero-Stäben mit eingehängten offenen Schaukästen, erinnern an Molekülketten.

2. Plan. Key: 1 Display units, 2 Information desk, 3 Office, 4 Telephone switchboard, 5 Sitting room, 6 Interview booths, 7 Central lounge, 8 Kitchen, 9 Catalogues and samples, 10 Lavatory.
3. The space between the display units and the information desk is separated from the central core by a projecting panel.
4. A view from the central lounge, near the internal corridor, across showcases and blinds towards the edge zone of the stand. The light fittings are mounted in the lattice work ceiling.
5. The display units are formed by two octahedrons and intermediately suspended display panels. The bearing structure consits of chromium-plated tubular steel. The joints of this structure are covered by light-metal globes painted in different colours. Vertical display panels were mounted between the bars of the octahedrons.

2. Grundriß. Legende: 1 Ausstellungselemente, 2 Information, 3 Sekretariat, 4 Telefonzentrale, 5 Aufenthaltsraum, 6 Besprechungsraum, 7 Zentraler Sitzbereich, 8 Küche, 9 Prospekte und Muster, 10 Waschraum.
3. Der Raum zwischen den Ausstellungselementen und der Informationstheke wird durch eine vorspringende Wand von der zentralen Raumgruppe abgeschlossen.
4. Blick vom zentralen Sitzbereich am internen Erschließungsgang durch Vitrinen und Jalousiewände auf die Randzone des Standes. Die mit Plexiglas abgedeckte Beleuchtung ist in der Rasterdecke untergebracht.
5. Die Ausstellungselemente werden aus zwei Oktaedern und der dazwischen eingehängten Ausstellungsfläche gebildet. Die Konstruktion besteht aus verchromten Stahlrohrstäben. Die Anschlußknoten sind kugelförmig mit farbig gestrichenem Leichtmetall ummantelt. Zwischen den Stäben der Oktaeder wurden senkrechte Ausstellungstafeln montiert.

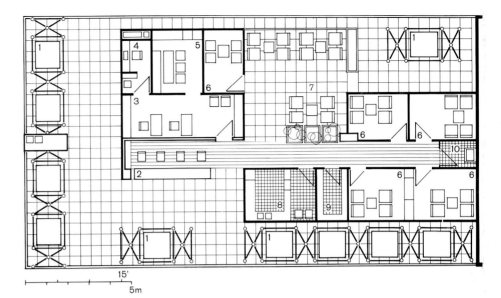

15'
5m

Exhibition Stand of the Kanthal Company

German Industrial Fair, Hanover, 1963
Architect: Walter Kuhn, Hanover
Associate: Rudolf Böling

Messestand der Firma Kanthal

Deutsche Industrie-Messe, Hannover,
1963
Architekt: Walter Kuhn, Hannover
Mitarbeiter: Rudolf Böling

This stand, erected for a Swedish company on a floor area of $34^1/_2 \times 28$ ft., was composed of a three-dimensional structure, consisting of a concatenation of cubic tetrahedrons and octahedrons with a standard side length of 2′ $1^1/_2$″. The structure was weld-assembled from $^1/_3$ in. thick steel tubes, and the horizontal octahedral pyramids and tetrahedral faces at the edges were covered with cocoon tissue. Fluorescent light fittings were mounted in the roof valleys. Along the sides, the central zones of the octahedral pyramids formed a line of showcases. The lighting for these showcases was installed in the tetrahedrons which were covered with white varnished metal sheeting on the outside and with cocoon on the inside. The whiteness of structure, walls and panels contrasted with the grey shade of the plastic flooring.

Der für eine schwedische Firma auf einer Grundfläche von $10,5 \times 8,5$ m errichtete Stand setzte sich aus einem räumlichen Tragwerk zusammen, einer kubischen Tetraeder-Oktaeder-Reihung mit einem Grundmaß von 65,5 cm Kantenlänge. Die Konstruktion war aus 8 mm starken Stahlrohren zusammengeschweißt, wobei die horizontalen Oktaederpyramiden und die Tetraederflächen der Randzonen mit Kokongespinst ausgefacht wurden. Die Rinnen der Deckenoberseite waren mit Leuchtstoffröhren bestückt. An den Seiten bildete der mittlere Bereich der Oktaederpyramiden eine Vitrinenreihe. Die Beleuchtung für diese Reihe war in den Tetraedern installiert, die nach außen mit weiß lackierten Blechen abgedeckt und innen mit Kokon bespannt waren. Die »Farbgebung« beschränkte sich auf sehr distinguiert wirkende Weiß- und Grautöne.

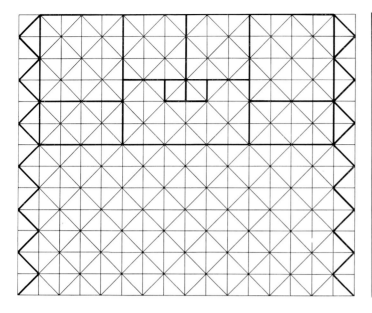

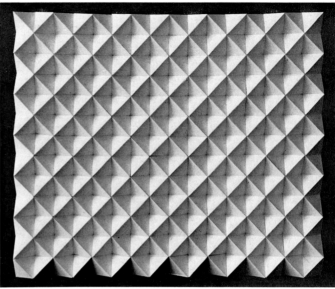

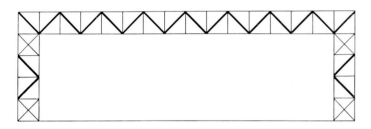

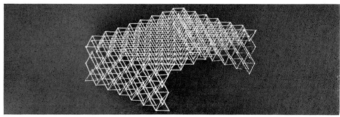

1. Side view of the stand.
2. Plan and longitudinal section of the structural system of tubular steel.
3, 4. Top view of the model, showing the cocoon-covered ceiling panels, and photograph of the model, revealing the filigree pattern of the structure as a whole.
5. This general view also shows the utility and conference rooms which were included in the cubic system behind solid wall panels.

1. Seitenansicht des Standes.
2. Das Konstruktionsraster des Stahlrohrgerüstes in Deckengrundriß und Längsschnitt.
3, 4. Aufsicht auf das Modell mit den Kokonausfachungen der Decke und Modellansicht der filigranen Gesamtkonstruktion.
5. Gesamtansicht. Die Wirtschafts- und Besprechungsräume waren hinter geschlossenen Wandflächen in das kubische System einbezogen.

1. This side view shows the simple module pattern of the load-bearing structure ("Abstracta" assembly tubing), interrupted in the centre by a full-height glass panel.
2. Through the wide opening in the main wall, the flexibility of the interior layout becomes apparent.
3, 4. The potentialities of this system comprise seclusion as well as open plan.

1. Die Seitenansicht zeigt den einfachen Raster des tragenden Skeletts (Abstracta-Anbaurohr), in der Mitte durch ein raumhohes Glasfeld unterbrochen.
2. Eine breite Öffnung in der Hauptwand gibt den Blick auf das variable innere Raumgefüge frei.
3, 4. Stärkere Abgeschlossenheit einerseits, Raumkontinuität andererseits gehören zu den Möglichkeiten dieses Systems.

Exhibition Stand of Messrs. Wagemans & van Tuinen

Utrecht Furniture Exhibition, 1961
Design: Kho Liang Ie, Amsterdam

This exhibition stand for "Artifort" furniture represents an interesting contribution to the important problem of developing structures which are, at one and the same time, optically unobtrusive, technically simple, sufficiently flexible and capable of being assembled within a very short time. Not accidentally, the designer has here combined the weightlessness of Far-East architecture with the functionalism of a simple trestlework structure assembled from tubular steel, painted black. The diaphanous wall panels were made of wooden lattice work or synthetic fibre netting. The flat-pitched saddle roofs, with valleys half-a-module above the top wall panels, were covered with bright cloth. By means of partitions, the internal layout can be modified at will so that the furniture sets can be displayed against varying backgrounds.

Messestand der Firma Wagemans & van Tuinen

Utrechter Möbelmesse, 1961
Entwurf: Kho Liang Ie, Amsterdam

Dieser Messestand für Artifort-Möbel ist ein interessanter Beitrag zu der wichtigen Aufgabe, optisch und technisch leichte Konstruktionen zu entwickeln, die flexibel sind und sich innerhalb kurzer Zeit aufbauen und demontieren lassen. Nicht zufällig hat der Entwerfer hier die Schwerelosigkeit fernöstlicher Architektur mit der Sachlichkeit einer aus schwarz gestrichenen Stahlrohrstäben zusammengesteckten Gerüstkonstruktion verbunden. Die diaphanen Wandfelder bestanden aus Holzstab- beziehungsweise Kunstfasergewebe; die im Abstand eines halben Rasters darüber beginnenden, flach verlaufenden Satteldächer waren mit hellem Stoff bespannt. Durch Zwischenwände konnte das innere Raumgefüge beliebig verändert werden, so daß sich wechselnde Hintergründe für die auszustellenden Möbelgruppen ergaben. Standpodest: gebeizte Fichtenbretter.

日本写真機工業会

Exhibition Stand of the Japanese Camera Industry

Photo Cine Fair, National Hall, Olympia, London, 1961
Design: Ian Bradbery, London

The stand of the Association of the Japanese Camera Industry provided information about the history and importance of this branch of industry. The structure, covering an area of approx. 65×12 ft., consisted of a scaffolding of 2″ square uprights and 2″ square horizontal tubes of mild steel, supplemented by an open ceiling grid of pine, supporting the light fittings. This open grid was covered by saddle roofs of canvas. The space between the uprights was taken up by display panels, glazed showcases made from teak veneered block board, and matting. Without wishing to over-emphasize Far-East exotics, the designer intended to convey something of the special atmosphere of Japanese architecture, but fusing it with the precision of modern technology so as to demonstrate the Japanese blend of tradition and efficiency.

Messestand der japanischen Kameraindustrie

Photo Cine Fair, National Hall, Olympia, London, 1961
Entwurf: Ian Bradbery, London

Der Verband der japanischen Kameraindustrie unterrichtete mit seinem Stand über Geschichte und Bedeutung dieses Wirtschaftszweiges. Das etwa 20×3,65 m große Ausstellungsgehäuse bestand aus einem Gerüst von senkrechten und waagerechten Vierkantstahlrohren, ergänzt durch horizontale, hochkant gestellte Kiefernholzbalken in Deckenhöhe. Über diesem offenen Deckenrost spannten sich die aus Stoffbahnen gebildeten Satteldächer. Zwischen die vertikalen Stützen waren Ausstellungstafeln, verglaste Schaukästen in Teakholzfassungen und Matten eingefügt. Es gelang dem Entwerfer, ohne vordergründige Fernostexotik etwas von der Atmosphäre japanischer Architektur einzufangen, sie mit der Präzision moderner Technik zu verbinden und auf diese Weise Tradition und zeitgemäße Aufgeschlossenheit der Japaner zu demonstrieren.

1, 2. The most variegated elements – Japanese and Latin scripts, enlarged photographs depicting Japanese arts, modern products of the Japanese optical industry, wall-mounted and low table-mounted showcases, sisal matting and teakwood tops – were combined with the load-bearing structure into an integrated whole.

1, 2. Die verschiedenartigsten Elemente – japanische und lateinische Schrift, Großfotos japanischer Kunst und moderner japanischer Erzeugnisse aus dem Bereich der optischen Industrie, Wand- und niedrige Tischvitrinen, Matten aus Binsengeflecht und Teakholzflächen – verbanden sich mit dem Grundgerüst zu einem einheitlichen Gesamteindruck.

**Exhibition Stand of Messrs.
Bang & Olufsen**

German Industrial Fair, Hanover, 1965
Design: Werner Neertoft, Birkerød

A floor area of no more than 300 sq. ft. was available, at the 1965 Hanover Fair, for this Danish company of radio and television manufacturers. Moreover, the stand had to be erected within 24 hours. This was achieved with the aid of a carefully considered layout plan which, apart from the open exhibition area, also included a conference room with tea kitchen, and by the prefabrication of all the necessary structural parts. The structure mainly consisted of pinewood frames and boarding, square timber supports, and batten ceiling. Two rows of spherical light fittings drew attention to the main display table. The same company had also used similar units for major stands at other exhibitions thus creating a characteristic image which made, at the same time, a specifically Danish impression.

Messestand der Firma Bang & Olufsen

Deutsche Industrie-Messe, Hannover, 1965
Entwurf: Werner Neertoft, Birkerød

Nur knapp 28 m² Ausstellungsfläche standen dem dänischen Unternehmen der Radio- und Fernsehbranche 1965 in Hannover zur Verfügung. Der Stand mußte zudem innerhalb von 24 Stunden aufgebaut werden. Dies gelang nach Ausarbeitung eines sorgfältigen Raumplanes, der außer dem Ausstellungsteil noch einen Besprechungsteil mit Küche einschloß, und dank der Vorfertigung aller notwendigen Konstruktionsteile. Das Standgefüge bestand in der Hauptsache aus Naturkieferrahmen und -verbretterung, Vierkantstützen und Lattendecke. Zwei Reihen von Kugellampen lenkten den Blick auf den wichtigsten Ausstellungstisch. Aus ähnlichen Elementen hatte das Unternehmen auch Stände für andere Messen zusammengebaut, so daß man von einem charakteristischen Firmengesicht sprechen kann, das zugleich ausgesprochen dänisch wirkte.

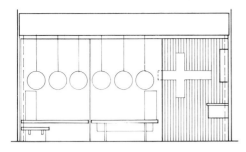

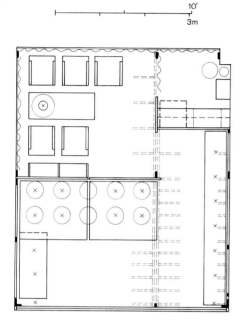

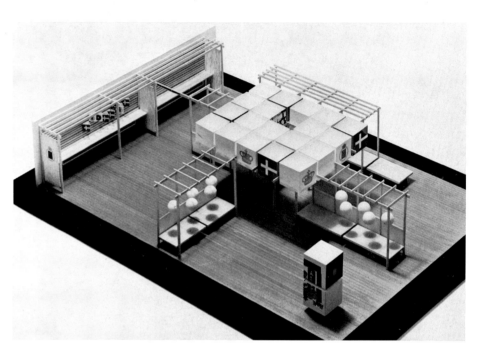

10'

3m

1. Hanover, 1965; main view of Bang & Oiufsen's stand. The main attraction was the display table with different radio and record player sets, lit by five spherical lamp fittings. Colour scheme: red backcloth with white Danebrog and black lettering; in the foreground, white wall with black lettering; dark-grey carpet.
2, 3. Elevation and plan of the same stand.
4, 5. Model photographs of the company's stand at the Firato Fair, the leading biennial Dutch radio and television show.
6. London, 1964; Carlton Towers. At all three exhibitions, the company made use of the same stand units, albeit in different composition.

1. Hannover, 1965; Hauptansicht des Standes. Blickfang war der von fünf Kugellampenpaaren beleuchtete Ausstellungstisch mit verschiedenen Radio- und Plattenspielermodellen. Farbgebung: rote Rückwand mit weißem Dänenkreuz und schwarzer Beschriftung, davor weiße Wand mit schwarzem Text; dunkelgrauer Teppichboden.
2, 3. Aufriß und Grundriß desselben Standes.
4, 5. Modellaufnahmen des Standes auf der Firato-Messe, der wichtigsten holländischen Ausstellung für Radio- und Fernsehgeräte, die alle zwei Jahre stattfindet.
6. London, 1964; Carlton Towers. Für alle drei Ausstellungen wurden gleiche Standelemente, wenn auch in unterschiedlicher Komposition, verwendet.

Exhibition Stand of the Walpamur Company Ltd.

Building Exhibition, National Hall, Olympia, London 1963
Design: David Iredale, London

Ausstellungsstand der Walpamur Company Ltd.

Bauausstellung, National Hall, Olympia, London, 1963
Entwurf: David Iredale, London

Two companies, manufacturers of wallpapers and paints who had formerly occupied separate stands, demonstrated their merger under a new name and symbol in a joint rotunda. The bearing structure consisted of a wooden scaffolding supplemented by display panels. The centre of the stand was occupied by offices and interview rooms. From this core radiated the segments of the exhibition booths which were lit by spotlights mounted in the pyramids of the ceiling panels. The display supports, partly consisting of three-dimensional arrangements of panels held together by wooden frames, were designed to inspire ideas for interior design, for combinations of wallpapers, curtains and furniture. A particularly interesting feature was the design of the central area ceiling structure, radiating in sixteen directions.

Zwei Firmen, Hersteller von Tapeten und Farben, die früher getrennt ausgestellt hatten, demonstrierten mit einem Rundstand ihren Zusammenschluß unter neuem Namen und Zeichen. Die Konstruktion bestand aus einem Gerüst flacher Balken und Bretter, ergänzt durch Tafeln, auf denen die auszustellenden Tapeten und Farben aufgebracht waren. Im Zentrum des Standes befanden sich Büro- und Verhandlungsräume. Von diesem Kern gingen strahlenförmig die Segmente der Ausstellungskojen aus, die jeweils von Punktstrahlern unter den Deckenpyramiden ausgeleuchtet wurden. Die Ausstellungselemente, zum Teil räumlich zusammengefügte, von Holzrahmen gehaltene Platten, gaben Anregungen für das Kombinieren von Tapete, Vorhang und Möbeln. Interessant war die sechzehnstrahlige Deckenkonstruktion über dem Mittelraum.

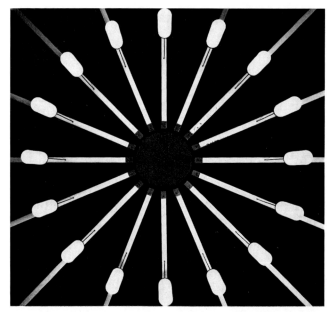

1. Model of the Walpamur stand which was divided into sixteen segments. The core, separated from the outside by a ring of panels, contained offices and interview rooms.
2, 3. Part-views of the finished rotunda. Each booth was lit by eight parallel spotlights.
4. Above the central area, the ceiling beams with their sixteen oval fittings formed a luminous star below the black textile covering.

1. Modell des in sechzehn Segmente aufgeteilten Firmenstandes. In dem nach außen durch Platten abgetrennten Kern lagen die Büro- und Besprechungsräume.
2, 3. Teilansichten des fertigen Rundstandes. Jeweils acht parallel geführte Spotlights leuchteten eine Koje aus.
4. Über dem Zentralraum bildeten die Deckenbalken mit den sechzehn ovalen Beleuchtungskörpern einen leuchtenden Stern unter der schwarzen Stoffbespannung.

Exhibition Stand of the ICI General Chemicals Division

International Aerosol Exhibition, Brighton, 1963
Design: C. S. Brown, Central Publicity Department, ICI, London

The great British chemical combine, Imperial Chemical Industries, demonstrated the various applications of their aerosol containers. The stand was, however, in marked contrast to the conventional, indifferent fair stands where any product might be on offer. It served not only as a frame for the display of the Arcton Products; its publicity appeal was mainly based on the design of the stand which was predominantly designed for prestige purposes. Six upright transverse panels, echeloned in two rows, were linked by arc-shaped display panels formed by enlarged photographs in angled juxtaposition. The rear displays on the inside consisted of narrow strips of photographs and texts. Below them, the rounded wall panels were lined by benches. Circular windows in the transverse panels permitted interesting vistas.

Messestand der ICI General Chemicals Division

Internationale Aerosol-Ausstellung, Brighton, 1963
Entwurf: C. S. Brown, Central Publicity Department, ICI, London

Der englische Chemiekonzern ICI demonstrierte hier die verschiedenen Verwendungsmöglichkeiten seiner Spraydosen. Von den üblichen neutralen Messeständen, in denen jedes beliebige Erzeugnis angeboten werden könnte, unterschied sich dieses Beispiel jedoch beträchtlich. Es diente nicht nur als Gehäuse für die Darbietung der Arcton-Produkte, sondern der Werbeappell wurde vor allem durch die Form des Standes ausgelöst, der vorwiegend der Repräsentation diente. Sechs aufrecht stehende Scheiben, in zwei Reihen gegeneinander versetzt, waren durch bogenförmig geführte Zwischenwände verbunden, die von gefächert nebeneinandergestellten Großfotos gebildet wurden. Im Inneren befanden sich auf den Rückseiten schmale Bildstreifen und Texte; darunter begleiteten Sitzbänke die Rundungen der Wände.

1. General view of the stand which was placed on a blue-carpeted platform.
2. The model clearly shows the echelon arrangement of the different panels. The 16 enlarged photographs were mounted on 1″ thick pressboard panels.
3. The view through the windows of the transverse panels was additionally enlivened by coloured aerosol container shapes mounted on each window.
4. The angled external panels with alternating light and dark photographs were illuminated by 50-Watt spotlights.

1. Gesamtansicht des Standes, der auf einem mit blauem Spannteppich bezogenen Podest stand.
2. Das Modell läßt die versetzte Anordnung der einzelnen Elemente gut erkennen. Die 16 Großfotos waren auf 2,5 cm starke Preßspanplatten aufgezogen.
3. Der Durchblick durch die Querwände wurde zusätzlich belebt durch auf die Verglasung aufgesetzte, farbige Flaschensilhouetten.
4. Die leicht gefächerten Außenwände, bei denen hellere und dunklere Fotos abwechselten, wurden durch 50-Watt-Punktleuchten angestrahlt.

Ante-room of the Rosenthal Stand

German Industrial Fair, Hanover, 1965
Design: Claus Cullmann, Selb

The design of this ante-room, covering an area of some 1000 sq. ft., was entirely attuned to the publicity for a new wine glass. The interior of the stand was reserved for clients so that the only part of the stand visible from outside was a set of glass shelves which was closely packed with different glass models, and also served as a screen. The emphasis was not so much on individual design but on the display of glass as a material. A similar design was adopted for the side wall on the left-hand side. The ceiling, illuminated by concealed lighting only, was formed by tulip glasses suspended by their stems from grooved battens. Recessed booths were used for wine tasting. Access to the display of the complete sample collection was along the rear wall of the ante-room, formed by a free-standing set of glass shelves.

Messestand-Vorraum der Rosenthal AG

Deutsche Industrie-Messe, Hannover, 1965
Entwurf: Claus Cullmann, Selb

Die Gestaltung dieses etwa 100 m² großen Vorraumes war ganz auf die Werbung für ein neues Rheinweinglas abgestimmt. Der Stand präsentierte sich nach außen – zugleich abschirmend, da nur Kunden zugänglich – durch ein Glasregal, auf dem die verschiedenen Modelle dicht gereiht standen. Es ging dabei weniger um die Einzelform als um die Demonstration des Werkstoffes Glas. Nach demselben Prinzip und von rückwärts durchleuchtet baute sich die von Schrifttafeln unterbrochene linke Seitenwand auf. Die nur indirekt erhellte Decke wurde aus Kelchgläsern gebildet, deren Füße in genuteten Leisten hingen. In die rechte Seitenwand waren Weinprobierkojen eingeschnitten. Der Weg zur eigentlichen Musterausstellung für die Gesamtkollektion führte vorbei an der Rückwand des Vorraums, einem frei stehenden Gläserregal.

1. View across the free-standing set of glass
shelves at the passage leading to the samples
display.
2. Glass shelves and photographic display wall
at the entrance.
3. On the left, the rear-lit glass wall; on the
right, the five semi-circular recesses for the tasting of wines from different viniferous areas; in
the background, the glass shelves screening
the entrance to the samples display. The light
emanating from the side wall on the left is reflected in the thousands of tulip glasses suspended from the ceiling.
4. Plan of the rectangular ante-room of the
exhibition stand.
5. On the glass shelves of the longitudinal wall
on the left, the different types of glasses form a
great variety of vertical and horizontal structures.

1. Blick durch das frei stehende Gläserregal am
Durchgang zu den Musterräumen.
2. Glasregal und Fotowand vor dem Eingang.
3. Links die von hinten erleuchtete Glaswand,
rechts die fünf halbkreisförmigen Probierkojen
der verschiedenen Weinbaugebiete, im Hintergrund das Gläserregal zur eigentlichen Musterausstellung. In der aus Tausenden von Kelchgläsern bestehenden Decke reflektierte sich
das Licht der linken Seitenwand.
4. Grundriß des rechteckigen Ausstellungsvor-
raumes.
5. Auf den Glasborden der linken Längswand
bildeten die Gläsertypen vertikal und horizontal
ständig wechselnde Strukturen.

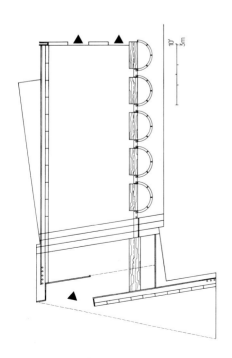

Exhibition Stand of the Phonola Company

Milan Fair, Milan, 1960
Architects: Ernesto Griffini and
Dario Montagni, Milan

In order to create an effective contrast between this representative stand and the conventional open stands in the vicinity, an oval core was created on a rectangular plan. This core was surrounded by walls covered with green billiard-table cloth and perforated with openings spelling out the name of the company in capital letters. The mirror-glazed ceiling made the room appear twice as high, and the oval shape of the core was emphasized by 17 spherical light fittings. In the centre of the room – a symbol rather than an exhibit – stood the casing of a wireless set. The other models representing the production programme were displayed in the corridor-like side booths. The floor of the stand proper was laid out with ceramic tiles. Walls and ceilings were either covered with cloth or mirror glass or consisted of stained boards.

Ausstellungsstand der Firma Phonola

Fiera di Milano, Mailand, 1960
Architekten: Ernesto Griffini und
Dario Montagni, Mailand

Um diesen Repräsentationsstand möglichst wirkungsvoll von den üblichen offenen Nachbarständen abzuheben, wurde über rechteckigem Grundriß ein ovaler Mittelraum geschaffen. Seine mit grünem Billardtuch ausgeschlagenen Wände waren von den Großbuchstaben des Firmennamens durchbrochen. Die spiegelverglaste Decke täuschte eine Höhenverdoppelung vor, und 17 Kugelleuchten zogen das Eirund des Standzentrums nach. In Raummitte war – mehr Symbol als Ausstellungsstück – das Chassis eines Radiogerätes aufgestellt. Die anderen Modelle des Fabrikationsprogramms wurden in den gangartigen Seitenräumen dargeboten. Während der Fußboden im Standbereich einen hellen Kachelbelag erhalten hatte, bestanden Wände und Decken, soweit sie nicht mit Stoff oder Spiegelglas verkleidet waren, aus gebeizten Holzbrettern.

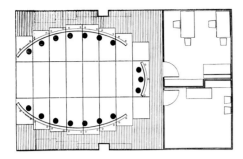

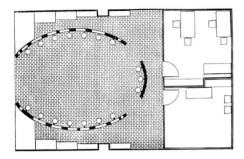

1. Axial view of the oval core, roofed by a mirror-glass ceiling.
2, 3. Under-view of ceiling, and plan.
4, 5. The larger-than-man-sized letters cut into the walls created a visual link between core and side corridors. The spherical light fittings were suspended from wooden brackets.

1. Axialer Blick in den ovalen, mit einer Spiegel-glasdecke versehenen Hauptraum.
2, 3. Deckenuntersicht und Grundriß.
4, 5. Die übermannshoch aus den Wänden aus-gesparten Buchstaben schufen die Sichtver-bindung zwischen dem Zentrum des Standes und den seitlichen Umgängen. Darüber hingen an hölzernen Wandarmen die ballonförmigen Leuchten.

**Exhibition Stand
of Vereinigte Drahtwerke AG**

Swiss Industries Fair, Basle, 1965
Design: Georg Vetter, Zurich

This stand was placed between two main passages, accessible from all sides. The designer adopted a system of narrow, upright display panels connected by horizontal strips which was, in deliberate contrast to the conventional right-angled stands in the vicinity, placed diagonally on the platform of the stand, measuring 40×52$^1/_2$ ft. The motif dominating the upright panels was provided by the contours which depicted the wide range of rolled steel products and were reminiscent of Op Art. Other products of this extensive production programme were displayed in actual size: wires and steel tapes in coils; steel bars in racks; pins, screws and fittings in flat boxes. The design of the stand was based on a 1 in 10 scale model which enabled the designers to try out all the detailed effects beforehand.

**Messestand
der Vereinigten Drahtwerke AG**

Schweizer Mustermesse, Basel, 1965
Entwurf: Georg Vetter, Zürich

Dieser Stand lag von allen Seiten frei zugänglich zwischen zwei Hauptpassagen. Der Gestalter entschloß sich zu einem System von schmalen, senkrechten Akzentflächen, verbunden durch waagerechte Blenden, das er, in bewußtem Gegensatz zu den rechtwinklig gereihten Nachbarständen, diagonal auf die 12×16 m große Ausstellungsplattform stellte. Die Konturen des umfangreichen Angebotes an Stahlprofilen erschienen als beherrschendes Moment auf den Akzentflächen, deren Grafik Anklänge an Op Art spüren ließ. Andere Erzeugnisse des vielseitigen Produktionsprogramms waren im Original ausgestellt: Draht und Bandstahl in Rollen, Stabstahl in Rahmengestellen, Stifte, Schrauben und Kleineisenwaren. Ausgangspunkt für die Standgestaltung war ein genaues Modell im Maßstab 1:10, an dem alle Detailwirkungen erprobt werden konnten.

1, 2. Views of the diagonally placed stand. The photographic and pictorial displays, even of small products, attracted attention from the distance. Outsize models of screws drew attention to another production branch.
3, 4. Two photographs of the model which had been prepared with such precision that the stand fitters had no need for drawings.

1, 2. Ansichten des großzügig wirkenden, diagonal gestellten Standes. Fototafeln und grafische Montagen warben auch auf größere Distanz für die zum Teil recht kleinen Produkte. Überdimensionale Schrauben machten auf einen weiteren Fertigungszweig aufmerksam.
3, 4. Zwei Aufnahmen des Modells. Es war so exakt ausgeführt, daß der Firma, die den Stand baute, keine Pläne geliefert werden mußten.

School Buildings of Brick

Fair stand of the Association of Swiss
Manufacturers of Brick and Artificial
Stone, Zurich
Swiss Industries Fair, Basle, 1961
Graphic artist: Ernst Sommer, Zurich

Schulhausbau in Backstein

Stand des Verbandes
der Schweizerischen Ziegel- und
Steinfabrikanten, Zürich
Schweizer Mustermesse, Basel, 1961
Grafik: Ernst Sommer, Zürich

Composed of simple yet impressive elements, this stand was designed to draw the attention of architects and authorities to the potentialities which that ancient building material, brick, has to offer even, and especially, to modern school building. Wall panels of exposed brick carried the lattice work of the ceiling. The brick wall panels were also used for the display of photographs of school buildings of particularly felicitous design. A wall panel decorated with a multi-colour painting served the dual purpose of ensuring privacy for an interview booth amid the otherwise rather open stand, and of providing a lively central accent. On the main display side, three over-lifesized sculptured figures of children, placed on a 20 ft. high steel scaffold surmounting the stand, formed an attractive feature visible from the distance.

Aus einfachen, doch einprägsamen Elementen setzte sich ein Stand zusammen, der Architekten und Behörden auf die Möglichkeiten aufmerksam machen sollte, die ein so altes Baumaterial wie der Backstein auch und gerade für den modernen Schulhausbau bietet. Wandscheiben aus Sichtmauerwerk trugen den Lattenrost der Standdecke, in der die Beleuchtungselemente installiert waren. An den Backsteinwänden hingen Großfotos besonders gelungener Schulanlagen. Ein farbiges Wandbild teilte einerseits einen Besprechungsraum von dem sonst recht offenen Standgefüge ab und wirkte andererseits als belebender zentraler Akzent, während an der Hauptschauseite drei überlebensgroße plastische Kinderfiguren, an einem 6 m hohen Stahlgerüst montiert, als weithin sichtbarer Anziehungspunkt die Standarchitektur überragten.

1. The open, main side of the stand is surmounted by the climbing frame of tubular steel with the figures of children. In the background on the right is the wall panel with the multi-colour painting. The lattice work of the ceiling was supported not only by the brick panels but also by a few steel tubes which likewise served as supports for the display panels.
2. The figures of children consisted of metal sheeting varnished in different colours.
3. Some of the panels in the large lattice work of the ceiling, consisting of vertical boards, were enclosed and fitted with spotlights.

1. An der offenen Hauptseite der Stahlrohrturm mit den Kinderfiguren, rechts dahinter die farbige Bildwand. Das Deckengitter lag nicht nur auf den gemauerten Wandscheiben, sondern auch auf einigen Stahlrohren auf, die ebenfalls zur Befestigung der Schautafeln dienten.
2. Die Kinderfiguren aus farbig lackiertem Blech.
3. In dem großen Deckengitter aus senkrecht stehenden Brettern waren einzelne Felder geschlossen und mit Punktleuchten bestückt.

Manuel de Falla Exhibition

Refectory of the San Jéronimo Monastery,
Granada, 1962
Architect: José M. Garcia de Paredes,
Madrid

This exhibition about the life and work of the Spanish composer de Falla was held in conjunction with the XIth Music Festival in Granada. To enable precious documents to be viewed with ease, yet without security risk, and to avoid any interference with the severe Renaissance architecture of the refectory by obtrusive mountings, the architect designed some flat domes made of slightly coloured transparent plastic, each covering an area of 3 ft. 3½ in. × 3 ft. 3½ in. The entire exhibition was concentrated in the centre of the room under two rows of twelve such dome-shaped showcases. The centre of each dome contained a mirror-glazed light fitting providing a direct, glare-free light. For security reasons, the edges of the domes were screwed to the table top.

Ausstellung Manuel de Falla

Refektorium des Klosters San Jéronimo,
Granada, 1962
Architekt: José M. Garcia de Paredes,
Madrid

Diese Ausstellung über Leben und Werk des spanischen Komponisten de Falla wurde im Zusammenhang mit dem XI. Musik-Festival in Granada veranstaltet. Um die teilweise recht kostbaren Dokumente übersichtlich, aber doch gut gesichert zu präsentieren und mit Rücksicht auf die strenge Renaissancearchitektur des Klosterrefektoriums, die nicht durch aufwendige Einbauten gestört werden sollte, entwickelte der Architekt flache Kuppeln aus leicht getöntem, durchsichtigem Kunststoff, die eine Fläche von 1×1 m überspannten. Die gesamte Ausstellung wurde in der Mitte des Raumes unter zwei Reihen von je zwölf solcher Kuppelvitrinen zusammengefaßt. Im Zenit jeder Kuppel war die Fassung für eine verspiegelte Lampe eingelassen, die ein direktes, blendfreies Licht gab. Zur Sicherung der Ausstellungsobjekte wurden die Kuppeln an ihren Rändern mit der Tischplatte verschraubt.

188

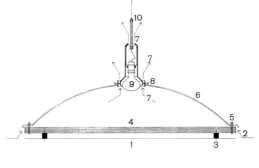

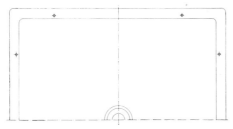

1. General view. The strict rhythm of the rows of domes was reinforced by the electric lead cables and the chromium-plated light fittings.
2, 3. Details of the light fittings and the screw-fastened edges of the domes.
4. Section and plan. Key: 1 Table top, 2 Air inlets, 3 Rubber buffers, 4 Display board, 5 Edge screw fastening, 6 Plastic dome, 7 Hot air outlets 8 Centering screws, 9 100-Watt bulb, 10 Intermediate steel tube for height adjustment.
5. A view of the domes. Compared with conventional displays of individual documents under flat glass plates, these domes have the advantage of being able to cover objects of different height.

1. Gesamtansicht. Die Kabel der Stromzuführungen und die verchromten Lampen steigern den strengen Rhythmus der Kuppelreihen.
2, 3. Detailansicht der Lampen und der verschraubten Kuppelränder.
4. Schnitt und Grundriß. Legende: 1 Grundplatte, 2 Luftzuführung, 3 Gummipuffer, 4 Ausstellungsplatte, 5 Randverschraubung, 6 Kunststoffkuppel, 7 Warmluftabführung, 8 Schrauben zur Zentrierung der Fassung, 9 Glühlampe, 10 Zwischenstück zur Höhenregulierung.
5. Blick auf die Kuppeln. Gegenüber flach aufliegenden Glasplatten haben sie den Vorteil, Gegenstände unterschiedlicher Höhe aufnehmen zu können.

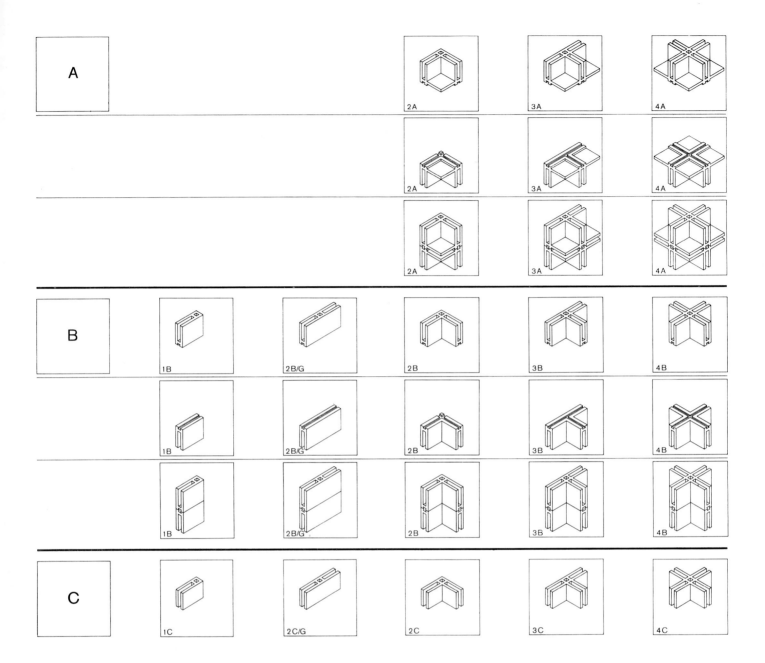

rts System
for Demountable Display Units

Design: Manfred Malzacher and
Hans Staeger, Stuttgart
Producers: Raumtechnik
Staeger & Co. KG, Stuttgart

This simple yet, in its applications, highly flexible system is based on the use of a number of well contrived joints. These include three groups of corner, longitudinal and transverse units made of grey plastics which can be duplicated by inserting dovetailed pieces. The deep hollows of these units can be used for inserting display panels of any desired size. With the aid of these unobtrusive units, entire walls as well as three-dimensional display supports can be rapidly assembled. The rts units are available in standard sizes of $16 \times 16 \times 1/6$ in. and $16 \times 8 \times 1/6$ in., made either of hard fibre, glass, Perspex or white-coated Finnish cardboard. The hard fibre units are available in raw condition, or with white spray coating, or glued with plywood.

rts-System
für demontable Ausstellungselemente

Entwurf: Manfred Malzacher und
Hans Staeger, Stuttgart
Herstellung: Raumtechnik
Staeger & Co. KG, Stuttgart

Eine gut durchdachte Reihe von verschiedenen Verbindungsstücken bildet die Grundlage dieses einfachen, in seinen Anwendungsmöglichkeiten jedoch sehr vielseitigen Systems. Es handelt sich um drei Gruppen von Eck-, Längs- und Kreuzverbindungen aus grauem Kunststoff, die durch eingeschobene Doppelschwalbenschwanzstücke noch verdoppelt werden können. In die tiefen Nuten dieser Verbindungsstücke werden Platten von beliebiger Größe eingeschoben. Mit Hilfe der unauffälligen Konstruktionsteile lassen sich ganze Wände ebenso wie dreidimensionale Ausstellungselemente schnell zusammenfügen. Bei den rts-Platten in den Standardgrößen $40 \times 40 \times 0,4$ cm und $40 \times 19,5 \times 0,4$ cm kann man zwischen verschiedenen Materialien wie Hartfaser, Glas, Plexiglas und weiß kaschiertem Finnischem Karton wählen. Die Hartfaserplatten sind roh, weiß gespritzt oder mit Holzfurnier verleimt lieferbar.

1. Schematic presentation of all the rts units
available. Each of the units belonging to groups
A and B is shown axonometrically from above,
from below, and in the doubled-up version obtained by dove-tailed inserts.
2. A simple glazed showcase with glass panels
and white hard-fibre panels.
3. A cross-joint duplicated by dove-tailed inserts.
4. 5. Examples of the application of these units,
with diagonal alternations of protruding cubes
and recesses.

1. Schematische Darstellung sämtlicher Verbindungsstücke. Die Teile der Gruppen A und
B sind jeweils in Draufsicht, Untersicht und
Verdoppelung mit Hilfe eingeschobener
Schwalbenschwanzstücke dargestellt.
2. Eine einfache Vitrine. Platten teils Glas, teils
weiße Hartfasertafeln.
3. Eine durch Doppelschwalbenschwanz-Stifte
verdoppelte Kreuzverbindung.
4, 5. Anwendungsbeispiele mit Schrägstaffe-
lung und vorspringenden Feldern bzw. ausge-
sparten Nischen.

1

Danish Exhibition System

Design: Jesper Tøgern and Thorkil Ebert,
Copenhagen, 1964

The predilection of Scandinavian designers for wood is well known; equally well known are the advantages of this material, its solid reliability in effect and construction. The system shown here makes use of squared timber of $2 \times ^7/_8$ in. cross-section which are assembled, with the aid of concealed hinges, to form collapsible cubic units of 2 ft. 2 in. side length. The corner joints are fixed by wooden pins which also serve to support the correspondingly perforated display panels – including those of plexiglass – so that the units can also be used for showcases. The units can of course also be combined vertically or horizontally so as to form podia, tables, shelves or other three-dimensional structures. The system is particularly well suited for the display of small arts and crafts objects.

Dänisches Ausstellungssystem

Entwurf: Jesper Tøgern und Thorkil Ebert,
Kopenhagen, 1964

Die Vorliebe skandinavischer Gestalter für Holz ist bekannt, und ebenso bekannt sind die Vorzüge dieses Werkstoffes, seine solide Zuverlässigkeit in Wirkung und Konstruktion. Das hier gezeigte System verwendet Vierkanthölzer von 50×22 mm Querschnitt, die mit Hilfe von verdeckt angebrachten Scharnieren zu zusammenklappbaren kubischen Elementen von 67,5 cm Kantenlänge zusammengefügt werden. Hölzerne Steckzapfen fixieren die Eckverbindungen und geben gleichzeitig entsprechend gelochten Ausstellungsplatten – auch aus Plexiglas – Halt, so daß die Elemente auch als Vitrinen verwendet werden können. Selbstverständlich lassen sich die Einheiten auf- und aneinandersetzen, so zu Podesten, Tischen, Regalen oder Raumkörpern. Das System eignet sich besonders für das Ausstellen kleinerer Exponate aus dem kunsthandwerklichen Bereich.

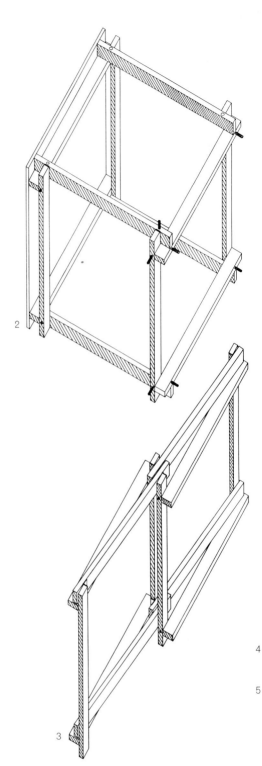

4

5

1. Corner joint of several units used as show-cases.
2. Isometric view of assembled unit.
3. Isometric view of a unit folded up for packing.
4. Corner joint of two vertically arranged, partially glazed units.
5. Danish Arts and Crafts exhibition at Gothenburg, 1964, where the system was used.

1. Eckverbindung mehrerer als Vitrinen benutzter Elemente.
2. Isometrie eines aufgebauten Elementes.
3. Transportbereites Element.
4. Eckverbindung zweier teilverglaster und aufeinandergestellter Elemente.
5. Aus dem System aufgebaute dänische Kunsthandwerks-Ausstellung in Göteborg, 1964.

1. The canted joints consist of (1) a 1¼ in. dia. joint body, (2) a 1¼ in. dia. joint lock, (3) ⅜ in. dia. rods, (4) ⅜ in. dia. adapter, and (5) countersunk screws.
2. Display rack for an architectural exhibition. On a tripod, the cubic elements are placed on edge and stayed by wires which also serve to hold the display panels.

1. Die schräggestellten Verbindungsstücke bestehen aus: (1) Verbindungskörper, Durchmesser 32 mm, (2) Verschlußstücke, Durchmesser 32 mm, (3) Gestänge, Durchmesser 9,5 mm, (4) Adapter, Durchmesser 9,5 mm, (5) Befestigungsschrauben.
2. Ausstellungsständer für eine Architekturausstellung. Auf einem Dreibein sind die Kubenelemente übereck gestellt und miteinander durch Drähte verspannt. Diese Spanndrähte halten auch die Ausstellungstafeln.

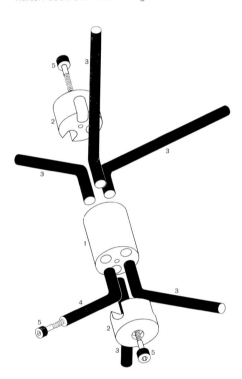

Collapsible Display System

Design: Paul E. Pate,
School of Architecture,
Texas A & M University, 1964

Faltbares Ausstellungssystem

Entwurf: Paul E. Pate,
School of Architecture,
Texas A & M University, 1964

Simplicity of design, a minimum number of components and manifold possibilities of application are the special advantages of this system. Metal rods and cylindrical joints consisting of three parts can be assembled into display frames, racks and entire structural systems of highly flexible shapes and sizes on which panels, showcases or table tops for display tables and desks can be fixed. The basic element, a cube composed of rods, is stabilised by the 'canted' joints so that no additional diagonal bracing is required. This tube can easily be folded up for economic storage and shipping. At the canted joints, special adaptors consisting of short pieces of rod can be inserted on which display panels can be fixed.

Einfache Konstruktion, ein Minimum an Teilen und vielseitige Verwendungsmöglichkeit sind die besonderen Vorteile dieses Systems. Aus Metallstäben und dreiteiligen, zylindrischen Verbindungsstücken lassen sich in sehr variablen Formen und Abmessungen Ausstellungsständer, -gestelle und ganze Konstruktionssysteme zusammensetzen, an denen Tafeln, Vitrinen, Schaukästen sowie Platten für Ausstellungstische und -pulte befestigt werden können. Das Grundelement, ein Gestängekubus, erhält durch die schräggestellten Eckverbindungen seine Stabilität, bedarf also keiner zusätzlichen diagonalen Verspannung. Dieser Kubus läßt sich ohne Schwierigkeit zusammenfalten und somit raumsparend verpacken und transportieren. In die Eckverbindungen können besondere Adapter, kurze Stangenstücke, eingesetzt werden, die zur Befestigung von Ausstellungstafeln dienen.

3. Display rack consisting of four parts, with display panels fastened to the adapters.
4. In the foreground, a more complex structure on which picture display panels are suspended; in the background, a rack similar to that shown in Fig. 3.
5. Schematic drawing of a cube built up from rods.
6. Drawings illustrating the folding sequence.
7. Folded cube.

3. Vierteiliger Ausstellungsständer mit an den Adaptern befestigten Platten.
4. Im Vordergrund eine umfangreichere Konstruktion mit eingehängten Bildtafeln, im Hintergrund Gestell ähnlich Bild 3.
5. Schemazeichnung eines Gestängekubus.
6. Phasenzeichnung des Faltvorgangs.
7. Zusammengefalteter Kubus.

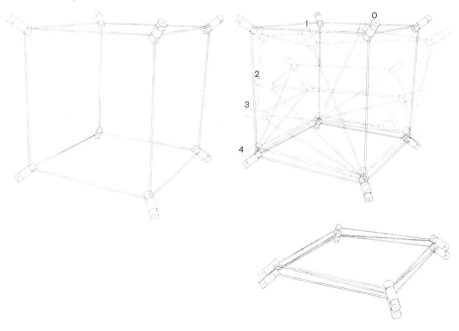

Demountable Exhibition System

Design: Otto and Peter Haupt,
Karlsruhe, 1963

This system, which can be packed in specially designed compact boxes, is particularly suitable for displays of arts and crafts products. Tables, showcases and display racks for textiles are composed of tubes, triangular frames and hexagonal boards. The low tables consist of hexagonal boards and three tubular legs which are screwed to the table tops by means of short terminal tubes. The two triangular frames, to which the textile display panels are fastened, are linked by three tubular supports, each consisting of three parts. Similar triangular frames are also used for bracing the three tubular supports of the showcases which extend beyond the hexagonal floor of the showcase to carry the top. Between bottom and top, panels of acryl glass may be inserted. A light fitting with transformer is mounted in the showcase top.

Demontables Ausstellungssystem

Entwurf: Otto und Peter Haupt,
Karlsruhe, 1963

Dieses in Spezialkisten kompakt verschickbare System eignet sich besonders zum Ausstellen von Kunsthandwerk. Tische, Vitrinen und Ständer für Textilien werden nach demselben Prinzip aus Rohren, Dreiecksrahmen und Sechseckplatten zusammengesetzt. Die niedrigen Tische bestehen aus sechseckigen Platten und drei Beinrohren, die auf den Tischflächen durch kurze Endrohre verschraubt sind. Drei dreiteilige Standrohre verbinden die beiden Dreiecksrahmen der Textilgestelle miteinander. An den Rahmen werden die mit dem Stoff bespannten Platten befestigt. Gleiche Dreiecksrahmen verspannen auch die drei Standrohre, die sich über dem sechseckigen Vitrinenboden fortsetzen und den Deckel tragen. Zwischen Boden und Abdeckung lassen sich Acrylglasplatten einfügen. Im Vitrinendeckel befindet sich eine Beleuchtungsanlage mit Trafo.

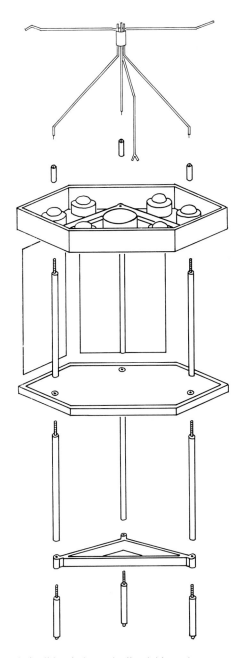

1. In this photograph, the tables, showcases and display racks for textiles form the technical equipment for an arts and crafts exhibition.
2. Schematic drawing of the showcase, consisting of tubular supports, triangular frames, showcase bottom and top and terminal pieces.

3. Group consisting of five showcases.
4–6. The showcase components are packed, layer by layer, in specially designed boxes.
1. Tische, Vitrinen und Textilständer bilden hier das technische Gerüst für eine Kunsthandwerksausstellung.

2. Schemazeichnung einer Vitrine, bestehend aus Standrohren, Dreiecksrahmen, Vitrinenboden und -deckel, Endstücken.
3. Gruppe aus fünf Vitrinen.
4–6. Schicht für Schicht werden die Vitrinenteile in Spezialtransportkisten verpackt.

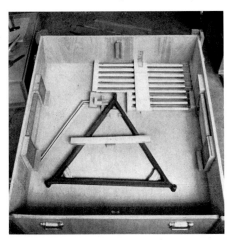

**"The Layton Awards" Exhibition,
C. & E. Layton Ltd.**

Stationers Hall, London, 1961
Design: F. H. K. Henrion, London

This system of easily assembled display panel units was developed for travelling exhibitions of specially interesting works – including prize-winning entries – which were also shown outside Britain. Each display unit is formed by three wood-framed, felt-covered display panels, held together at the top and bottom by two three-pronged spiders made of wood. The bottom spider is supported by rubber buffers while the one on top serves to hold light fittings, likewise designed in accordance with strict geometrical rules, and radiating their light in two directions. The prize-winning entries were displayed in special boxes, split into two hinged triangles mounted on casters. The system can be adapted to the most variegated space conditions and arranged in any desired groupings.

**Ausstellung »The Layton Awards«
der C. & E. Layton Ltd.**

Stationers Hall, London, 1961
Entwurf: F. H. K. Henrion, London

Dieses System einfach montierbarer Plattenelemente wurde für Wanderausstellungen besonders interessanter, zum Teil preisgekrönter Arbeiten entwickelt, die auch außerhalb Englands gezeigt wurden. Je ein Dreistrahl aus Holzlatten verbindet oben und unten drei Schautafeln, holzgerahmt und mit Filztuch überzogen, zu einer Ausstellungseinheit. Das untere dreischenklige Holzgestell steht auf Gummipuffern; am oberen Teil werden ebenfalls nach einem geometrischen Prinzip entworfene, in zwei Richtungen strahlende Beleuchtungskörper befestigt. Die mit dem Layton Award ausgezeichneten Arbeiten wurden in besonderen Schaukästen präsentiert, in dreikantigen Prismen, die paarweise auf Rollen montiert sind. Das Ausstellungssystem läßt sich den verschiedensten Raumverhältnissen anpassen und zu beliebigen Gruppierungen ordnen.

1. View from the gallery of Stationers Hall, London, on the stellated assemblies of display panels, placed at angles of 120°.
2. The demountable display boxes can be stored in a very confined space. They are assembled by means of simple pins.
3. The prismatic caster-mounted display boxes, which are fitted with interior lighting, can be combined for easy transport.
4. The dimensions of the boxes displaying the prize-winning entries exactly match those of the stellated assemblies of display panels.

1. Blick von der Galerie der Stationers Hall auf die sternförmigen Plattenkombinationen, die von 60°- beziehungsweise 120°-Winkeln ausgehen.
2. Die demontierten Ausstellungselemente lassen sich auf engstem Raum stapeln. Der Aufbau geschieht mit Hilfe einfacher Steckverbindungen.
3. Die auf Rollen fahrbaren, prismenförmigen Schaukästen, die von innen beleuchtet sind, können zur Transportvereinfachung zusammengeschlossen werden.
4. Die Schaukästen für die preisgekrönten Arbeiten passen in ihren Abmessungen genau zu den sternförmigen Plattenkombinationen.

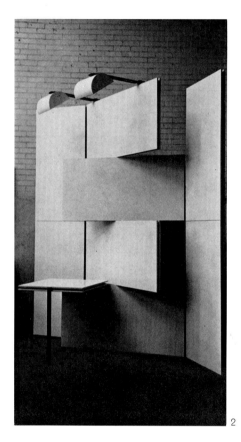

"X-Blok" Exhibit System

Designers: August Sak and Edison Price,
New York
Manufacturers: Edison Price Inc.,
New York

Ausstellungssystem »X-Blok«

Entwerfer: August Sak und Edison Price,
New York
Herstellung: Edison Price Inc., New York

The standard panel size of this system is 4×4 ft., but the panels can also be supplied in any other size. An exhibition can of course only be assembled from panels of identical size which then becomes a module. The 1½'' thick panels are covered with Formica on both sides and surrounded by extruded aluminium channels which act as a guide for sliding the panels onto a track inside the shipping case and house the electric wiring for the lighting. They also contain the connectors by which the panels can be locked through a quarter turn with a normal spanner. With these connectors, the panels can be firmly locked at any angle so that an amazing number of different combinations of display units can be obtained.

In der Regel haben die Tafeln dieses Systems eine Größe von etwa 120×120 cm, doch können sie auch in jedem anderen Format geliefert werden. Selbstverständlich läßt sich eine Ausstellung nur aus Platten von gleichem Grundmaß zusammenbauen, das dann zum Modul wird. Um die knapp 4 cm starken, mit Kunststoff furnierten Platten laufen aluminiumverkleidete Nuten, die einmal den Tafeln festen Halt in den Transportkisten geben und zum anderen die elektrischen Leitungen für die Beleuchtung aufnehmen. In ihnen sitzen schließlich die Verbindungszapfen, die durch die kurze Drehung eines normalen Schraubenschlüssels befestigt werden. Die Verbindungszapfen stellen in jedem gewünschten Winkel eine starre Verbindung mit den anderen Platten her und ermöglichen so auf einfache Weise erstaunlich vielfältige Kombinationen von Ausstellungselementen.

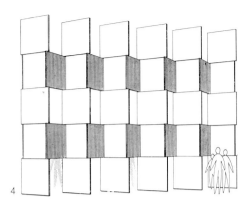

1. Simple concatenation of table and desk units.
2. A complex display unit, consisting of rectangular panels supplemented by a table top and light fittings.
3. Four-part unit with top lighting, consisting of rectangular panels and table tops.
4. A composition of display panels placed at different angles.
5. Pillar built up from staggered cubes.
6. Three-part unit placed on a special type base.
7. A further variant with inserted feet and a table-cum-desk unit.
8. S-curved display wall with window-like openings.

1. Einfache Reihung von Tisch- und Pultelementen.
2. Ein komplizierteres Ausstellungselement aus Rechteckplatten mit angefügter Tischplatte und Beleuchtung.
3. Vierteilige, beleuchtete Einheit aus Rechtecktafeln mit angesetzten Tischplatten.
4. Eine gefaltete Ausstellungswand.
5. Pfeilerelement aus versetzten Kuben.
6. Dreiteiliges Element auf Spezialfuß.
7. Eine weitere Variation mit eingesetzten Füßen und Tisch/Pult-Element.
8. S-förmige Ausstellungswand mit fensterartigen Aussparungen.

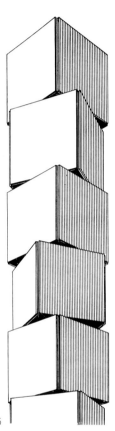

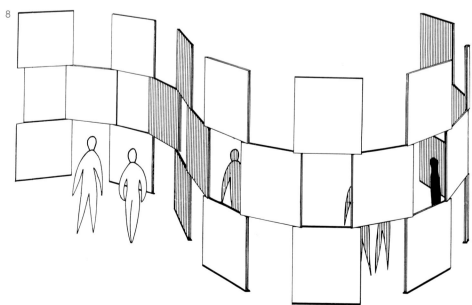

"Hyspa"
Exhibition of Hygienics,
Gymnastics and Sport in the 20th
Century

Berne, 1961
Graphic artist: Hans Neuburg, Zurich

»Hyspa«
Ausstellung über Gesundheitspflege,
Turnen und Sport im 20. Jahrhundert

Bern, 1961
Grafiker: Hans Neuburg, Zürich

In some sections of this exhibition, ⁴/₅ in. thick softwood panels lined by hard Pavatex on each side were used. These panels, 7 ft. 3 in. high and 3 ft. 7 in. wide, were supported by frames of square steel tubes with feet angled at 90°, bolted to the floor. Instead of the panels, the supports may also be used for the suspension of showcases. The arrangement of the supports can be varied freely. For the section "Gymnastics and Sport" designed by him, Neuburg adopted an arrangement which he called "a picture book in exhibition form": a simple grid of squares and rectangles separated by gaps of ⁴/₅ in. width. On the panels which had been painted with a white dispersion paint, this grid permitted a tidy and at the same time lively arrangement of the exhibits which, in this case, mainly consisted of photographs.

Für einige Abteilungen dieser Ausstellung wurden 20 mm dicke Tafeln mit Weichholzkern und beidseitiger Hartpavatex-Kaschierung verwendet, die – jeweils 220 cm hoch und 110 cm breit – von Ständern aus Vierkantrohr gehalten werden. Die abgewinkelten Ständerfüße werden auf dem Boden festgeschraubt; statt Platten können auch Vitrinen in die Ständer eingehängt werden. Die Anordnung der Plattengestelle läßt sich beliebig variieren. Neuburg fand für die von ihm gestaltete Abteilung »Turnen und Sport« ein Schema, das er »ein Bilderbuch in Ausstellungsform« nannte: einen einfachen Raster aus Quadraten und Rechtecken, die durch 2 cm breite Leerstreifen getrennt waren. Dieser Raster gestattete auf den mit weißer Dispersionsfarbe gestrichenen Platten eine klare und zugleich lebendige Verteilung des Ausstellungsmaterials.

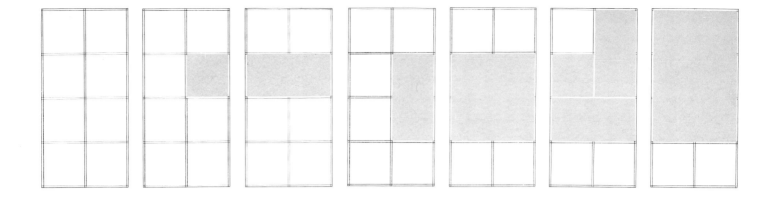

1, 3. The panel system is best suited for documentary displays for which easy and rapid mounting is essential. The system permits three-dimensional as well as fan-shaped arrangements. Alternatively, as Fig. 3 shows, the panels can be echeloned on either side of the passageway. As a distinguishing mark, the tops of some of the panels were marked with square patches of contrasting colours.
2. Different ways of using the panels.
4. A show case of the same depth as the tubular steel support was attached to the photographic display panels.

1, 3. Das Tafelsystem eignet sich am besten für dokumentarische Ausstellungen, die leicht und schnell montierbar sein müssen. Verschachtelte räumliche Gliederungen sind damit ebenso möglich wie fächerartige Aufstellungen. Die Plattenwände können auch, wie in Bild 3, beiderseitig gestaffelt den Weg der Besucher begleiten. Einige Tafeln wurden zur Unterscheidung der Begriffe oben mit Quadraten in Kontrastfarben versehen.
2. Schema der Plattenaufteilung.
4. Eine in ihrer Tiefe dem Stahlrohrständer angepaßte Vitrine ordnete sich der geschlossenen Fotowand ein.

Cocoon Spraying Method for Exhibition Buildings

Design for an exhibition ceiling without solid supports: Institute for the Development of Plastics in Building Construction
Director: John Zerning, Frankfurt/M

The cocoon spraying method, based on the use of PVC, for insulations, packaging, lamp shades, etc. has been known for a long time. In recent years, however, further applications have been found which are particularly suitable for the creation of temporary lightweight structures, i. e. especially for exhibition buildings with ceilings of complex design. The essential requirement is a lattice frame composed of wires, slats or the like, with a maximum mesh of 2 ft. Once the frame has been coated with an adhesion primer, the plastics can be freely sprayed on to the lattice frame, forming thin interweaving threads. Subsequently, this tissue is used as a base for a plastic coat of any desired thickness – even $1/_{32}$ in. would be sufficient – which, depending on the spraying method employed, may be made transparent or opaque and, as far as its surface is concerned, smooth, dull or rough. It may even be dyed.

Kokonspritzverfahren für Ausstellungsbauten

Entwurf für eine stützenfreie Ausstellungsdecke: Entwicklungsstätte für Kunststoffe im Bau
Leitung: John Zerning, Frankfurt/Main

Seit langem ist das Kokonspritzverfahren auf PVC-Basis für Isolierungen, Verpackungen, Lampenschirme usw. bekannt. In den letzten Jahren wurden weitere Möglichkeiten gefunden, die sich vor allem für die Herstellung leichter provisorischer Architekturen eignen, also gerade für Ausstellungsbauten mit kompliziert geformten Decken. Voraussetzung ist ein Gitterrahmen aus Drähten, Latten oder dergleichen mit einem Rasterabstand von maximal 60 cm. Nachdem der Rahmen mit einem Haftgrund bestrichen wurde, kann man den Kunststoff frei in dünnen Fäden webend auf das Gitter spritzen. Auf dieses Gewebe wird anschließend eine Kunststoffschicht von beliebiger Stärke – schon 0,8 mm genügen – aufgebracht, die je nach Spritzverfahren durchsichtig oder opak und in der Oberfläche glatt, matt oder rauh wirkt. Auch Einfärbungen sind möglich.

1. The weaving plastic thread is sprayed directly onto the lattice frame.
2. One of the many 'honeycombs' forming part of the ceiling shown in Fig. 4, which has a diameter of 100 ft. Each individual honeycomb is composed of a plywood frame, a trestle (four iron bars converging on top), and a sprayed skin of plastics which, in the centre, has an aperture of 16 in. diameter, reinforced by a metal ring. At this aperture, the plastic skin is pulled up by a span wire and fastened to the trestle. In this way, the roof laminations are given a sculptured shape. The aperture can also be utilised for the mounting of light fittings.
3. Plan of the ceiling structure designed for an exhibition stand. The alignment of the rib-shaped edges of the honeycombs is based on an orthogonal network of curved lines.
4. A view of the model of the ceiling which, with its fan-shaped structure, is reminiscent of medieval ribbed vaults.

1. Der webende Kunststoffaden wird unmittelbar gegen den Gitterrahmen gespritzt.
2. Eine der zahlreichen »Waben«, aus denen sich die in Bild 4 gezeigte Decke mit einem Durchmesser von 30 m zusammensetzt. Jede einzelne Wabe besteht aus Sperrholzrahmen, Bock (vier in der Spitze zusammengeführte Eisenstäbe) und gespritzter Kunststoffhaut, in deren Mitte eine metallringverstärkte Öffnung von 40 cm Durchmesser ausgespart ist. Diese Öffnung wird mit einem Spanndraht hochgezogen und am Bock befestigt. Dadurch erhalten die Lamellen des Daches eine plastische Struktur. In die Öffnung können auch Beleuchtungskörper montiert werden.
3. Grundriß der für einen Ausstellungsstand bestimmten Deckenkonstruktion. Die Linienführung der rippenartigen Wabenkanten beruht auf einem orthogonalen Netz von gekrümmten Linien.
4. Modellansicht der Decke, die in ihrer fächerartigen Struktur an mittelalterliche Rippengewölbe erinnert.

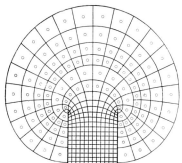

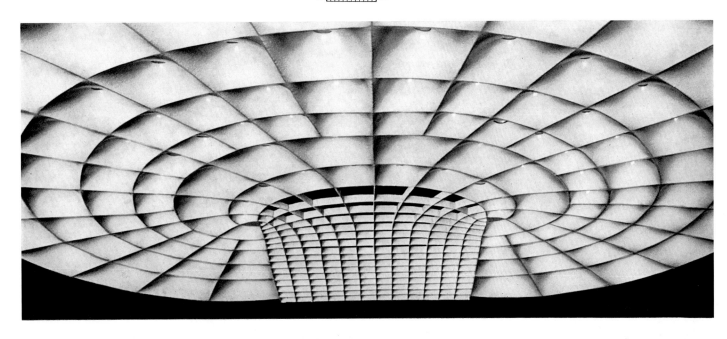

Index of Architects and Designers

Verzeichnis der Architekten und Entwerfer

Photo Credits · Fotonachweis

Aldo Ballo, Milano 73 (3), 76, 77 (2), 78 (6–8), 79 (9), 142, 143 (3, 4), 144 (5, 6), 145 (7, 8)
Manfred Barth, Kemnat 191 (5)
Hilla Becher, Düsseldorf-Wittlaer 40, 42 (5), 43 (9, 10), 93 (10)
Pierre Berdoy, Morainvilliers, Seine et Oise 124, 125 (3) 126 (4–6), 127 (7, 8)
Claus Boeckler-Siemens, München 92 (6)
Eddy Posthuma de Boer GKF, Amsterdam 154, 155 (2)
Erika Brande, Hannover 166, 167 (3–5)
Studio Casali, Milano 50 (5), 51 (8–10)
Ronald A. Chapmann, Enfield 198, 199 (3)
Color Service, Vevey 39 (3)
Commercial & Industrial Photography, Chichester Rents 199 (2)
Hans G. Conrad, Frankfurt/Main 20
Jerry Cooke, New York 139 (2–4)
Dagens Nyheter (Ronny Karlsson) 134, 135 (2–5)
Yves Debraine, Le Mont sur Lausanne 15
John Donat 130, 131 (2, 3), 132 (4–7), 133 (8)
Ehmann 117 (4)
Foto Eidenbenz, Basel 184, 185 (2)
David Farrell, London 175 (6)
Hannes Fehn, Hannover 46 (5)
Olga Gueft, New York, 106, 107 (3, 4)
Peter Guggenbühl, Zürich 156, 157 (3–6)
Foto + Grafik Alfred Hablützel, Bern 57 (4)
Hartwig Hammerich, Hannover-Badenstedt 162 (2)
Hansen 100 (5)
H. J. Hare & Son Ltd., London 179 (2)
Peter G. Harnden Associates, Orgeval S. et O. 129 (2)
Allan A. Hedges, Crows Nest 121 (2)
Foto Hoffmann, Basel 186, 187 (2, 3)
Wolfgang Hub, Duisburg 47 (8–10)
Edgar Hyman, Gipsy Hill 108 (2), 109 (5), 110, 111 (2, 4, 5)
Industrial Design 63 (5)
Foto-Kessler, Berlin 52 (3), 53 (6, 8), 54 (9, 10), 55 (11–14), 122, 123 (5)
KLP Film Services Ltd. 176 (1, 2), 177 (3, 4)
Studio André Lafolie, Johanneshov 69 (7)
Bedford Lemere & Co Ltd., Croydon 178, 179 (3, 4)
Hans Lux, Karlsruhe 112, 113 (2–4)
W. Lyrmann, Köln-Ehrenfeld 168, 169 (5)
John Maltby Ltd., London 104 (1–3), 105 (4)
Italo Martinero, Biella 82, 83 (3–5)

Erich T. Middendorf, Berlin 162 (1, 3), 163 (4, 5)
Paolo Monti, Milano 148, 149 (2–4)
Mulas 72, 74 (6, 7), 75 (9)
Sigrid Neubert, München 66, 67 (4, 5), 90 (1, 2), 91 (3, 4), 92 (7–9), 94
Neuendorff 116, 117 (2)
Foto d'Oliveira, Amsterdam 171 (4)
Lennart Olson, Bandhagen 11, 98, 99 (2)
Reinhold Palm, Frankfurt 95 (2–4), 96, 97 (2–5)
Photobild, Berlin-Wilmersdorf 147
Gottfried Planck, Stuttgart-Botnang 58, 59 (4–6)
Alfredo Pratelli, Milano 115 (3, 4), 150, 151 (3, 5), 152 (6)
Presseabteilung des tschechoslowakischen Pavillon, Montreal 70, 71 (2–5)
Pius Rast, St. Gallen 38, 39 (2, 4)
Simo Rista 100 (6–8), 101 (9)
Rosenthal-Porzellan AG, Presse- und Informationsbüro, Selb/Bayern 180, 181 (2, 3, 5)
Roslund-Nordin Studios 193 (5)
Foto-Röbenack, Hannover 174
Robert Ruthardt, Karlsruhe 196, 197 (3)
Sangermann, Köln 21 (18)
Schurig, Remscheid-Lennep 86 (1, 2), 87 (3, 5–7)
Carroll Seghers II 200 (3)
Nathan H. Shapira, Middletown/Conn. 8 (3)
Louis Singy 14
Peter Stähli, Küsnacht 36, 37 (3–6)
Steinmetz 102, 103 (2, 3)
Ezra Stoller Associates, Mamaroneck, NY. 136, 138, 140, 141 (2–6)
Walter Studer, Bern 202, 203 (3, 4)
Studio 22, Milano 85 (2, 3), 88
Strüwing 175 (4, 5)
Ufficio Fotografico, Montecatini 151 (4), 152 (7), 153
USIS, Bad Godesberg 8 (4), 9, 10 (6, 7), 25 (2), 27 (9, 10), 62
Foto Jan Versnel, Amsterdam 64, 65 (4, 6), 170, 171 (2, 3)
Georg Vetter VSG, Zürich 185 (3, 4)
Vogue Studio (James Mortimer), London 118, 119 (2, 3), 172, 173
Hans Wagner, Hannover 44, 45 (2), 46 (6)
Robert Zumbrunn 37 (2)
Zwietasch, Kornwestheim 25 (3), 27 (11, 12)